The Road to the Rapids

Parks and Heritage Series

Where the Mountains Meet the Prairies
A History of Waterton Country
by Graham A. MacDonald

Guardians of the Wild
A History of the Warden Service of Canada's National Parks
by Robert J. Burns with Mike Schintz

The Road to the Rapids
Nineteenth-Century Church and Society at St. Andrew's Parish, Red River
by Robert J. Coutts

The Road to the Rapids

Nineteenth-Century Church and Society at St. Andrew's Parish, Red River

Robert J. Coutts

UNIVERSITY OF
CALGARY
PRESS

University of Calgary Press. Parks and Heritage Series, no. 3

University of Calgary Press
2500 University Drive NW
Calgary, Alberta
Canada T2N 1N4

Canadian Cataloguing in Publication

Coutts, Robert.
The road to the Rapids

 (Parks and heritage series, ISSN 1494-0426 ; 3)
 Includes bibliographical references and index.
 ISBN 1-55238-024-6

 1. St. Andrew's Church (St. Andrew's, Man.) — History. 2. St. Andrew's
(Man. : Rural municipality) — History. 2. Red River Settlement — Social
conditions. 3. Anglican Church of Canada — Manitoba — History. I. Title. II. Series.
BX5617.S17C68 2000   283'.71274   C00-910457-7

Canada  We acknowledge the financial support of the Government of Canada through the Book Publishing Industry Development Program (BPIDP) for our publishing activities.

The Canada Council for the Arts
Le Conseil des Arts du Canada

 Printed and bound in Canada by Hignell Book Printing.
 ∞ This book is printed on acid-free paper.

Cover and page design by Kristina Schuring.
Front cover illustration adapted from "St. Andrew's Church, 1860," by Nanton Marble
(Provincial Archives of Manitoba). Back cover photograph "School Days, Selkirk, 1886"
(Provincial Archives of Manitoba).

For my parents and for my wife Catherine with whom I have travelled many roads, always with laughter and love.

Contents

List of Figures viii

Foreword x

Preface xii

1. Introduction 1
2. CMS Ideology and the Red River Mission 11
3. Establishing the Mission at St. Andrew's 39
4. Church and Company in Red River 65
5. The Mission and the Community 91
6. St. Andrew's and the Agricultural Economy 131
7. Anglican Mission to Rural Church 153
8. Conclusion 181

Notes 195

Bibliography 221

Index 229

List of Figures

1. The Red River settlement in 1835 5
2. Plan of the Selkirk Settlement, 1857 9
3. Rev. John West 27
4. Rev. John West's home at the upper settlement, c. 1822 29
5. Church and mission school at the upper settlement, 1820s 31
6. The Rev. William Cockran 35
7. The CMS mission at St. Peter's, Red River, 1844 36
8. St. Andrew's Church. Photographed by H. L. Hime, 1858 60
9. St. Andrew's Rectory. Photographed by H. L. Hime, 1858 60
10. The Red River Academy, 1852 61
11. Birds-eye view of the mission at St. Andrew's, c. 1850 62
12. Duncan McRae, c. 1880 63
13. George Simpson 66
14. Rev. David Anderson, first Anglican bishop of Rupert's Land 66
15. Catherine Truthwaite 75
16. Sarah McNab 76
17. Eden Colvile 84
18. Andrew McDermot 85
19. Lower Fort Garry, c. 1880 89
20. Thomas Sinclair 92
21. Letitia, a Métis woman of the lower settlement 93
22. Thomas Norquay 94
23. John McKay, Métis resident of Red River.
    Photographed by H. L. Hime, 1858 95
24. Annie McDermot 96
25. Going to church in Rupert's Land, c. 1875 98
26. James Ross, c. 1860 99
27. Captain William Kennedy 107
28. Donald Gunn 108
29. Ojibwa bark lodges on the banks of the Red River, 1858 113
30. View of settlement at St. Andrew's looking south
    from the Rectory, 1858 115
31. Typical Red River frame home, c. 1870 117
32. Buildings of the "industrial complex" at Lower Fort Garry, 1858 ... 119
33. The "Big House" at Lower Fort Garry, 1858 124
34. St. John's Anglican Church, Red River, 1858 125
35. St. Paul's Anglican Church, Red River, 1858 126
36. Rectory at St. Peter's Dynevor, c. 1880 127
37. Kildonan Presbyterian Church, 1858 128
38. Miss Davis's School, St. Andrew's Parish, c. 1880 128
39. Settler's house and cart, c. 1870 133
40. Modern depiction of a typical St. Andrew's riverlot farm 135
41. Farm homes, windmills, and cultivated acreage
    in the middle settlement, 1858 140
42. Farm along the Red River, c. 1870 147
43. Metis farm in the Red River area, 1882 150

44. Rev. James Hunter and wife Jean Ross 155
45. Rev. William West Kirkby, c. 1875 156
46. Rev. Henry Budd 160
47. Archbishop Robert Machray, c. 1895 169
48. Sketch of St. Andrew's Church, 1860, by Nanton Marble 171
49. The Red River Settlement in 1870 173
51. Church picnic at St. Andrew's Rectory, c. 1880 179
52. St. Andrew's Church and Rectory, 1899 184
53. St. Andrew's School, 1907 185
54. River Road, 1922 193

Foreword

Some one hundred and fifty years ago, on 19 December, 1849, The Rt. Rev. David Anderson, the first Anglican bishop of Rupert's Land, came to St. Andrew's to consecrate the new stone church. One of the participants in the service, the Rev. Robert James, recorded the proceedings that day:

> Today the new stone church at the Grand Rapids was consecrated by the bishop. Five years it has been building and a wonder on to many. About £1500 has been expended upon it, a marvel to all who know our abilities. I doubt not the real fact that God was honoured by the magnificence of the design and carried us through without loss of life or credit. Several individuals contributed in a princely way, especially Mr. Cockran. Perhaps the most pleasure of all and to myself this day was to see for the first time in God's house my whole congregation, young and old. Long and anxiously have we laboured and I looked for this day. The service was shared by the bishop [Anderson], Mr. Cockran, Mr. Smithurst, Mr. Hunt and myself. The spacious church was filled. It was the first consecration they had ever witnessed. I will not attempt a description of what my people this day felt.

The consecration of St. Andrew's church was an important event for the Anglican Church in western Canada. A bishop was now resident in the country and a group of scattered missions was evolving into an organized diocese. For St. Andrew's parish the consecration of the church marked an important stage in the life of this Christian community. By 1849, the original mission had evolved into a settled agricultural community, with the church, cemetery, rectory and mission buildings surrounded by farms.

A century and a half later, on Sunday, 19 December 1999, St. Andrew's parish celebrated the 150th anniversary of the consecration of the church. The Rt. Rev. James Allan, formerly bishop of the Diocese of Keewatin, celebrated the Eucharist and preached. As Bishop Allan represented Bishop Anderson, so too did the congregation that day represent the congregation of 150 years ago and indeed all the people who have worshipped inside the walls of this church. One hundred and fifty years of history were recalled in an act of thanksgiving to God.

Now, to further honour St. Andrew's and it's anniversary, Robert Coutts has written this history of the parish. *The Road to the Rapids* is a work of careful scholarship and the product of years of research. The book tells the story of the mission on the banks of the Red River, its evolution into a prosperous farming community, and then into the community that we know today. It is the story of the people who built the church, and of their successors. They worshipped within its walls and rest in the cemetery that surrounds it. This is the account of their lives and their faith as well as the story of their priests, beginning with Archdeacon Cockran who founded the mission and parish, built the church, and now rests next to the pathway that leads to its front doors.

The parish has evolved a great deal since those early days. The farms, market gardens and feed lots have given way to subdivisions and homes. The once narrow country roads are now paved. In the midst of this community, the church, cemetery, and rectory still stand, and the church bells continue to call the people to worship. The Red River still flows past on its way to Lake Winnipeg.

And I am Archdeacon Cockran's successor. I live in the rectory that he helped build and preach from his pulpit. I celebrate the Eucharist at the altar that he placed in this church, and my congregation, like his, continues to travel the road to the rapids.

The Rev. S. C. Sharman
Archivist, Diocese of Rupert's Land
and Rector, St. Andrew's Parish

Preface

This study focuses upon the impact of the Anglican Church on the European and English-speaking Métis communities that lived in St. Andrew's Parish in the Red River settlement in the nineteenth century. Founded in 1829, St. Andrew's was one of the prominent and most populous communities in nineteenth-century Red River, and the story of the complex interrelationship of clergy and society there reveals a great deal about Red River history and the lives of the settlement's aboriginal peoples. The study explores the evangelical basis of the church's approach in the parish, its attitudes towards indigenous populations, and the relationship between Anglican missionaries and the Hudson's Bay Company in Red River. Within these larger themes, it tells the story of the establishment of the mission at the Rapids (as St. Andrew's was originally known) and traces the development of the parish from a frontier mission to a rural Anglican outpost. The history of the mission is also contextualized within a broad analysis of the St. Andrew's community in the nineteenth century, with a focus upon the role of education and agriculture in its development.

An earlier version of this study was written in support of the Parks Canada planning and interpretive programs at St. Andrew's Rectory and Lower Fort Garry national historic sites. The present work is a much-revised version of that earlier study and incorporates the relevant work that has been published in the fields of Native, fur trade, Red River, and mission history over the last decade.

A variety of archival sources were examined in the course of my research on St. Andrew's. Located, for the most part, at the Provincial Archives of Manitoba, they include the papers of the Archives of the Ecclesiastical Province of Rupert's Land, Red River census data, private journals contained in the Red River Settlement Collection, and the journals, letters, and accounts found in the Hudson's Bay Company Archives. The most significant sources for this study, however, were the letters and journals of Church Missionary Society clergy, microfilmed copies of which are also located at the Provincial Archives of Manitoba. This vast collection of private journals and correspondence not only provides commentary on daily occurrences within the community, but offers invaluable insights into missionary philosophy and attitudes. The daily journals and lengthy annual letters of clergymen such as William Cockran, Robert James, David Anderson, James Hunter, and Joseph Gardiner, among others, provide an almost unbroken account of the mission experience at St. Andrew's in the years between 1829 and 1887. Information on the history of the church for the period after 1887, when the parish became entirely self-supporting, was contained in the St. Andrew's vestry minutes, which begin in 1890 and carry through to the present day. These minutes are now in the custody of the Archives of the Diocese of Rupert's Land of the Anglican Church of Canada, located in Winnipeg.

I am indebted to a number of colleagues and friends for their assistance in the preparation of this study, especially to Margaret Burnip of Parks Canada, who edited an earlier version of the manuscript. I would also like to thank the Keeper of the Hudson's Bay Company Archives for permission to quote from the documents, and the staff at the Provincial Archives of Manitoba for pointing me in the right direction in my researches and for allowing access to the Church Missionary Society records, the Archives of the Ecclesiastical Province of Rupert's Land, and the Red River Settlement Collection. For permission to use material located at the Archives of the Diocese of Rupert's Land, I am indebted to Mr. D. A. Thompson, legal custodian of the collection. I would also like to thank Parks Canada and the parish of St. Andrew's whose generous financial contributions helped make the publication of this book possible.

Lastly, a brief comment on some of the terminology used in this study, specifically the designation "English-speaking Métis" to describe the mixed-blood residents of Cree or Ojibwa and (predominantly) Orkney ancestry who lived in Red River. The English-speaking Métis of Rupert's Land were part of what John Foster has called "the Bay tradition" and were the children of English, Scottish, and Orcadian traders and First Nations women who were raised around the fur posts of the Hudson's Bay Company. Their ancestry and traditions differed from those of the French-speaking Métis, who historically were attached to the North West Company and the old St. Lawrence-Great Lakes trading tradition. A variety of historical terms were used to designate this English-speaking group, or were used by the people themselves, including such words as 'Halfbreeds,' 'Hudson Bay English,' 'Rupertslanders,' and 'Country-born.' Some of these terms (i.e., 'Halfbreed') are pejorative, while others (i.e., 'Country-born') are ambiguous, so

I have chosen instead to use the more precise term 'Métis,' attaching the prefix 'English-speaking,' or sometimes simply 'English' to distinguish Native peoples in St. Andrew's from their French-speaking brethren in the Red River settlement and throughout the fur-trade country. Although differing in language and patrilineal ancestry, both shared the cultures of their aboriginal mothers and the traditions of life within a fur-trade economy.

Chapter One

Introduction

Approximately twenty kilometres north of Winnipeg, in the municipality of St. Andrew's, lies River Road, a local byway with a long history. Curving along the west bank of the Red River, the road first appeared on maps of the Red River settlement in 1836, linking the narrow lots that angled back from the river's edge. For a century thereafter, River Road (or the "Inner Road," as it was once known) served as a local landmark to the people of old St. Andrew's parish, a "thoroughfare for an extended village, a kind of back street for a parish that had no proper main street because it possessed too little commerce to require anything so grand." [1] Some distance along this now popular country drive, at a sweeping bend in the Red River, modern travellers get their first glimpse of St. Andrew's Church, its familiar steeple rising prominently above the low horizon of the shallow river valley. Reproduced in innumerable paintings and photographs instantly recognizable to many Manitobans, St. Andrew's-on-the Red, as it has become known, stands today a pastoral reminder of a time when church and community were among the integral constituencies of everyday life.

What is no longer visible to modern-day sojourners along River Road, however, is the set of rapids that in an earlier time presented a formidable impediment to river traffic in the region. Once located adjacent to the old stone church, the rapids, like River Road, were a prominent local feature that defined not only the geography of the region but its nomenclature as well. The first church in the area, once located immediately behind the site of the present stone building, was known as the "Rapids" or "Grand Rapids" church, and the settlement of the region as the "Rapids Parish." The rapids are now gone, the result of high water caused by the construction of a dam at Lockport early in the twentieth century. And while the rapids have disappeared, and the old river edge thoroughfare that once linked the lower settlement to the forks of the Red and Assiniboine rivers was eventually replaced by the "King's Road," located a kilometre or so to the west, River Road was, for much of its history, "the road to the Rapids."

* * *

Throughout the nineteenth century, St. Andrew's parish played a prominent role in the economic, religious, and social life of the old Red River settlement – a unique European and aboriginal community that has provided a focus for generations of Canadian historical writers. In recent times, much of this writing has emphasized the many internal factors that shaped both the fur trade and Red River society in the nineteenth century. In their analysis of the social and cultural patterns of the fur trade, and the colony that it spawned, and, more precisely, in considering reasons for the historical continuity and change that was experienced within these communities, writers have tended to focus attention upon such subjects as ethnicity, kinship, and the establishment of racial and sexual hierarchies.[2] Demographic studies, the analysis of ethnic and cultural persistence, and the pursuit of racial or ethnic roots – what cultural historians and anthropologists call "ethnogenesis" – have in large measure dominated these perspectives.[3] This emphasis upon internal social and cultural forces, of attempting to define the nature of Native and fur-trade societies as a key to understanding the history of the West over two centuries, was motivated in part by the reaction against the traditional views inherent within the old metropolitan and frontier schools of Canadian history, and against their attempts to view the fur trade within the context of Confederation and Canadian expansion.[4] To some degree, the reaction to these traditional perceptions has led Red River research (and Métis studies in general) in the direction of racial origins, and focussed growing attention upon Métissage and kin group relations, the search for ethnic boundaries, and a focus upon the interrelationship of the settlement's European and Métis communities in the nineteenth century. Within these parameters, the tensions that character-ized the history of the settlement are viewed from the context of the Métis en-deavour to adapt and survive culturally while being marginalized politically.

In the process of studying the internal dynamics of a community such as Red River, however, there is a danger that historians may ignore the broad pat-terns of economic organization that had such a defining impact upon the history and development of the settlement that grew from the forks of the Red and Assiniboine Rivers. Though the study of ethnicity remains an interesting field of analysis, historians should not lose sight of the role of nineteenth-century European colonialism and its role in shaping the West for its own purposes. The study of one such colonial institution, the Anglican Church Missionary Society (CMS) – a London-based organization that funded mission outposts in various parts of the world, including the Red River colony – reveals a great deal about the role of mission societies in the expansion and consolidation of the British empire in the nineteenth century. Motivated by spiritual goals, the Anglican Church promoted an Anglo-Christian ethic that fulfilled an important socializing role at St. Andrew's and throughout English-speaking Red River and facilitated the extension of European cultural and economic influence over an indigenous Native culture.

The arrival of the Church Missionary Society in 1820 had a profound effect upon the Native peoples of Red River. Much has been written about early mis-sions and missionaries in the West, but until recent decades most studies have simply chronicled the extension of Christian influence through out the fur-trade country, avoiding the consideration of mission work within a larger political and cultural framework.[5] In recent times, however, scholars have been more willing to examine the motivations that lay behind this process and have attempted to assess the social and cultural role of the missionary, as well as the impact of mis-sions upon indigenous societies. They have become increasingly sensitized to these impacts and have explored how early missionaries challenged traditional world views and belief systems. At mission outposts such as St. Andrew's, the Anglican Church emphasized the themes of education, religious observance, and European agricultural practices as key components in communicating an Anglo-Christian ethic and in advocating spiritual "rebirth" and cultural change among local peoples. The missionary challenged traditional customs and behaviours and encouraged the creation of a new society of settled agriculturalists and a Christian community divorced from the economic and social traditions of the fur trade. For the missionary, the victory of "civilization" over "barbarism" was critical to the survival of the community and required conformity at a number of levels. If European, Métis, and Indian settlers were not encouraged to till the soil and send their children to mission schools, the missionary believed, they could never become truly Christian. It was this ethic that represented the motivating principle behind the establishment of the mission at St. Andrew's. Yet, the success of the Red River mission was dependent upon more than simply hard work and persistent proselytizing. Although disputes between trader and missionary inevitably arose, the CMS realized that it could do little without the tacit approval of the Hudson's Bay Company. To be effective in the colony, the Church Missionary Society had to establish a viable working relationship with the HBC – a relationship that was based upon a degree of trust and a shared vision of social and political leadership. At Red River, it was these two organizations, along with the Catholic clergy and the "principal" settlers, who formed the basis of the governing framework in the colony throughout much of its history.

Setting the Stage in Red River

Established in the heart of the North American continent, and within the fur-trade territories that the Hudson's Bay Company called Rupert's Land, the Red River Colony began as a home for Scottish settlers dispossessed by the Highland clearances of the eighteenth century. In 1811, under the direction of the philanthropic Earl of Selkirk, a majority shareholder in the company, the colony was established on the banks of the Red and Assiniboine Rivers. It was part of a land grant of over 300,000 square kilometres, known as the District of Assiniboia, an immense area that covered parts of modern-day Manitoba, Saskatchewan, North Dakota, and Minnesota. The establishment of the new colony was a critical development in the long-standing conflict between the HBC and the North West Company for control of the fur trade. Aside from altruistic motives, the London based company saw the settlement as potentially disruptive of the Nor' Wester's pemmican supply line, while at the same time providing a source for provisions and labour for its own operations in the West.

4

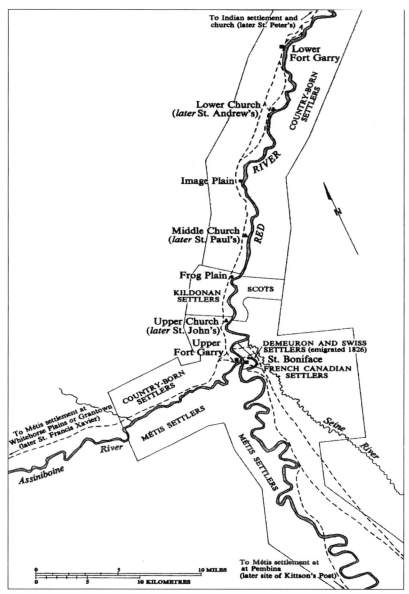

To Indian settlement and
church (later St. Peter's)

Lower
Fort Garry

COUNTRY-BORN
SETTLERS

Lower Church
(*later* St. Andrew's)

RIVER

Image Plain

RED

Middle Church
(*later* St. Paul's)

Frog Plain

KILDONAN
SETTLERS

SCOTS

Upper Church
(*later* St. John's)

Upper
Fort Garry

DEMEURON AND SWISS
SETTLERS (emigrated 1826)

St. Boniface
FRENCH CANADIAN
SETTLERS

N

COUNTRY-BORN
SETTLERS

Seine

River

To Métis settlement at
Whitehorse Plains or Grantown
(later St. Francis Xavier)

MÉTIS SETTLERS

River

MÉTIS
SETTLERS

Assiniboine

To Métis settlement at
at Pembina
(later site of Kittson's Post)

0   5   10 MILES
0   5   10 KILOMETRES

The Red River settlement in 1835, from L. G. Thomas, *The Prairie West to 1905.*

Within the homeland of generations of Cree and Assiniboine peoples, the Forks of the Red and Assiniboine Rivers was occupied in the late eighteenth century by Ojibwa (*Anishinabe*) peoples as part of a larger westward relocation from their ancient territories around the Great Lakes. Early in the nineteenth century, a handful of French-speaking Métis *gens libres* – retired NWC engagés who worked as contract freighters and hunters travelling between Red River and the settlement at Pembina near the present U.S. border – also settled near the junction of the two rivers. When the first group of Selkirk's colonists arrived in Red River in 1812, they occupied riverlots below the Forks on the west bank of the Red River. Later, on the opposite side of the river, a handful of French-Canadian émigrés who had accompanied Rev. J. N. Provencher to the West in 1818 settled in the area that came to be known as St. Boniface. Nearby were located the remnants of the Demeuron regiment – mercenaries recruited by Selkirk for service in Red River – and a large group of Swiss families who arrived in the colony in 1821.

With the merger of the two competing fur-trade companies in 1821, the face of the colony changed dramatically. When almost 1,300 fur-trade employees – largely French and English-speaking Métis labourers and Scottish-born personnel – lost their jobs in the newly restructured company, many relocated to the young colony. Orkney Scot and English Métis families were drawn to the area north of the tiny remnant of Selkirk settlers, while French-speaking Métis families who had once been attached to the NWC settled at the southern end of the colony. In 1824, approximately one hundred Métis families from the Pembina area south of Red River relocated to the colony, settling in the region known as the White Horse Plain along the Assiniboine River west of the Forks. The new colony was now largely Native in origin, especially with the departure of the Swiss settlers shortly after the great flood of 1826, and grew rapidly as the influx of Métis settlers continued into the 1830s.

The Red River settlement was organized geographically around the riverlot and the parish. Farm lots up to twelve chains in width, and two miles in length, stretched along the banks of the Red, Assiniboine, and Seine Rivers. The geographic separation of the various racial groups was emphasized by religious affiliation, and by the presence of Christian missionaries in the colony. Roman Catholic and Anglican missionaries were invited to the colony by the HBC early in its history:

Father J. N. Provencher, who arrived in Red River in 1818, ministered to the Catholic French-speaking population, while two years later Rev. John West took up duties with the Protestant English-speaking population and served as company chaplain. Their missions helped create the parish system of administrative authority within Red River. By 1835, Ojibwa and Cree peoples, who had entered into treaty with Selkirk in 1817, were either living at the parishes of St. Peter's and Baie St. Paul (Wabassong) or were visiting the settlement on a seasonal basis. Orkney Scot and English-speaking Métis families were located at St. Andrew's (or the Grand Rapids) parish. The descendants of the original Selkirk settlers were settled at St. John's and Kildonan, while the Métis and Canadians lived at St. Boniface, St. Vital, and St. Norbert parishes, and at the White Horse Plain, or Grantown, as it came to be known. Hudson's Bay Company operations in the settlement were centred at Fort Garry (and later at Upper Fort Garry) located at the Forks, and at Lower Fort Garry situated on the banks of the Red some thirty kilometres to the north.

A blend of production strategies characterized aboriginal life in Red River by 1830, although in the early years of the settlement the pemmican industry and seasonal work on the company's York boat brigades predominated. Cree and Ojibwa peoples who frequented the colony exchanged country provisions such meat, fish, maple sugar, and manufactured articles to the company and local settlers in return for foodstuffs and material goods, while Métis inhabitants traded pemmican and hides, or earned wages as cart drivers and hunters or as boatmen on the brigades that left annually for Norway House and Portage La Loche. When not engaged in such seasonal work, many local settlers tended their small farms, selling any excess produce to the HBC. Only the Selkirk settlers were full-time farmers, though even they were often forced to hunt or trade for fresh provisions.

The governing structure of the Red River colony lay in the hands of the Governor and Council of Assiniboia, initially appointed by Lord Selkirk and his heirs (under the auspices of the Hudson's Bay Company), but after 1835 by HBC Canadian governor George Simpson and his Northern Department Council. An unelected body, the Council of Assiniboia exerted nominal authority within a region radiating fifty miles out from the Forks and was made up of individuals selected by the HBC from the commercial and clerical elites of the colony. Until

1835, the council had direct responsibility for the administration of justice within the colony. That same year, a general quarterly court was established by the company under the authority of the chief recorder, who was also appointed by the HBC. District magistrates were designated throughout the settlement in order to hear minor cases that did not come within the purview of the quarterly court. Court proceedings in Red River were based on an amalgam of practices from other British jurisdictions, including procedures from Scottish and Quebec courts and allowed the chief recorder to act as the Crown's representative in laying the case before the jury.[6] Although the council appointed a number of special constables to police the settlement, it was the quasi-military organization of the Métis buffalo hunt that served as the *de facto* constabulary within the colony, at least during its early years.[7]

By the middle of the nineteenth century, the Red River settlement bore little resemblance to the colony first envisioned by Lord Selkirk. The tiny community of displaced Highland Scots and Irish that settled on the west bank of the Red in 1812 was soon eclipsed by subsequent waves of Métis and Canadian settlers who would dramatically alter the character and history of the settlement. The arrival of Christian missionaries in Red River within a decade of its founding would also influence the course of settlement history, with the interrelationship of church and society in the colony emerging as an enduring feature of this unique frontier community of varied cultures and economic strategies.

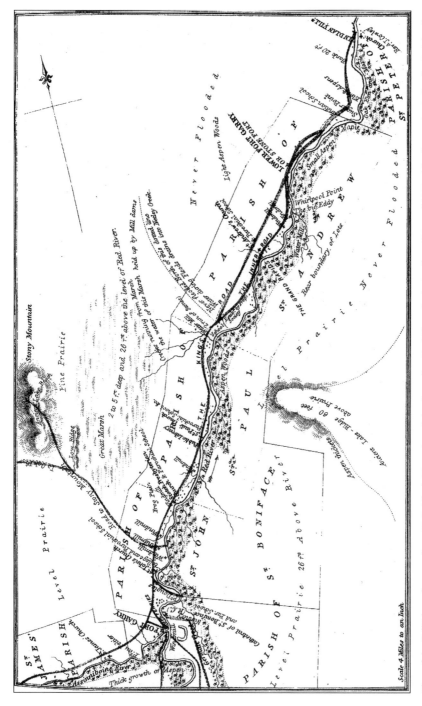

Plan of the Selkirk settlement, from H. Y. Hind, *Narrative of the Canadian Red River Exploring Expedition of 1857.* Hind's map includes the Parish of St. Andrew, St. Andrew's Church, the Grand Rapids, and the "Inner Road," later known as River Road.

Chapter Two

CMS Ideology and the Red River Mission

"Conditions of Civilization and Barbarism"

Recent decades have witnessed considerable scholarly writing and debate concerning the early history of Christian missions and their impacts upon the cultures of North American aboriginal peoples. In the United States, authors such as Francis Jennings, Robert Berkofer, and James Axtell, among many others, have re-examined the early mission experience and the nature of Native-missionary contacts in that country.[1] Similarly, in Canada, the writings of historians and ethnohistorians such as Cornelius Jaenen, Bruce Trigger, Jean Usher, James Webster Grant, and Olive Dickason (to name only a handful) have used a variety of analytical frameworks to put forward differing perceptions of Native-missionary contact on the northern side of the border.[2] In western and northern Canada, more recent studies by Frits Pannekoek, Kerry Abel, Martha McCarthy, Raymond Huel, Robert Choquette, Winona Stevenson, and Earle Waugh have looked at the histories of particular missionary orders, the experiences of individual aboriginal nations, and the lives of particular missionaries.[3]

These studies follow upon a lengthy tradition of historical writing on early Christian missions, works that were frequently authored by clerical historians or by those who, it could be argued, wrote largely from a religious perspective. The story of the establishment of the Anglican Church in western Canada, in particular, has been well chronicled in various books and articles by such authors as Thomas Boon, Frank Peake, and Arthur Thompson.[4] Boon's study of early Anglican missions, entitled *The Anglican Church from the Bay to the Rockies,* provides a comprehensive, if largely uncritical, overview of the history of the Church of England throughout much of western Canada and has remained a standard reference work for church history. But as historian Frits Pannekoek has noted, the writings of clerical historians, and in particular their use of religious archival sources, remained outside the scope of early mainstream interpretations of the pre-confederation west as set by G.F.G. Stanley, A. S. Morton, and Marcel Giraud.[5] And if the old dominant discourse has been successfully challenged by succeeding generations of historians, religious history remains largely peripheral to professional historical writing in Canada, and for the most part restricted to inwardly focussed and denominational histories. Despite this lack of explicit attention to the role of religion and its influence in early western Canadian society, the relationship of religious institutions, movements, and ideas to such things as political conflict, social protest, and cultural identity has implicitly informed a good deal of literary, sociological, and historical scholarship in the West and throughout Canada.[6]

As Canadian historical writing has shifted away from nation-building or "national" themes (much to the chagrin of historians such as J. L. Granatstein and Michael Bliss) to the study of regional communities, ethnic groups and various aspects of social and intellectual history, organized religion has once again become the focus of research, not so much as part of institutional history, but for its impact upon communities and groups. To "secular" historians, as they are sometimes referred to, religious institutions become important when they are viewed as having influenced the character of the society or community within which they operate. Historical writing on Red River is a case in point. Early accounts of the Anglican Church in this isolated nineteenth-century community – such as the work of Thomas Boon – are more concerned with the history and development of the institution than they are with the church's impact upon it parishioners, or the part that the mission played in influencing the development of the wider community.

This approach to mission history in western Canada was about to change. Historical writing on the history of Red River, and the relationship between Natives and non-Natives and between elites and non-elites – a venerable theme in western Canadian historical writing – was largely transformed in the 1970s with the work of John Foster and Frits Pannekoek. Both authors examined the impact of the Red River churches and their clergy upon the Métis inhabitants of the colony and concluded that these religious institutions had a profound effect, not only upon the lives of their parishioners, but on the ultimate direction of the colony.[7] For Foster, the influence of the Anglican Church Missionary Society upon the English-speaking Métis of the colony was, for the most part, positive. The migration of large numbers of Métis to the settlement after the amalgamation of the Hudson's Bay and North West Companies in 1821 threatened to engulf what he called "the few vestiges of British civilization that existed" in Red River.[8] At this point, Foster argued, the arrival of the CMS "tipped the balance in favor of Christianity and civilization in the Protestant community in the Settlement," and ultimately prepared the English Métis to better withstand the great changes that occurred in the West after 1850.[9] Pannekoek's views are also familiar to students of Red River history. Rather than serving as a catalyst for the Métis to adjust to the new order in the West, the Anglican Church, according to Pannekoek, helped to divide the community along ethnic and religious lines, precipitating, in effect, a civil war in 1869-70.

To some extent, the views of Foster and Pannekoek are not completely dissimilar as both eschew an anticolonialist interpretation of the church's role in Red River society in the nineteenth century. Referred to by some as a "secular" interpretation, the anticolonialist perspective views the missionary as generally disruptive of traditional Native culture and spirituality. For Pannekoek, the adverse impact in Red River of the Anglican Church, which advocated not only religious objectives for its parishioners but economic and political ones as well, had little to do with its role as an external agent of social control. Rather, he argues, it "accentuated the struggle for status within the [Red River] elite, and intensified racial and religious differences"; differences which had existed within the colony virtually since its inception.[10]

In examining the impact of the Anglican Church and the Church Missionary Society on Red River society in general, and on the community at St. Andrew's in particular, it is important to look at the attitudes and principles that the missionaries brought with them to the settlement. Although their approaches were ultimately tempered by the unique realities of life in Red River, Anglican missionaries, like missionaries everywhere, carried with them the considerable cultural baggage that was the result of their training, their attitudes toward aboriginal peoples, and indeed their whole nineteenth-century world view. It was the introduction of this particular world view to western Canada in the early decades of the nineteenth century that succeeded in changing the nature of contact between aboriginal and non-aboriginal peoples, especially in Red River. It transformed what had once been a period of non-directed cultural contact, as represented by the fur trade, into one of direct contact where the efforts of missionaries and teachers were marshalled towards bringing about major social and cultural change among aboriginal groups.[11] The Protestant missionary was in the forefront of this campaign. The product of a worldwide organization concerned with the promotion of an Anglo-Christian social theory, the missionary was trained in dealing with "exotic" cultures and in the handling of large and small-scale adaptations of Protestant Christianity.[12] Through the framework of the Church Missionary Society, an organization that enjoyed financial and spiritual support from a large cross-section of wealthy and powerful English business leaders, the missionaries received spiritual and emotional motivation, training, and financial aid in their efforts to carry British values and civilization to the "heathen" peoples of the world.

The Christian missionary movement that gave birth to such groups as the Church Missionary Society was the product of an evangelical revival that emerged in Great Britain at the close of the eighteenth century. The roots of Protestant evangelicalism can be traced to the middle decades of that century and were largely a reaction to the rationalist intellectual philosophies that prevailed in the Anglican Church during the post-Puritan age in Britain and, indeed, as British historian Ian Bradley has argued, it represented a return to the central ideas of the Reformation and the traditions of seventeenth-century Puritanism.[13] To its proponents, emotion and "evangelicalism" – literally to be seized with the spirit of the Gospel – were preferred to the rational, intellectual theology of the established church. For the evangelical, personal salvation was achieved through an inward transformation that was demonstrated through the "witnessing" of one's faith by outward acts of belief and compliance.

As with many popular crusades, the theme of conversion, of giving over one's life to God through spiritual rebirth, played a pivotal role in the evangelical movement. According to Walter Houghton, evangelicalism represented a "reaction against the High-Church 'evidences'; the insurrection of the heart and conscience of man against an arid orthodoxy." It portrayed itself as a "vital Christianity," which protested the intellectual character of eighteenth-century apologetics as the "Christianity of Books."[14] But as Houghton also suggests, it was characterized by an anti rationalist approach and had "no intellectual basis, no internal ideas, no principle of unity [and] no theology."[15]

While representing a significant change of direction for elements within the Anglican Church, evangelicalism posed no threat to the established institutions that formed the social, economic, and political structure of the nation (although a number of evangelicals were in the forefront of the anti-slavery campaign during the late eighteenth century). In many ways, they represented a strongly conservative force that attempted to solve the social problems of the world, not by revolution in the French tradition, but by personal reformation. The ills of an industrializing British society, theoretically ripe for class warfare and revolution, were partly diffused by an evangelical philosophy that taught that all social problems were the result of individual or collective shortcomings, rather than inadequacies inherent within the country's political or economic institutions. If individuals only lived their lives according to a few simple theological truths, the evangelicals believed, society would enjoy peaceful coexistence, mutual benefit, and law and order. The evangelical message, one the Victorians took to heart, was this sense of personal responsibility. It was what Ian Bradley has called "a perpetual call to seriousness."[16]

The Clapham Sect was the most important evangelical group of the period.[17] Its members helped translate evangelical theory into political and commercial reality. The evangelicals were generally men of wealth, and many within the sect held positions of power in parliament or in commerce.[18] Emphasis among the Claphams was on works of charity and philanthropy: combating the slave trade, establishing foreign missions, and distributing Bibles. With their concern for values that were both British and Christian, the Clapham Sect and its missionary representatives helped support the philosophical basis of English imperialism in the nineteenth century. The conversion of "heathen" peoples and the inculcation of British values of civilization and morality were seen by these men and women as the greatest charge God could give to his people.

The Church Missionary Society for Africa and the East was formed from the Clapham Sect in April, 1799. Its organizing committee was headed by evangelical John Venn and was comprised of both clergy and laymen. The Church Missionary Society, as it later came to be known, grew slowly. Its first missionary, Henry Martyn, was sent to India in 1805, a full six years after the founding of the society. Three more missionaries were sent to West Africa the next year, but, by 1809, the CMS had enlisted only a total of five missionaries in its cause. Thereafter, the society experienced increased growth, focussing its evangelical endeavours on missions in Africa, India, and China. In 1814, its first bishop, Rev. Dr. Middleton, was consecrated at the Calcutta mission in India.

The Church Missionary Society had originally been established to challenge the London Missionary Society and the Society for the Propagation of the Gospel in Foreign Parts, as neither was felt to reflect the particular views of the evangelicals within the Anglican church. The London Missionary Society, the CMS believed, conducted its activities too far outside the control of the episcopacy, while the Society for the Propagation of the Gospel was dominated by the Anglican Church establishment, some of whom looked with disfavour upon the evangelical cause.[19] Although the Church Missionary Society remained strongly allied with the established church, there was little sympathy within the society with the high church view that the episcopacy should direct and control missionary endeavours. This was not simply an anti-Episcopalian bias, but rather a fear that non-evangelical elements would dominate the missionary field. The society experienced some problems in the first few decades of the nineteenth century, primarily in getting its ministers ordained for foreign service. Greater co-operation between the CMS and the church episcopacy occurred, however, after the enactment of the Colonial Service Act in 1819. This act empowered the Archbishops of York and Canterbury and the Bishop of London to ordain missionaries for the colonies.[20] Although it appeared that control by the episcopate over the affairs of the society had been strengthened, the actual administration of the organization remained in the hands of the CMS committee and its secretaries. In the early years of the society's missionary enterprise, missionaries in the field were subject to very little control from the local Church of England bishops. Frequent communications with the society's secretarial office helped maintain a high degree of piety and zeal at the expense of established church liturgy and ritual.[21] In its official "Regulations and Instructions to Missionaries," the CMS warned its members: "Beware of the temptation to omit or abridge devotional exercises for the purpose of giving more time to intellectual study. Do not be discouraged by any sense of deficiency in natural ability or mental furniture." [22]

The direct contact between missionaries in the field and their superiors on the CMS committee was the key to the society's organizational effectiveness. Aside from correspondence dealing with specific issues, the committee sent each worker in the field annual letters containing general directives as well as advice and information on particular problems.[23] More importantly, the letters generally contained emotional support for the missionaries that were stationed in isolated locations, exhorting them to ever greater heights of evangelical zeal. This link with the committee in London, according to H. A. Cairns, "enhanced the missionary's feelings that he was an emissary with a specific task, a representative of a religious society whose moral and spiritual values it was his function to spread."[24]

Another source of communication within the CMS was the *Church Missionary Intelligencer,* its house journal, founded in 1849. The magazine published extracts from missionary journals and correspondence (The Rev. William Cockran at St. Andrew's often complained that his writings were not "exciting" enough for publication), sermons, mission histories, and information on CMS policy. The committee used the *Intelligencer* to raise money for the missions and to solicit recruits for its ever-expanding operations throughout the world. The publication helped support the notion within the mind of the missionary that his work was divinely inspired and that ultimately and inevitably his labours would be rewarded.

The evangelical world view of the Church Missionary Society, and like-minded religious groups, helped formulate Victorian society's attitudes toward aboriginal peoples in an age of colonial and imperial expansion. For Victorians, exotic cultures and peoples were an increasing source of fascination and curiosity, as well as the object of religious and paternalistic "conversion fever." Missionary societies promoted the notion of a world wide community and, according to the

Intelligencer, it was this community that formed the basis of their mission. "Christian ethnography," its editors wrote, "the scattered portions of the great human family; the places of their habitation; the condition to which sin has reduced them; or the benefits they have received from the ... Christian Missions – this is our subject."[25]

The Church Missionary Society, like most Christian mission groups, attempted to recast aboriginal culture. Canadian historian Cornelius Jaenen has identified three aspects of the conversion process. Firstly, missions were active promoters of European values, moral assumptions, and religious culture, as well as some form of nationalism or imperialism. The Church Missionary Society reflected the particular British-Christian values of its homeland and remained attached to its institutions and philosophies. A colonialist attitude governed most Native-newcomer relations throughout the nineteenth century. Missionaries operated, for the most part, on the assumption that one set of cultural stand-ards – the one shared by churchmen and politicians – promoted both spiritual progress and stability.[26] Secondly, missions were the result of social change. The evangelical movement, along with changing perceptions of aboriginal peoples, played key roles in the form and direction of nineteenth century Protestant mis-sionary endeavours. Thirdly, according to Jaenen, Native religions, when brought into contact with European Christianity, were neither static nor passive. They continued to evolve and to adapt new and varied ways of dealing with the intro-duction of such elements as the fur trade and settlement.[27]

The fundamental attitude of the CMS missionary toward aboriginal peoples was influenced by their conviction that all individuals represented a part of the divine image and were therefore members of a single human family.[28] According to the *Intelligencer*, humanity was "one species, derived from one common parentage, yet under the varying influences of climate, habits of like, etc., pre-senting itself under a variety of modifications."[29] This intrinsic notion of the human family fit comfortably into the world-view of culture and progress as forming a continuum that evolved through time in an essentially linear fashion. Cultural evolutionary theory was first accepted and popularized in the early nine-teenth century by anthropological societies throughout Europe such as the Ethnological Society of London.[30] An offshoot of the Aborigines Protection Society, this group promoted the idea that different levels of civilization, in the words of Victorian anthropologist Edward Tylor, were more "differences of development than of origin, rather of degree than of kind."[31] Social evolution for the Victorians was intrinsic to the notion of "progress." Each age, they believed, possessed and profited from a constantly increasing body of positive truth. Control of the environment, faith in the new technology, and the accumulation of knowledge signalled an end to the superstitions of the past and the victory of civilization and reason over barbarism. For the missionary, theories of social evolution provided a comfortable intellectual resting place, where the need for certainty and the need to accommodate diverse cultures, and more subtle ways of understanding them, reached a kind of temporary equilibrium.[32]

Cultural evolution provided a cognitive foundation for the missionaries of the CMS. It was an optimistic theory, enabling aboriginal peoples to be seen as potential Europeans; as a culture that simply lagged behind on the path of civilization. A social theory that held that mankind represented different stages in a process called "progress" was then translated into a moral and political imperative.[33] By bringing the Christian gospel to the "savage" races, they too might eventually achieve the level of civilization found in Great Britain. Rev. William Cockran, a product of CMS training, was therefore able to excuse the shortcomings of his Native congregation at Red River by saying that, while "the Indian has a good eye and a dexterous hand," if he learned the habits of "sober industry and economy, his character would soon rise in the judgment of the European."[34] For Cockran and his colleagues, "the European, having the fixed habits of full 1,800 years of civilization, views with contempt the tardy march of the Indian in the first generation, forgetting that his own ancestors were under similar circumstances."[35] Such an opinion provided the missionary with both an optimistic view of the future and a certainty in the legitimacy of his own moral duty. British society, the Victorian missionary believed, was morally bound by virtue of its superiority to aid in the development of what it considered more primitive cultures. God gave empires for the good of the governed, and as Christians they were bound to pass on to other societies the benefits and advantages of Anglo-Christian civilization. The conviction that Native peoples lagged behind British civilization, and the optimistic portrayals of their future under the guiding hand of the missionary found throughout mission journals and corre-spondence, helped to justify the treatment of Natives as subordinates. Before the arrival of the church in Rupert's Land, the CMS believed, Native people had been condemned to a life of privation and depravity. Even as late as 1920, William Heeney in his book, *Leaders of the Canadian Church*, described western Canada before the founding of the first missions as undergoing a period of "long neglect ... [where] civilization ... withheld the touch of its soothing hand and the dynamic of its redemptive force."[36]

Although the Anglican missionary in Red River believed in the evolutionary theory of progress, he held no romantic view of the noble savage. According to the *Intelligencer:*

> *Old Books ... may describe the simple pastoral life of the North American Indian.... But we know that, on more accurate inspection, these pleasant imaginations shift into dark and horrible realities; and cruelty and cannibalism and human sacrifice tell us too plainly that Heathenism is everywhere and always the same accursed thing.*[37]

Anglican missionaries in Red River reflected this viewpoint in their own correspondence. Writing to the secretaries of the CMS, William Cockran described Native peoples in Rupert's Land as "immoral, capricious, intractable, indolent, callous, prideful, wayward, extravagant, ungracious, improvident and careless."[38] Such an opinion by Cockran and the society was not surprising. To consider the Native as noble and unspoiled would expose the missionaries to criticism for attempting to destroy such an idyllic culture.

CMS missionaries also considered the Native to be childlike. Like children, they were regarded as emotional, immature, and impulsive. The missionary as parental figure and the Native as child was an image constantly re-enforced by the society. In its "Regulations and Instructions to Missionaries," the CMS cautioned its workers that "the missionary cannot love the Native Christians too much, but this love should be rather tender, grave and respectful, than free and familiar."[39] The paternalism of the missionary-aboriginal contact situation was an almost universal characteristic, helping to justify any enterprise at the Natives' expense. If children could be successfully molded into adults in the Victorian world view, the Native too could be educated and trained in the ways of civilization. But just as with children, the missionary believed, increased affluence posed certain risks for Native people. Worried that the Cree and Ojibwa living in the Red River parish of St. Peter's would be spoiled by their newly found prosperity, Richard Davis and the CMS committee cautioned the Rev. John Smithurst, the minister in charge, that "the dangers ... resulting from their increased worldly prosperity must be made the subject of earnest prayer."[40]

In the mind of the Victorian, Christianity and civilization were considered inextricably bound within a belief in the superiority of the British way of life. The pre-eminence of the empire, for most, was based upon the soundness of its Christian moral values. Any transference of Christian principles necessarily involved the teaching and communication of the basic creed of nineteenth-century British civilization. Within missionary circles, however, the issue of whether civilization came before Christianity, or vice versa, remained contentious. While the Anglican CMS was concerned with a total re-organization of aboriginal social and political structures, the Methodist Church, on the other hand, claimed only to be interested in the communication of the gospel. "Christ first to the heart, and then the after blessings of civilization" was the comment of Rev. James Evans, the first Methodist missionary in Rupert's Land.[41] It was a policy that stressed itinerary over settlement and agriculture, and one that endeared that sect to Sir George Simpson, the overseas governor of the Hudson's Bay Company. Simpson mistrusted the CMS, suspicious of its intention to remove the Native from what that society believed was the destabilizing influence of the fur trade.

From the very beginning of the mission to Red River in 1820, representatives of the CMS placed heavy emphasis upon the pursuit of the crucial components of British civilization – education and agriculture.[42] William Cockran, stationed at St. Andrew's and later at the Indian settlement, constantly exhorted his congregations to give up their hunting and gathering traditions and to learn to farm. As well, schools were established in the settlement to teach Red River children, not only scripture, but mathematics, history, geography, and domestic skills. For Cockran and his colleagues, these elements were absolutely crucial to the communication of the Gospel. "I think," he wrote to the CMS in 1828, "there is no other way of conveying the knowledge of the Gospel to the Indians of Hudson's Bay but through the medium of civilization."[43] Even John Smithurst, who was occasionally critical of Cockran's preference for practical skills over academic subjects, wrote that "if the Indian cannot be induced ... to lay aside his erratic mode of living and attach himself to one place where he can be regularly instructed in the Word of God I do not think there is much prospect of his becoming Christian."[44] As with Cockran, and almost all CMS clerics, agriculture for Smithurst held the key to this process. "A great advantage arising from the farm," he wrote in his journal, "is the employment it gives the Indians, leading them almost insensibly into the habits of civilized life."[45]

The Church Missionary Society's emphasis upon the dual role of Christianity and civilization played a part in the expansion of the British empire in the nineteenth century. Aboriginal cultures in direct contact with European culture, the CMS believed, were doomed to destruction unless Christianity was introduced to help facilitate the transition. In 1860, the *Intelligencer* commented:

> *Is it possible that two distinct portions of the human race in the opposite conditions of civilization and barbarism, can be brought into immediate contact without the destruction of the uncivilized race? We believe it to be quite possible, if only Christianity in its purity and power be on the spot.*[46]

In Rupert's Land, Anglican missionaries viewed contact between Native peoples and the Hudson's Bay Company as helping to exacerbate the problem, "scarring the body afresh and pour[ing] in vials of moral disease."[47] Only the introduction of Christianity, they believed, could equip the Native to withstand the onslaught of European society. The economics of the fur trade, which saw Native peoples as commercial trappers increasingly tied to foreign markets, was thus accompanied by Christian missions that demanded a complete and unwavering compliance to a new and foreign morality.

CMS attitudes toward the Métis peoples of Red River and throughout the West were not markedly different than their views toward Indian peoples. The emergence and history of the Métis, of both French and English-speaking traditions, has been the subject of much scholarly writing in recent decades.[48] The intermarriage of Hudson's Bay Company fur traders with Native women in the eighteenth and nineteenth centuries created a new mixed community in Rupert's Land. These English-speaking Métis, the sons and daughters of company officers and servants of largely Scots/Orkney background and Cree and Ojibwa mothers, were culturally distinct from those Métis whose origins could be traced to the French-speaking personnel of the North West Company and the old St. Lawrence-Great Lakes trading system. With the union of the competing fur companies in 1821, many of the fur-trade personnel declared redundant by the HBC were encouraged to move to Red River with their Métis families in order to provide the company with a docile workforce of tripmen and provisioners while dissuading its ex-servants from remaining near its interior posts and trading in furs outside of the company's self-declared monopoly. At the colony (first established by a small number of Métis freemen in the very early years of the nineteenth century and augmented by Lord Selkirk's Scottish settlers some years later), the HBC hoped that Métis would come under the direction of churches, schools, and company-controlled government.[49]

Beginning in the 1820s, a period of cultural adjustment awaited the former HBC employees and their Métis families as they left company fur-trade posts for the Red River colony. The influence of the Church of England missionaries and the HBC were factors in determining the ultimate role of Native peoples in the settlement. For historian John Foster, two divergent strains could be identified within what he called the "Country-born" (or English-speaking Métis) community in Red River; one stemming from the century-old traditions of the trading post; the other the European traditions of British-born fathers and grandfathers.[50] These varying legacies, however, did not pose any real tension within the community, at least not in the early years. Rather than demonstrating a clash between "civilization and barbarism," parishes such as St. Andrew's prior to 1850, reflected the economic and social reality of Red River, where the traditions of separate cultures were adapted and integrated into a way of life unique to the colony.

Anglican missionary attitudes toward the Métis reflected much of the same paternalism that they reserved for Indians. In general, they considered the English Métis lower than Europeans on the evolutionary scale of civilization. The British ancestry of the English Métis, however, allowed Anglican cleric Abraham Cowley to admit that they "will fare much better [than the Indians]. Being nearer European full descent, they have an advantage and many endure if not forever, for a longer space."[51] However, in a description of Métis tripmen to the CMS committee in 1833, Cockran was far more critical, remarking that

> *the Voyageur's progeny are the offspring of the adulterer and the whore....*
> *They have to be brought exceedingly low before God will condescend to*
> *bestow his renewing grace to change their characters. The voyageur's very*
> *bones must be broken; wearisome months must be appointed as his portion,*
> *to give him time to remember the transgressions of 30 or 40 years.*[52]

Some of his parishioners, Cockran charged, "are still in the possession of all the manners and customs of the Indians, and ... live very profane, licentious, intemperate lives."[53] Similarly, the Rev. Robert James found his congregation at St. Andrew's Parish, "frank and simple minded ... deceitful ... selfish, improvident and unthankful."[54] The CMS believed that most aspects of the behaviour of the English Métis required rehabilitation. At St. Andrew's, missionaries attempted to discourage the involvement of their parishioners in the buffalo hunt and the annual York boat brigades, or any of the other traditions of the fur-post environment, viewing these activities as antithetical to their development as Christians. It was only through the Christian gospel and the plough, they concluded, that the Métis settler might create "a little Britain in the wilderness."

The first Protestant missionary in Rupert's Land, the Reverend John West, arrived at York Factory on the 13th of August 1820. The Hudson's Bay Company was instrumental in his appointment by virtue of the changing attitude of its governing body (known as the London Committee) towards missionary work within its territories. Originally the HBC's Royal Charter of 1670 had made no mention of religious obligations either to the aboriginal peoples within its territories or to the servants in its employ. By the early part of the nineteenth century, however, a number of evangelical and religiously motivated Anglicans had come to occupy influential positions on the London Committee and lobbied for the introduction of Protestant missions to the company's territories. The growing colony at Red River, they felt, provided an excellent location for a company chaplain and missionary to minister to the retiring traders and voyageurs. Benjamin Harrison, a member of the London Committee since 1809, belonged to the evangelical Clapham Sect, while Nicholas Garry, another influential company director, was devoutly religious. Company Governor Andrew Colvile, the "moving spirit of the Committee," was supportive of the scheme and asked the CMS to supply a minister for Red River in 1819.[55]

A number of business factors were also involved in the Hudson's Bay Company's support for the creation of a Protestant mission in the Northwest. During the period of intense rivalry between the HBC and the North West Company, the Cree and Ojibwa trappers who occupied the zones of greatest competition had begun to suffer privation and food shortages due to over-trapping of the fur-bearing population.[56] The company, which had now shifted a great deal of its attention to the prime fur areas of the Mackenzie and Athabaska districts, was concerned that these groups, without the ability to purchase ammunition for hunting, had grown reliant upon company food and resources.[57] As well, the HBC had begun retiring a number of its now redundant servants to Red River and felt that the presence of the church would provide both a disciplinary and social welfare role for the growing population of Métis settlers. In its directive to George Simpson, the London Committee stated: "These people form a burden which cannot be got rid of without experience; and if allowed to remain in their present condition, they will become dangerous to the peace of the Country and the safety of the trading posts."[58] Consequently, the committee recommended that the Métis freemen and their families be encouraged to settle at Red River,

> *where the Catholics will naturally fall under the Roman Catholic Mission, which is established there; and Protestants and such Orphan children ... may be placed under the Protestant Establishment and Schools under the Revr. Mr. West.*[59]

A third factor, perhaps the most crucial, helped prod the company into encouraging settlement and missionary work at Red River. At a time when the evangelical movement in England was helping to turn public opinion against the slave trade, monopolies such as the East India Company, which practised the trade, were declining in popularity. That company's refusal to allow missionaries into its territories had been successfully overruled in the House of Commons.[59] The action served as a warning to other British monopolies. The new evangelical spirit, which had infused the British population with the desire to see the Christianization and civilization of aboriginal peoples, no longer tolerated a monopolistic and strictly secularist exploitation of resources. In 1821, the British parliament passed "An Act for Regulating the Fur Trade, and Establishing a Criminal and Civil Jurisdiction Within Certain Parts of North America." This act legally bound the Hudson's Bay Company to support both permanent settlement outside the fur trade and missionary work among the inhabitants of the territory.[60] The company's " License for Exclusive Trade," granted at the time of coalition in 1821, was subject to renewal every twenty years by parliament. It instructed the company to address itself to a program that would promote "the moral and religious improvement" of the inhabitants of the country. Unwilling to risk public disfavour, or even official censure, Andrew Colvile wrote to George Simpson:

> *It is incumbent upon the Company ... to have a chaplain in their country and at least to allow missions to be established at proper places for the conversion of the Indians, indeed it would be extremely impolitic in the present temper and disposition of the public in the Country to show any unwillingness to assist in such an object.*[61]

John West was appointed to the dual role of Hudson's Bay Company chaplain and representative of the Church Missionary Society. Unlike many of the missionaries to follow him, West was a member of the British upper class, an Oxford graduate and an experienced parish vicar.[62] He collected a salary of £350 a year; £200 from the CMS and £150 from the Hudson's Bay Company. Immediately upon his arrival at York Factory, the missionary formulated a plan for the education of a certain number of Indian and Métis children so that they could be "maintained, clothed and educated upon a regularly organized system." Although ambitious, John West lacked the acumen and tact necessary for the delicate negotiations that were often needed to bring his plans to fruition.

The Church Missionary Society's first representative in Rupert's Land wasted little time in communicating his view of the aboriginal population. The paternalism which was to characterize the work of the society in the West over the next sixty-five years is evident in West's publication entitled *Substance of a Journal* in which he described the Native peoples as being in a "sad condition, so degraded and emaciated, wandering in ignorance."[63] After departing on the company boats for Red River on 7 September, 1820, West cited his voyageurs as exhibiting "horrid imprecations ... [and] ... a degeneracy of

The Rev. John West, a member of the Church Missionary Society and the first Anglican missionary in Western Canada (Provincial Archives of Manitoba).

character in the Indian country."[64] Their "blasphemy" and "barbarous treatment of women," he lamented, made them "slaves to their arbitrary inclinations."[65] Arriving at Red River on the 14th of October, West pronounced the inhabitants to be in a "wild and hunter like state." He constructed a cabin a little distance below Fort Douglas and with George Harbidge, a schoolmaster who had come out from England, began teaching "from twenty to twenty-five children."[66]

During his tenure in Rupert's Land, John West spent a good deal of his time outside the settlement. Early in 1821, West journeyed to the Qu'Appelle region, where he preached the evils of drunkenness and licentious living to both company servants and the local Native people. "I explained to them," he wrote, "the nature and obligations of marriage and baptism; and distributed among them some Bibles and testaments and religious tracts."[67] In the spring of 1821, West travelled to Pembina where he claimed he became "depressed in mind ... at the spectacle of human depravity and barbarism I was called to witness."[68] In the next two years, he visited York Factory twice, Fort Churchill, as well as the post at Bas de la Rivière. The small log structure that West had built north of the forks of the Red and Assiniboine Rivers in Red River served as a combination church, schoolhouse, and residence for a number of local aboriginal children.

Almost from the very beginning, John West succeeded in alienating some of the critical elements of early Red River society: the Hudson's Bay Company, the Catholic Church (whose mission had been established in Red River in 1818), and the Kildonan Presbyterian settlers. West's exhortations regarding Christian marriage, drinking, and working on Sunday particularly rankled company officers who resented his attempts to undermine the fur trade. The missionary viewed the trade as contributing to the "barbarous culture" of Rupert's Land and faulted it for maintaining Native peoples, and the company's own voyageurs, in a state of "depravity." Moreover, his attempts to extend missionary work outside of Red River disturbed George Simpson, who described West as "extremely unpopular."[69] West was unable to align the aspirations of his mission with those of the fur trade. He viewed himself, according to church historian Arthur Thompson, as the harbinger of civilization in Rupert's land that would remove the Indians from trapping and ultimately destroy the fur trade.[70] Not surprisingly, HBC officers in the settlement looked upon West and his mission with some contempt, and Simpson accused the missionary of being motivated more by "the prospect of gain and self interest ... than the pure love of doing good."[71]

Apart from his relations with the HBC, West also experienced difficulties in his association with the Presbyterian community in Red River. When Selkirk established his colony in 1811, he promised his Scottish settlers a minister of their own denomination. They strongly resented the presence within their community of an Anglican clergyman who expected them to adapt to the traditional English liturgy. For his part, West confessed that he was "disappointed in my sanguine hopes of their [the Presbyterians'] cheerful and preserving assistance."[72] In his dealings with the Catholic Church in Red River West, maintained an uneven relationship with the local clergy. He deeply resented Catholicism, labelling it a "dry system of ecclesiastical statutes. They lightly regard the Sabbath and sanction the practice of spending the evenings of this sacred day at cards, or in the dance."[73] West generally preferred not to interfere with Catholic affairs in the settlement, however, and at one point even offered to teach English to the local priests if they would return the favour and instruct him in French.

It was John West who, with the assistance of the Hudson's Bay Company, instituted the first Anglican Indian School at Red River. Education for the Church Missionary Society was crucial to Christian evangelization. Through education,

John West's home at the upper settlement, c. 1822 (Provincial Archives of Manitoba).

the basic tenets of British civilization could be communicated to the Native and, according to West, he could be removed from "the influence of those savage-taught habits in that he has been nurtured."[74] For West, Native people were to be educated in order to comprehend the benefits they received from civilization, a process which would lead to an understanding and appreciation of Christianity.[75] Agriculture, West believed, held the key to this undertaking. "As agriculture was an important branch in the system of instructions," he wrote in his journal, "I have given them [his pupils] some small portions of ground to cultivate."[76] He went on to describe:

> *We often dig and hoe with our little charges in the sweat of our brow as an example and encouragement for them to labour; and promising them the produce of their own industry, we find that they take great delight in their gardens.*[77]

Unfortunately for West, the reality of events in Red River belied his romantic portrayal of the Indian School. In the first year of operation, only seven children were actually registered at the school, and the schoolmaster, George Harbidge, described by Simpson as "ignorant, self-conceited and without system or authority" proved unfit for the position.[78] The Hudson's Bay Company had little sympathy with West's schemes. Simpson pronounced the undertaking as simply "filling the pockets and bellies of some hungry missionaries and schoolmasters and rearing the Indians in habits of indolence." The scheme, as he commented to HBC Governor Andrew Colvile, would "do harm instead of good to the Fur Trade."[79] Education for the Métis of the country was for Simpson a wasted enterprise. He uncharitably labelled them as "blackguards of the very worst description, they not only pick up the vices of the Whites upon which they improve but retain those of the Indian in their utmost extent."[80] Aside from the Indian School, West also initiated a day school for the children of the local settlers. A Sunday School was established for the benefit of the Native wives and older Métis children, although some of the Kildonan Scots attended as well. During his three years in the settlement, it was in the area of education where West's contribution to the future of the mission was most significant. He clearly delineated the goals of the Indian School as well as the nature of the curriculum needed to reach them. His journal reveals the template for an educational philosophy that would help guide Anglican missionaries in Red River for many years to come.[81] West returned to England in the fall of 1823 in order to bring his wife and family to the settlement. While there, Simpson moved quickly to have the HBC chaplaincy taken away from the missionary, and the CMS, unwilling to force an open disagreement with the company so early in the life of the mission, withdrew their support from West.

John West's troubles in Red River can be easily traced to his failure to establish a viable working relationship with the officers of the Hudson's Bay Company and to his inability to appreciate the realities of fur-trade society in Rupert's Land. His constant preaching against the behaviour of traders and Native peoples, particularly the traditional custom of country marriages, as well as his desire to expand mission work and agricultural schools to other company posts, put West in a most difficult position within the small colony. Disliked by Simpson and most of the other company gentlemen, West was considered a liability by the Church Missionary Society.[82] They had hoped he would have been more tactful in his dealings with both fur-trade officers and the so-called principal settlers in Red River.

West's replacement, David Jones, arrived at York Factory in the late summer

The church and mission school at the upper settlement built by the Rev. John West, 1820 (Provincial Archives of Manitoba).

of 1823. Unlike his predecessor, Jones was originally from a rural parish and had been priested only four months prior to his arrival in Rupert's Land.[83] Although evangelically motivated, he proved more tactful in his dealings with both the Hudson's Bay Company and the principal settlers. Jones was instructed by Josiah Pratt, the corresponding secretary of the Church Missionary Society, to be flexible and to confer with the governor of the settlement, Andrew Pelly, "freely and confidentially." Personality conflicts between Jones and the leaders of the company, Pratt cautioned, were to be avoided. "Friendly persuasion" was to be employed in all negotiations and dealings.[84]

Publicly, Jones got along better with the leading elements in Red River, though privately he grew frustrated with his role as company chaplain. In his journal, he complained that:

> [a]s a Company Chaplain I occupy a very important and prospectively useful sphere of action, but as I am now, I may be here twenty years and be able to do hardly anything as a Missionary to the Indians, for I never see any of them, excepting now and then one that is straggling from the Band.[85]

The response of the CMS recognized the dual role of the Red River missionary. While considering missionary overtures to the Indian still their "sole interest," the society encouraged Jones to concentrate his efforts on the Métis and European community in Red River. "The ties that bind a missionary to his people," the directors wrote, "are of a nature not to be lightly broken ... his residence at any particular spot ... is not needlessly to be relinquished."[86] Effectively restricting the efforts of the society to the colony at Red River no doubt pleased Simpson, who viewed Jones's role in the settlement as being one of social and political control. Ultimately, the missionaries were able to shift the focus of their attention to the settlement only when the directors of the CMS saw the clergy's efforts there as an integral part of Christianity and civilization in Rupert's Land.[87]

The Hudson's Bay Company reacted favourably to Jones's mission at Red River. Although Jones was often critical of fur-trade marriage practices and "illicit connexion[s] with Native women," he confined his work to the boundaries of the settlement.[88] Simpson, for his part, assured Jones of the "high esteem and regard I entertain for you" and even appointed him to the Council of Assiniboia, the quasi-governing body within the settlement.[89] Jones was politically astute in his relations with the company. "I am aware of the tender ground," he wrote to Simpson in 1825, "on which a missionary treads, and of the absolute necessity of maintaining a good understanding with the Hon. Company's Agents in the country."[90]

In the area of education, David Jones continued West's initiatives at the Indian School, day school, and Sunday School. As attendance at the Indian School stagnated – the number of children registered at the school increased by only seven in 1824 – Jones elected to place greater emphasis upon the education of the English-speaking Métis children in the community.[91] Educating the Métis was, according to Jones, the key to missionary work in the country. "The Halfbreeds," he remarked in his journal, "are the uniting medium between us and the Indians"[92] The increasing interest of the company's chief factors and traders in having their offspring educated at Red River swelled the number of pupils under the care of Jones, his wife, and the new teacher, William Garrioch, a retired HBC officer.[93] At the school, students received a religious education as well as learning agricultural skills, although Jones advised that "moderation must be used."[94] The success of the Red River school, however, was short-lived. The death of some students at the school brought into question its treatment of Métis children, and Jones's intention of using Métis graduates as catechists among the larger Native population proved unrealistic when it became increasingly obvious that these pupils were not ready for the ministry.[95] The school's problems were compounded by the difficulty in finding qualified teachers. School teacher George Harbidge and his wife were considered grossly inadequate, and Garrioch lacked the education necessary for such a position. Jones's difficulty in collecting donations from the local settlers, including the Presbyterian Scots, who, according to the missionary, made excuses "notoriously distant from the truth," made it difficult to attract educated persons to teach in the settlement. For a number of years, the Church Missionary Society's school in Red River operated under severe financial restrictions, unable to attract the widespread support and patronage needed to guarantee its success.

If Jones encountered problems in establishing a viable system of education in Red River, he was more successful than his predecessor in demonstrating the "religious means of persuasion." Jones moved away from West's reliance on established rites and sacraments, or what he called the "formulary" that made up the church service.[96] For Jones, an evangelical approach made greater sense within the context of Red River society. His use of church liturgy, slightly modified to suit the large Presbyterian population, as well as prayer meetings and pastoral visits all contributed to the acceptance of his mission among the local English Métis and Scottish populations. By emphasizing sermons and extemporaneous prayer over established rites, Jones was able to relate church services to the social and cultural reality of the settlement.[97] Prayer meetings helped to circumvent the dry ecclesiasticism of the traditional Church of England liturgy and appealed to those who were not among the community's social and political elite. Pastoral visits also promoted evangelical values by attempting to establish religious observance as part of the daily lives of the settlement's inhabitants. John West had travelled throughout much of Rupert's Land attempting to attract Indian children to his school with very little success. Jones, on the other hand, fashioned his ministry after the style of the country parson, focussing his energies upon a more or less stable, settled population within the boundaries of the colony. His initiatives marked a significant change of direction for the Red River mission. Over the next sixty-five years, Anglican missionaries in the settlement more or less followed Jones's path, modelling their endeavours upon the English country pastorate and, in the words of Frits Pannekoek, "struggled to recreate [in Red River] the English rural parish, a little Britain in the wilderness."[98]

In 1825, a CMS recruit who would have a profound effect on religious life within the settlement and the lives of the English Métis of St. Andrew's Parish arrived in Red River. That year the society sent twenty-nine-year-old William Cockran to Red River as an assistant to David Jones, and over the next forty years this "rough-hewn north country Anglican of practical bent" ministered to settlers at the parishes of St. John's, St. Andrew's, Portage La Prairie, and the Ojibwa and Muskego Cree communities at St. Peter's.[99] Usually considered the founder of the Anglican Church in western Canada, Cockran's influence on the people of settlement, and St. Andrew's Parish in particular, was significant. More than any other Anglican missionary in the West, he has been the been the focus of much research and commentary by historians over the last century. In a 1997 article, historian Raymond Beaumont traced the widely diverging historiography relating to William Cockran, "the man and the image."[100] Early historians, as Beaumont wrote, generally viewed the longtime missionary in eulogistic terms. Alexander Ross, Red River's first historian, for instance, described Cockran as the most popular of all the Church of England missionaries "due to his earnestness, his candour, and his zeal as a minister."[101] Writing in 1920, the former Sheriff Colin Inkster praised Cockran as "a great preacher, teacher, a master builder, a master organizer and farm instructor."[102] A. C. Garrioch's 1923 book, *First Furrows,* did the same, while Thomas Boon's history of the Anglican Church in western Canada repeated a number of these positive assessments and added that Cockran's impact on Native-trained catechists even influenced the conversion of aboriginal peoples as far west as the Columbia River valley.[103] Beaumont contrasted these positive statements with the negative characterizations of Cockran to be found in more recent works, specifically those of Frits Pannekoek and George van der Goes Ladd. Where Pannekoek described Cockran as a negative force within the settlement whose racist views of aboriginal people contributed to the disintegration of Red River society,[104] van der Goes Ladd went further, characterizing the Anglican missionaries as "ideological cadres of British colonialism," and Cockran, in particular, as a "poisonous pedagogue," who employed physical intimidation to discipline his unruly parishioners.[105] Attempting to forge what he hoped to be a middle ground, Beaumont effectively sided with historian John Foster, who viewed Cockran as an important catalyst in the "successful adaptation of English-speaking mixed-bloods to the changes which engulfed them during the nineteenth century." [106]

Clearly, William Cockran's impact upon the development of the church in Red River and upon the development of the colony's English-speaking peoples – either positive or negative depending upon one's perspective – is evident in the passionate tones exhibited by his supporters and detractors. If Pannekoek's and especially van der Goes Ladd's assessments are unduly harsh and overstated, the traditional views of

The Rev. William Cockran, a member of the Church Missionary Society and the founder of the Anglican mission at St. Andrew's (Provincial Archives of Manitoba).

Ross, Garrioch, Inkster, and Boon provide little more than hagiography and shed only a dim light on the role of this controversial missionary and the conversion experience of Native peoples in Red River. On the other hand, it remains to be seen whether, as Foster argued, the English Métis were successful in their adaptation to the "changes which engulfed them, " or if they were either swept aside or effectively absorbed into the Anglo-Protestant society that gained ascendancy in Red River after 1870. Within this interpretive framework, it is instructive to examine the history of the Anglican Church in the settlement and the important role of a man like William Cockran.

Born in Northumberland and raised with a strong background in farming, Cockran was considered a second-rank candidate by CMS Director J. W. Brooks. "He would not suit a congregation in England," Brooks wrote, "his origin is low – his wife, though a discreet and pious woman, was a servant maid – his manners unpolished and indicate his origin.... His dialect [is] broad and vulgar even as a Scotchman."[107] Priested less than one week before his departure for Red River, Cockran was appointed assistant chaplain to the Hudson's Bay Company at an annual salary of £50. This stipend was supplemented with £200 from the society, a salary Cockran admitted to be "adequate."[108] Soon after his arrival at the Upper

A romanticized depiction of the CMS mission at St. Peter's, Red River, in 1844. From
G. J. Mountain's *Journal of the Bishop of Montréal*, 1846 (Provincial Archives of Manitoba).

Church, Cockran put his training in agriculture and animal husbandry to good
use by teaching the rudiments of farming to English Métis children. Although
his plan to enlarge the size of the mission farm met with some opposition from
Jones, Cockran successfully increased cultivated acreage at the mission from only
three and a half acres in 1825 to twenty-four acres by 1829 and constructed an
ambitious irrigation system.[109] The energetic missionary instructed both pupils
and local farmers in the care of farm animals, as well as in the proper techniques
of planting, harvesting, and storing vegetable and grain crops. Cockran was a
firm believer in the necessity of communicating practical farming skills to the
Métis inhabitants of the settlement. Agriculture represented the cornerstone of
an Anglo-Christian world view, according to Cockran, and promoted a sedentary lifestyle that enabled its practitioners to achieve a higher level of civilization
and spirituality. For Cockran, example provided the greatest teaching tool. "Let it
not be thought," he wrote to his friend Rev. Bickersteth in London, "that it detracts
from the dignity of a clergyman in Red River to be found holding the Plough–it increases his value. It is our example," he maintained, "that gives weight to our precepts."[110]

In the latter part of 1828, Cockran began making pastoral visits to the growing community of English Métis who had left the service of the HBC at its

interior posts and had begun to settle along the Red River at the rapids located a short distance north of Image Plain, near the present site of St. Andrew's Church. The area came to be known as "The Grand Rapids," or among locals as simply "The Rapids." This pastoral work, which brought him to the area about once a week, usually involved the holding of services in private homes, visiting the sick, and conducting marriages, funerals, and baptisms. In 1829, eager to begin his own Red River mission after his conflict with Jones regarding the extent and importance of the mission farm at Red River, Cockran departed the upper settlement for the Grand Rapids, where he hoped to establish a church, school, and extensive farm.[111] During the tumultuous decades before mid-century, Cockran's name was to become synonymous with the development of "The Rapids" (later St. Andrew's) mission and the largely Native community that surrounded it.

Chapter Three

Establishing the Mission at St. Andrew's

"*A Great Many Temporal Discouragements*"

If the first years of the Anglican mission in Red River colony were characterized by poor leadership and direction, the tenure of David Jones and his assistant William Cockran helped to put the church on a more solid footing within the settlement. Where the goals of the mission had remained ambiguous for John West, who saw himself as ministering to the wider population of aboriginal peoples throughout the territory rather than being confined to the role of company chaplain, they were less uncertain for Jones, who restricted his ministry to the borders of the settlement and was able to ally himself with a governing elite in Red River made up of "principal settlers" and the company squirearchy. The religious means of conversion had been developed and, under the direction of Cockran, were successfully twinned with the pedagogical attractions of the mission farm. By 1829, the mission was on a more or less solid footing, its goals successfully redefined and the institution now part of the colony's governing class.

After the severe flood of 1826, the number of Métis families who relocated to Red River from the fur-trade territories increased remarkably. Many of these families, some headed by Orkney-born officers, servants, and others of mixed-blood parentage, chose to settle on the lands available in the lower region of the settlement adjacent to the rapids, or "Grand Rapids," as they were known locally.

As settlement expanded northward from the Forks of the Red and Assiniboine, so did the influence of the Anglican mission. Jones's 1825 church at Image Plain, some six miles down river from what was called the "Upper" church (later St. John's), soon became the "Middle" church with the establishment of the Grand Rapids parish in 1829.

The arrival of Métis families in the settlement and the establishment of farms along the Red and Assiniboine Rivers was regulated by the Hudson's Bay Company and its policy of land grants for retiring servants. The application of the policy was based on rank.[1] The size of grants ranged from as little as twenty-five acres to upwards of two hundred. As the depths of the riverlots remained constant at two miles, river frontage could vary from one and a half chains to twelve chains for retiring chief factors. As well, grants of 25 acres were often given to a settler's eldest son. But for many retiring servants, the grants of land were too small to farm effectively. William Cockran, writing to the secretaries of the CMS in 1833, identified the problem. The settler, according to the missionary, "received gratis a piece of land, 33 yards in breath, and two miles in length. This is too narrow to fence and to make a farm of."[2] By the 1830s, the price of land had risen to ten shillings an acre, and, coupled with high seed, equipment, and livestock costs, the problem of acquiring additional lots proved almost insurmountable for many incoming settlers.[3] Cockran outlined the difficulty of the situation:

> *The people of this Lower part of the Settlement are exceedingly poor, and meet with a great many temporal discouragements emerging from the nature of the soil and climate and their inexperience in providing for future contingencies. They scarcely ever succeed in raising as much grain as will serve their families throughout the year. Few are so rich as to possess a plough and yoke of oxen; therefore all that they can plant and sow in the Spring has to be done with the hoe.*[4]

The missionaries viewed the initial disadvantages facing the Métis settlers as limiting in their attempt to become successful farmers. In keeping with their belief in an individualistic, racially based Victorian moral ethic, the missionaries also saw a great deal of this inability as the result of "barbarism" and the absence of a civilized ethic. The Métis were poor farmers, Cockran argued, because of natural as well as structural disadvantages. However, it was the evangelical view that individual initiative, both moral and economic, was always preferable to the structural transformation of the social and economic system.

Without church or residence at the Rapids, Cockran began his ministry there by visiting the local settlers and holding services in their homes. With a grant of land from the HBC, Cockran, citing HBC London governor Andrew Colvile's promise to the CMS that the company would "grant every facility" to the new mission, also hoped that the company would help to offset the cost of building a church and school. George Simpson, however, opposed the missionary's plan. Publicly, according to Cockran, Simpson exhibited "disinterested kindness" towards the success of the endeavour, though privately, the missionary charged, he paid only lip service to London directives regarding company assistance to the church.[5] Simpson generally viewed Anglican expansion as a threat to HBC interests in Rupert's Land, no doubt fearing that the church might succeed in turning away some from the provisioning and labour services that were critical to the company's success there. Notwithstanding the antipathy of the company's overseas governor, Cockran, who was often critical of the fur trade, rarely reproached Simpson himself, faithfully complimenting his "unwearied attention ... to our welfare."[6] Cockran was above all a pragmatist and realized early on that Simpson was a better ally than foe. The two men enjoyed a synergistic relationship with each realizing that some form of accommodation was no doubt the most expedient and desirable course of action.

Not long after he had established a church and residence in the lower settlement, Cockran decided to use his own financial resources to purchase four plots of land adjacent to Jackfish Creek at the Rapids. These included two lots on the west side and two on the east side opposite. A copy of the Deed of Purchase dated the 1st of May, 1832, and signed by George Simpson (as agent for the estate of the Earl of Selkirk whose heirs still owned the land), confirmed the sale of the four lots of eight chains frontage each totalling four hundred acres. At 7s.6p. per acre the cost amounted to £150. A further 150 acres adjacent to the property were reserved for the Church Missionary Society and the new church.[7] The CMS grant included a riverlot on the east side of the Red and, like Cockran's east side property, was used primarily as a wood lot. Cockran's decision to purchase his own property at the Rapids was based largely on his fear of eviction by Simpson, should the land remain under HBC ownership, and his concern that if the CMS ever decided to abandon its Red River mission, he would be left without a home. Cockran eventually sold a portion of his property to a local farmer in 1841 and the balance of his estate at the Rapids to the CMS in 1846.

In the summer of 1829, shortly after his arrival in the lower settlement, Cockran advised the CMS secretaries that: "[o]ur new Establishment at the Rapids is now rearing its head in the wilderness." A stone and mortar foundation was laid, and Cockran hurriedly attempted to complete the log Red River frame house before the onset of winter. The following spring, upon finding his new residence too small for the number of parishioners who attended services, the missionary began to

> ... collect as much wood in the Winter as would build a room 42 feet by 20 (intended to be divided into three apartments: a kitchen, store and Dairy). As soon as the weather grow so mild as to allow the Carpenters to work out in the open air, we commenced building.[8]

Cockran's new structure served as a church and school, with services held Sunday mornings and Tuesday evenings, and operated as a day school for local Métis children.

In July of 1830, Cockran informed the CMS that he had initiated plans to build a log church at the Rapids. Wood was floated down the river sufficient to erect a frame building approximately fifty feet long, twenty-two feet broad, and eleven feet high.[9] Though Cockran admitted that the building would not be finished that year (1830), he did inform the society that stones would be collected from the riverbank and a foundation laid that summer. According to the missionary, the building effort would be collective:

> There is a Mason among us [he wrote] who promises to assist us in laying it. The rest of us can do anything that is requisite to be done.... Some will go to the pines for sawboards, others will have got an axe, a saw plane, and chisel will come and assist in putting up the frame, and others who have a spade and hoe will dig mud, and those who have oxen will haul it.[10]

The following summer, Cockran reported the outside walls of the partially constructed church to be fifty-two feet by twenty-three feet. The use of oak rafters coupling the walls and thatched roof created a cathedral-like ceiling over the small wooden structure. Although Cockran's journal for 3 August, 1831, declared the building to be "finished," there are numerous entries over the next year referring to further work on the church.[11] On the 7th of September, 1831, Cockran's workers commenced laying the floor of the church, finishing two weeks later on the 21st.[12] Over the course of the winter, work continued on the interior of the building. A group of directors, comprised of the heads of seventy-six families in the parish, were appointed by Cockran and were responsible for the provision of materials and labour for furnishing the new edifice.[13] A stove was purchased from the Hudson's Bay Company, as were such articles as window glass, sheet iron and lime for plastering. The construction of the forty-two pews for the church was the responsibility of individual heads of families. Although each family would own their own pew, in the Church of England tradition, they were instructed by Cockran to "welcome strangers and sojourners into their seats, and allow none to stand in the alley."[14] Lots were to be cast for the location of each pew inside the church and "none to be allowed any preference." The Grand Rapids Church opened the 1st of May, 1832. In his journal, Cockran notes that he had hoped to have the building ready for services eight days earlier, but the "abyss of sorrow into which the Governor [Simpson] and family had been plunged by the sudden and unexpected death of [their] little boy caused us to defer it."[15] David Jones described the new church as able to accommodate 350 people and possessed of "a degree of elegance never hitherto attempted in the settlement."[16] If the latter part of Jones's claim was true, it is somewhat doubtful that a fifty-two by twenty-three foot structure could hold 350 people.

Evidently, the greater part of the costs associated with the construction of the church and parsonage were absorbed by Rev. Cockran. The financially troubled Church Missionary Society had refused Cockran a financial grant, informing the missionary that the society was contemplating the reduction of funds to Red River so that it might focus greater attention on its work in Africa and Asia. The society's plan did not sit well with Cockran. In a forthright letter to the secretaries in July of 1833, the missionary reminded the society that it had "refused to grant a single shilling" towards the building of the mission in 1830. Lashing out at the committee, he wrote: "You seem not to have the growth of the Church of God so much at heart as your own ease, the growth of your own ease [and] the growth of your own purses and families."[17] Moreover, he charged, if the society, "which has £40,000 a year at its disposal ... had a zeal for God equal to the despised missionary, there can be little doubt ... they had the power of saving more for the establishing of the Mission on the bank of Jackfish Creek than he [Cockran] who was upon a salary of £300 a year."[18] Cockran blamed much of his predicament upon David Jones. He accused his colleague of never recommending his projects to the society and of failing to help solicit funds from the gentlemen of the Hudson's Bay Company.[19] Jones, Cockran believed, was more concerned with maintaining a comfortable life at the Forks than with interesting himself in the work of evangelism. Despite the antagonism that existed between the two missionaries, and the apparent lack of commitment by the CMS to the mission at the Rapids, Cockran's new church helped raise the profile of the Anglican Church in the lower community. It facilitated the process of acculturation through which former company servants were integrated into a new local economy that added farming to the traditions of the fur trade and the buffalo hunt.

As the "civilizing" benefits of agriculture were integral to Cockran's proselytism, he lost little time in establishing a farm at his new mission. He strongly believed farming to be a major catalyst in the introduction of Anglo-Christian culture to the English Métis and hoped it would lead them away from what he called the "vagaries of the hunt." In the spring of 1830, Cockran cleared and ploughed seven acres and sowed fourteen bushels of wheat as well as thirty bushels of potatoes. The results of that first planting were disappointing. The wheat turned out to be of greatly inferior quality, while the potatoes rotted in the ground. The poor crop led Cockran to lament in his journal that he had "never been so unsuccessful [as a farmer] since I came to Red River."[20] The determined missionary persevered, however, and by 1833 the farm was expanded to twenty acres. The harvest that year yielded 353 bushels of potatoes, 200 bushels of wheat and sixty bushels of barley.[21] A grist mill, built the previous summer near the creek that ran through the mission property, was used for grinding the grain from the mission farm and the meagre returns from the farms of the local settlers. The traditional method of grinding grain between the two flat stones of simple handmills called "querns" was time-consuming, and Cockran hoped the new mill would greatly improve the quantity and quality of flour produced in the parish.[22] The year 1833 also saw the construction near the parsonage house of a small fenced enclosure in which thirty head of cattle were grazed the year round.[23] The mission farm enjoyed another successful crop the following year. Wheat, which had been planted in May of 1834, was calculated by Cockran to have reached a height of five and a half feet by mid-August. The harvest that year resulted in a crop that, according to Cockran, was "excellent, free from smut and promising to yield great returns."[24] Although the Grand Rapids mission enjoyed successful harvests between 1833 and 1835, Cockran still accused his reapers, generally Métis children from the parish school, of being "the most awkward beings that ever laid hold of a sickle. Sometimes they tried to reap sitting, at other times kneeling."[25]

Events conspired against the continued success of Cockran's farm during the remainder of the decade. In the late summer of 1837, heavy rains caused much of the wheat and potato crop to rot in the ground. The only potatoes that survived were those growing along the riverbank, and they provided much of the food for Cockran and his family over the ensuing winter.[26] Early frosts and prairie fire were other elements that threatened the mission farm. Severe frosts in 1839 and 1840 heavily damaged the wheat and barley crops, while a destructive prairie fire in October of 1839 succeeded in wiping out a good deal of the hay used to feed the livestock.[27] Prairie fires were greatly feared by the early farmers in Red River. Whole fields of ripening hay and grain were lost while homes could be set ablaze in minutes. When fuelled by strong winds, these fires could wreak devastation for miles in every direction, often claiming livestock or some unfortunate human victim. Frequent mention of prairie fires and their destructive power is made in the journals of a number of the Red River missionaries.

Although the farm at the Grand Rapids mission experienced difficulties, Cockran remained indefatigable in his efforts to expand his agricultural operations in the lower settlement. Working tirelessly, often from morning till nightfall, the missionary succeeded in eking out a living from the mission farm. As well, he used the farm to help teach agricultural techniques to the local aboriginal population. Heavy rains throughout the late 1830s and early 1840s doomed much of Cockran's wheat, barley, and potato crops. Efforts in those years to dig drainage furrows were unsuccessful, and much of the grain simply rotted in the soggy fields. Cockran's journal for the period reflected his growing despondency:

*When I reflect on the many inconveniences which this mission has been
subjected to, and the galling disappointments which providence has permitted
to arise, I am lost in wonder at the ways of God – that this should be necessary
in laying the foundation of good work.*[28]

It was not until 1845 that Cockran could again report a successful harvest, the dry conditions that year resulting in a "very weighty crop," according to the missionary.[29]

After establishing the farm at the lower church, William Cockran turned his attention to the Ojibwa and Swampy Cree who resided at the northern extremity of the settlement in the area around Netley Creek. It was the belief of the CMS, at least in this early period, that the conversion of the Indians of Rupert's Land remained an important goal of the organization and its missionaries in Red River. Cockran, in particular, believed in the urgency of this task. The establishment of an agricultural colony among the Ojibwa and Cree, he believed, would act as a vortex and eventually draw people from all over the region to adopt a sedentary, agricultural, and Christian way of life.[30] The key to the success of the project was, of course, the establishment of an agricultural economy. Knowledge of the gospel and the inculcation of Anglo-Christian values among Native peoples could only be achieved, the missionary believed, through a repudiation of the hunt and the adoption of an agrarian model of self-sufficiency. For William Cockran, such a pastoral existence was the way these individuals might "procure their livelihood in an honourable honest manner."[31]

In 1832, with the reluctant approval of the Hudson's Bay Company, Cockran convinced a handful of families led by Chief Peguis to settle at Sugar Point, a location on the Red River near the present town of Selkirk. Cockran's plan involved the development of a small village and adjacent farmland situated around a central church, school, and mission farm. In 1833, a log school was built, and, in October of that year, the missionary reported in his journal that:

*I am happy to say that we have now got nine small houses built at the Indian
Settlement for the accommodation of those families who intend to have their
children educated. The houses are about 24 feet in length and 15 or 16 in
width: they are sufficiently large to admit of a cellar in the centre of the room
to deposit the potatoes.*[32]

In 1836, a wooden church (later named St. Peter's) was constructed by Cockran and his small Native congregation at the Indian settlement. Claiming the new structure could accommodate almost 300 people, the missionary boasted to the society that the Indians "have been taken from the chains of heathenism and are now brought under the sound of the Gospel."[33] In 1854, this wooden church was replaced by a larger stone structure that still stands.

It is evident from Cockran's journal and correspondence between 1832 and the arrival of the Rev. John Smithurst in 1839, that the establishment of the mission at St. Peter's remained uppermost in the missionary's mind. Numerous entries provide commentary upon the building of houses at the settlement, the expansion of mission farmland, and the spiritual and temporal welfare of the Native peoples residing there. Cockran's attitude during this period vacillated considerably. At times, he wrote in glowing pastoral terms of the "little whitewashed cottages shining through the trees," while at others he grew discouraged and described his work as "strewn with thorns and pregnant with sorrows."[34] During this period, the missionary seemed to pay little attention to the mission at the Rapids for which he was still responsible. For Cockran, at least, evangelizing among the settlement's Cree and Ojibwa population was viewed as having priority over the duties of HBC Chaplain.

In 1835, Cockran's mission farm at St. Peter's occupied thirty-five acres of cultivated land, while a further eighteen acres were being farmed by local people. By 1840, they had increased this amount to fifty-six acres under cultivation, by 1849 to 200, and by 1856 to over 300 acres.[35] The average acreage per person had also increased in this period from 0.1 in the early 1830s to 0.5 in 1843.[36] Although cultivated acreage at St. Peter's averaged between two and a half and three acres per farm after 1843, this statistic does not indicate the wide variation in cultivated acreage among the parish's seventy-nine farms. While one farm had eight cultivated acres, most had only one or two acres under the plow. Nineteen of these St. Peter's settlers cultivated no land at all.[37] Cereal grains such as wheat and barley, along with corn and potatoes formed the basis of the crop at St. Peter's, as they did elsewhere in the settlement. The number of livestock in the parish had also increased by 1838, the Red River Census for that year listing a total of 138 horses, cattle, pigs, sheep, and oxen in the parish. Eleven years later in 1849, the census lists 375 domestic animals in the parish, a further increase of 237.[38]

Mindful of the extra burden placed on the limited resources of the Anglican Church in Red River by the St. Peter's mission, Jones and Cockran petitioned their parent committee in London for the services of another missionary for the colony. Cockran's work at St. Peter's, they argued, could not possibly survive unless greater assistance was forthcoming. To this end, Jones sent a letter to the secretaries that he claimed was dictated to him by Chief Peguis (although Jones probably penned it himself), pleading with the society to not forget its recent converts in Rupert's Land:

> *We now like the word of God [Peguis stated, according to Jones]; and we have left off getting drunk, left off adultery ... cast away our rattles, drums, idols and our bad heathen ways.... Must we turn to our idols and gods again? or must we turn to the French Praying-Masters for protection and assistance.*[39]

In order to promote their endeavours in Red River, Jones and Cockran often portrayed Native peoples in the settlement as being in a state of childlike dependency, reliant upon the favours of the Church Missionary Society for both their moral and physical salvation. While the mission was often painted in glowing terms, it was always made clear to the society that their converts in Red River could very easily slip back into the abyss of "heathenism," if additional aid was not forthcoming.[40] This was pretty much standard mission society practice; glowing reports of great progress were frequently tempered by disparaging accounts of barbarism and heathen behaviour intended to maintain the flow of donations and funding. The society responded to the requests from Red River and, in 1839, sent the Rev. John Smithurst to take over the mission at St. Peter's. David Jones had departed the settlement the year before – his wife died in 1837 – and Cockran was left with the pastoral care of the Upper, Middle and Lower churches, as well as St. Peter's. Smithurst, a graduate of the society's Islington College, was characterized by the principal of the college to be "not a man of shining talent" but of "decided piety" and, in the words of Frits Pannekoek, willing to "commit ... [himself] ... to the frozen wastes that were thought to be Rupert's Land."[41] Smithurst continued Cockran's agricultural endeavours at the Indian settlement and succeeded in expanding the mission farm, while introducing a number of new crops such as cucumbers, melons, and kidney beans.[42] Between 1839 and Smithurst's departure in 1851, the population of the Indian settlement increased, as did the total number of acres under cultivation.

For Cockran and his successors at St. Peter's, agriculture was in essence a metaphor for the conversion and transformation of aboriginal beliefs and culture. They wanted their Native settlers to grow European crops such as wheat rather than "Indian corn," to plant in straight furrows, and above all to be "industrious," as they defined it. The mission involved more than just transforming religious belief; it centred upon a redefined work ethic, a European-style nuclear family, and European gender roles that would see men, not women, as farmers. The mission at St. Peter's embodied a fundamental change for Native peoples and represented, according to ethnohistorian Laura Peers, "a transformation of culture, of language, of family structure, of patterns of personal interaction, of social expectations, and of religion and world view as well as economy."[43] But, as Peers adds, the precarious state of agriculture in the parish, and indeed throughout the settlement, where crops failed with regularity, made it necessary for aboriginal settlers – or those she refers to as the "Christian Indians" – to maintain aspects of the traditional seasonal round of hunting, fishing, and trapping.[44] This combination of old and new produced a lifestyle that was little different from that of the English Métis of St. Andrew's.

Like the mission farm at St. Peter's, the Grand Rapids farm continued to play a key role in the communication of agrarian, Christian values to the parish's Métis residents during the 1840s. In 1846, William Cockran decided to leave Red River with his family for a much-needed rest. The Rev. Robert James, who had been sent by the Church Missionary Society to Red River in 1845, assumed Cockran's duties at the lower church. The CMS, acting on the advice of John Smithurst, had purchased the house and property at the Rapids from Cockran and turned it over to James. In a letter to the committee in October of 1847, Smithurst described the property at the Grand Rapids and included a survey of the property by W. D. Moody of the Royal Engineers. The mission property amounted to thirteen chains of river frontage on both sides of the Red River. This land included the CMS property, which contained the church, a school, and private woods on the east side of the river. The adjacent land previously owned by Cockran included the farm with approximately thirty acres under cultivation, a large barn and stable, a house and various smaller outbuildings, or "cow-houses."[45] Though James, who did not have an agricultural background, was initially reluctant to continue Cockran's farming operation in the parish, he did admit in a letter to the CMS in August of 1847 that, "I have found from experience that here we must provide for ourselves."[46] James realized the necessity of the farm in providing a reliable food supply for the mission, but did not completely share Cockran's devotion to an agrarian ethic and its use in communicating the elements of "civilization." To this end, he stated his intention to farm only half the property and lease the rest "to a respectable tenant."[47]

Given the restrictions of climate and technology that hampered agriculture in Red River in the years before mid-century, the church farm at the Rapids could be considered reasonably successful, though it never reached the level of production that Cockran first envisioned. Frits Pannekoek has suggested that, in general, Protestant agricultural missions in the West enjoyed only marginal success. He concluded that they were never able to achieve the ultimate goal of developing self-sufficient and predominantly agricultural Native communities. Farming was backward, only in a few cases spontaneous, and always ancillary to work on the boat and cart brigades. The reasons for this failure, according to Pannekoek, lay in the church's belief in the inferiority of Indian and Métis peoples, especially as farmers, and in the missionaries' inability to change their idyllic concepts of agriculture to suit the harsh environment of the West.[48] An unfavourable climate, the absence of up-to-date agricultural technology, the availability of wild game within the general vicinity of the settlement (at least before 1860), and the lack of any substantial market for produce combined to keep mission farms small and unproductive. While agriculture played an important part in the communication of the Christian ethic at missions such as Grand Rapids and at St. Peter's, the existence of church farms in these communities remained fragile at best.

Just as agriculture was considered by some missionaries to be the foundation for a settled Christian way of life, education too played a major role in the church's approach to proselytism in Rupert's Land. As mentioned above, Rev. John West's first school was established at the Forks in 1820 with George Harbidge as teacher, and, under David Jones and William Cockran, the Indian school, day school, and Sunday school were continued. In 1827, a school for the daughters of company officers was established at Red River under the tutelage of Cockran's wife, Anne. Mrs. Cockran was not held in high esteem by Governor Simpson, who, in an oft-quoted passage, described her as a "Dollymop ... who ever prays and cooks and looks demure." Mrs. Cockran," he wrote, "whose assumed Puritanism but ill conceals the vixen, shines only when talking of elbow grease and the scouring of pots and pans."[49] Company officers wanted their daughters to be taught the ways and manners of "proper" young ladies, including instructions in deportment, music, and dancing. Mrs. Cockran's apparent difficulties in communicating such ornamental skills resulted in only eighteen girls being enrolled in the school by 1829. Her husband considered the fur traders' desire to have their daughters educated in such refined skills to be pretentious. Red River society, he concluded, "not being so highly polished as to meet their approbation, they wish to make the offspring of the Indian Wives accomplished Ladies all at once."[50] When David Jones's wife arrived in 1830, she took over duties at the school for girls, while Anne Cockran moved with her husband to the lower settlement.

In the summer of 1831, a day school was established for Métis children living in the new Grand Rapids parish. A two-room building was erected by Cockran, who reported to the CMS in August of 1831 that seventeen boys and six girls were in attendance.[51] "They are learning very fast," wrote schoolmaster W. K. Smith, "and have adopted the fashion and customs of Europeans: they have cropt their heads."[52] Two years later, the number of students had risen to over sixty, approximately half of whom were female.

In undertaking his educational initiatives, Cockran realized that a traditional, British public school style of education would serve little purpose in the communication of Christian values at the Rapids mission. Instead, he devised a plan to establish an industrial school in the parish, where children would be taught such "practical" skills as carpentry, farming, animal husbandry, spinning, weaving, and knitting. The missionary considered these skills more appropriate to Red River than academic subjects. Their importance being akin to the centrality of agriculture and its affiliated skills in the process of conversion, they would, Cockran believed, lay the critical foundation for the religious instruction of parishioners. He claimed that his plan presented the only legitimate alternative to the fur trade. If the scheme failed, Cockran wrote to the society in 1833;

> our present Congregations must return again to their woods, and seek for
> clothing from the back of the beaver. There is no general market for anything

except furs. Therefore, a man must either clothe his family by manufacturing the material raised by his own industry, or hunt furs to clothe them.[53]

As Cockran was establishing his school at the Rapids, David Jones was founding the Red River Academy near the Forks in 1832. Jones's intention was to provide a more refined education to the sons and daughters of Hudson's Bay Company officers. Tuition was set at £35 per student per year to cover the cost of education and board. John Macallum, a graduate of King's College in Aberdeen, was sent to Red River by the Church Missionary Society in 1833 (though he was not ordained until 1844) and was appointed master at the academy. For the position of school governess, company officers hoped that they could find a woman who could teach "the ornamental as well as useful branches of Education; in short an accomplished well-bred lady, capable of teaching music, drawing, &c &c, of conciliating disposition and mild temper."[54] Mary Lowman, a widow described as a " clever, unsurpassed woman," served in the position for two years and was well liked by company officers. The course of instruction embraced such subjects as "reading, writing, arithmetic, geography, the use of globes, history ... catechetical information ... bookkeeping, algebra, mathematics, Latin [and] Greek."[55] While the Red River Academy was initially successful, a number of company gentlemen took issue with their children receiving education under the same roof as the Indian students that Jones still maintained at the settlement. Earlier, George Simpson had made his views known to Jones when he wrote the missionary that "we consider it very desirable that the young ladies should have as little discourse with the native women in this country as possible."[56] Consequently, Jones, who was the senior missionary at Red River and deferential to Simpson and the company, decided to have the Indian school re-established at the Rapids Church. Cockran took exception to Jones's action and ended up sending the children on to his school at the Indian settlement. The Red River Academy declined after 1840. Mary Lowman had left the school in 1835 to marry Chief Factor James Bird, while Macallum was accused of employing overly severe measures in the disciplining of his students. Letitia Hargrave, the wife of Chief Factor James Hargrave at York Factory, described the nature of the academy's troubles:

*They say that Mr. Macallum's school is going to wreck. Children who have
had duck, geese and venison 3 times a day are supposed to suffer from
breakfasts of milk and water with dry bread, severe floggings and confinement
... the boys and girls are constantly feinting.*[57]

As well, Macallum became embroiled in a dispute with the new governess, a
Miss Allen, described by Letitia Hargrave as "really very queer and foolish."[58]
Enrollment dropped considerably during the 1840s, and the academy, after "declining
in popularity and usefulness for some time past" according to George Simpson, closed
its doors in the summer of 1859.[59]

In their 1835 "Report on the State of Religion," Jones and Cockran described
the status of education in Red River. The Grand Rapids school, under schoolmaster
Donald Gunn, had seventy Métis and twenty-five Indian children enrolled. The average attendance, according to Cockran, totalled between fifty and fifty-five as "at
certain seasons the grown up children are required to assist their parents in their
farming operations."[60] Other Protestant schools in Red River included a day school
and Sunday school under teacher Peter Garrioch at the upper church, a school at Frog
Plain under John Pritchard, a school at Image Plain (Middlechurch) under Richard
Stevens, and the Indian school at St. Peter's under Joseph Cook and John Smith, two
Métis catechists. As well, David Jones administered the Red River Academy at the
upper parish. In 1837, Cockran complained to the CMS that the schoolhouse at the
lower church was badly in need of repair. During the winter months, he noted, the
cold weather forced the children to wrap their blankets around themselves while "the
ink often congeals in the pen."[61] Cockran superintended a group of twenty men from
the parish who completed renovations to the log structure in the fall of 1837. Their
improvements, it was noted, substantially increased the structure's ability to withstand the harsh elements of a Red River winter.[62]

The school at the Grand Rapids enjoyed a slow growth in the period between
1831 and 1840, despite a crop failure in the parish in 1836 and a serious influenza
outbreak that occurred in the spring and summer of 1835, killing a large number of
young children in the parish.[63] Attendance declined in the decade that followed,
however. Other Anglican schools in Red River also experienced a drop in enrollment
in this period. This decline was most likely the result of the serious economic malaise

that affected the settlement in the 1840s. In the previous decade, the lower settlement had experienced a certain economic vitality and social homogeneity, though its settlers shared a growing disenchantment among the Métis of Red River with the leadership of the HBC and their control of all aspects of settlement administration and prices. (To some degree, these concerns were alleviated in 1835 by the company's expansion of the Council of Assiniboia to include more representatives from the Métis communities, and by the creation of a new judicial administration.) A diversified economy based upon small scale agriculture, the buffalo hunt, the fisheries, and the fur trade, seemed to offer a measure of economic security within the settlement. During the 1840s, however, events occurred in Red River that seriously challenged this outlook. Limited employment with the Hudson's Bay Company, growing opposition to the company's monopolistic economic control, and hardening social lines contributed to the rise of the free-trade movement as well as to growing tensions between the classes within Red River society. The decline of the buffalo hunt as the dwindling herds moved further from the settlement had its impact on many in the parish, as traditional sources of income came under threat. As Red River endured this period of economic and social transformation, interest in education, or at least in the kind of education offered by the Church Missionary Society, waned. After 1860, at St. Andrew's, and after the transition from a society that had once paralleled the environment of the fur-trade post to a community that was evolving more or less into "a little Britain in the wilderness," education would once again play an important role in the development of the parish community.

Throughout the 1830s, the numbers of retiring company servants and their families arriving in Red River increased. The parish at the Rapids witnessed a steady rise in the English-speaking Métis population during this period. In his correspondence with the society, Cockran noted that, by 1833, his congregation averaged 250 people, though many were "erratic" in their attendance at church. Less than one half of the families in the parish were headed by European males, most of whom were characterized by the missionary as having come into the country when they were youths "without any fixed principles."[64] This population was scattered along both sides of the Red River for a distance of approximately twelve miles in a "country without roads, full of swamps and miry creeks."[65] Cockran spent a good deal of his time travelling by horse in the summer and carriole in winter, visiting the homes of his parishioners, baptizing both children and adults, visiting the sick, and generally lecturing on the evils of the fur trade. The missionary fulfilled many roles in the lower settlement, acting in his own words as "priest, clerk, schoolmaster, arbitrator, agricultural director, [and] funeral manager."[66] Services were scheduled every Sunday and Tuesday evening at the Rapids church, while prayer meetings were held every Wednesday. Cockran himself maintained a busy schedule, preaching Sunday mornings at the Rapids, Sunday afternoons at the middle church and Tuesday evenings back at the Rapids.[67] In a seven-month period in 1841, he claimed to have baptized 122 individuals, married fifteen couples, buried twenty-one parishioners, and admitted twelve people as communicants.[68]

In 1834, Cockran wrote the CMS asking that David Jones take over preaching duties at the middle church so that he might devote more attention to the Indian settlement. His efforts there, he claimed, had been confined to weekdays "when mens' minds are full of secular concerns."[69] Later, Cockran pointed out to the secretaries the necessity of acquiring another minister for Red River to take over duties at the Indian settlement. This missionary's plan was to see a resident minister located at each of the upper, middle, lower and Indian parishes. When John Smithurst was sent to replace the departed David Jones in 1839, Cockran took over responsibility for the upper and middle churches. Clerical duties at the lower church were shared between Cockran and Smithurst, with the latter missionary assigned the task of administering the church, school, and mission farm at St. Peter's. In September of 1842, the Rev. Abraham Cowley arrived in Red River and was stationed at the Rapids. Between 1842 and 1846, Cowley shared responsibility with Cockran for the upper, middle and Rapids parishes.[70] Cowley, a product of the CMS training school at Islington College, eventually became Cockran's assistant at the Indian settlement in 1854. He remained in Rupert's Land until his death in 1887.

Life could be difficult for the European missionary in Red River, especially during the long winter months. The intense cold presented a formidable barrier to travel, lodging, and construction in the settlement. Even short trips by carriole could produce severe frostbite, while log buildings were difficult to heat and subject to the shifting and heaving of ground-frost. Cracks and fissures running below mission buildings at the Rapids often split the walls and floors, allowing in the harsh winter cold. Bread and vegetables stored in the parsonage cellar froze "solid as stones,"[71] according to Cockran, and "silvery particles of ice," caused by the congealed breath of the congregation, coated the interior of the church, giving it the appearance of a "temple cut from a rock of ice."[72] Combating the cold proved to be an expensive proposition. Aside from the cost of repairing damaged buildings, Cockran outlined to the society the added expense of food, clothing, and firewood during the winter months. Food consumption, he claimed, doubled in winter, while the price of firewood rose to between £9.10 and £14 for one season's supply.[73] The extra clothing necessary for winter also proved costly. Along with leggings and moccasins, the missionary was forced to purchase a "duffle capote which we wear over 3 shirts, viz. one flannel, another of linen and another of leather, [and] a cloth coat and vest."[74]

Despite the severity of the climate and Cockran's belief that "it is the intense cold of winter which produces the peculiar apathy of the Indian character,"[75] the missionary remained optimistic throughout the 1830s regarding the future of the church's efforts at the lower settlement. By the end of the decade, however, much of his zeal had disappeared. He expressed disappointment that his parishioners had not adopted British practices to the extent he felt was necessary for both temporal success and spiritual salvation. Though the settlement might give the appearance of a rural English village, the people were still actively involved in hunting, trapping, and tripping for the company. Agriculture represented a portion of the seasonal economic cycle at the Rapids and was viewed by the Métis community as simply an adjunct to traditional ways of making a living. The missionaries' glowing reports of packed churches and increasing numbers of communicants and baptismal candidates often belied the reality of religious life in the lower settlement. Without public structures, the local church served as a meeting hall for inhabitants of the lower settlement. Church services were seen as an occasion for socializing and in favourable weather could attract large congregations. Moreover, comments by Cockran on the state of religion and mortality in the settlement often contradicted the enthusiasm of the statistical reports. Disparaging remarks regarding the "immorality" of Métis behaviour were frequent. "Heathenism surrounds us everywhere," Cockran wrote, often characterizing his work at the Rapids as "burdensome, tedious and gloomy."[76] Reflecting on how his admonitions to his parishioners "produced no effect," the missionary admitted in 1838 to being possessed of "an empty head and a shriveled heart."[77]

Throughout his journals and letters, Cockran often complained of ill health.

"My health has been sinking for some time past," the missionary wrote in August of 1838. "I cannot at present see anything that will inspire me with courage to persevere."[78] His complaints ranged from a hernia and nervous exhaustion to headaches, "stoppages in urine," and "flatulence in bowels."[79] The Church Missionary Society became concerned for the missionary's well-being and offered him a furlough to England. Cockran decided to stay on at the Rapids, however, until a suitable replacement could be found. In 1846, the Rev. Robert James was dispatched to the Red River, and Cockran, sensing that he would not be happy in England, decided to leave with his family for Toronto. One year later, his health restored and his spirits apparently rejuvenated, Cockran returned to Rupert's Land. He served at St. John's until 1851, whereupon he moved to the Indian settlement to replace John Smithurst.

Building the Stone Church

In late 1844, Cockran announced his intention to replace the wooden church at the Rapids with a new stone structure. The old church, he argued, was much too small, and very often people were excluded from services because of the lack of space. To expand the wooden church would not be economical, Cockran informed the society. The relatively short life-span and constant upkeep of wood structures in Red River ended up "costing ... more than houses of the best materials in Europe."[80] The cost of the project was estimated at £1,180. Money and materials raised by the congregation would account for a portion of the budget, while it was hoped the balance would be forthcoming from the society.[81] A committee was formed to superintend the gathering of materials and the actual construction of the building. Cockran felt buoyed by the response of his parishoners. "Silver and gold they have none; but stones, lime, shingles, boards, timber and labour were cheerfully contributed," he wrote in his journal in 1844.[82] The new church was to measure 81.5 feet by 40 feet and contain a bell tower and a "commondious porch [which would] exclude the cold air from the body of the Church in winter."[83] The first order of business in the summer of 1845 involved quarrying stones from the river edge. This process was superintended by Cockran and ended up costing more than was initially budgeted. Limestone used in the building of the church was generally quarried in the late summer and fall when river levels were low and workers could get at the shallow rock outcrops. The masons, under the direction of Duncan McRae, the Scottish-born stonemason who is known to have built many of the stone churches and houses in Red River, split and dressed the large slabs at the building site adjacent to the log church before they were assembled into the walls and tower. The large quantity of lime mortar required for the work was produced at a nearby kiln. Wood for the large timbers used in the construction of roof trusses came from a wooding camp at nearby Bird's Hill. The quantity of materials and labour services donated by local people shows up in a list contained in the Anglican Diocesan Archives in Winnipeg entitled *Materials furnished by Subscribers towards payment of their Subscriptions.* One hundred and five individuals are listed in the document, and beside each is their material and/or labour contribution as well as the monetary value of each. Materials provided include a specific quantity or *toise* (i.e., a French linear measurement of just under two metres) of stone, planks, bushels of lime, shingles, rations, draught oxen, tools, and nails. Donated labour included masonry work, carpentry, hauling stones, hewing wood, and manufacturing lime. John Tait, for instance, did much of the carpentry and built the pulpit, the reading desk and the box pews. James Corrigal provided 150 bushels of lime mortar, and one *toise* of stone, as well as £29-worth of labour. Donald McDonald, another local settler, provided 334 bushels of lime, a mortar-box, thirty-six pounds of dried meat, and fifteen days of labour, all valued at £110.10.6. The total monetary value of material and labour amounted to £355.3.11.[84] In late 1845, Cockran expressed his concern that the existing funds might be inadequate to finish the new structure. It was decided, therefore, to continue the work at a more leisurely pace as resources became available, and, by June the following year, Cockran reported the walls to have reached a height of ten feet, six inches.[85] Cockran, however, did not remain in the settlement. One month later, in July of 1846, he left Red River for his sabbatical in Toronto.

Cockran's successor, Robert James, seemed to place a low priority on the completion of the new stone church, perhaps because of his added duties as pastor at the middle church. Work on the structure progressed slowly over the next year until Cockran assumed superintendency on the project upon his return to the settlement in 1847.[86] In the late summer of 1848, James reported the roof to be finished and promised that the building would be open within a few months.[87] One year later, however, work was still continuing on the interior of the church. "The ceiling is finished," James declared in August of 1849, "and the windows are all in. The flooring is being laid and the pews are all made. John Tait, our active and ingenious carpenter is going on with the pulpit and desk."[88] A grant of £100 toward the completion of the church was received in 1849 from the Hudson's Bay Company. As well, £50 was given by David Anderson, the recently appointed bishop for the new diocese of Rupert's Land.[89] Anderson had planned to reside at the Big House at Lower Fort Garry, just north of St. Andrew's, which would make the lower church the new Anglican diocesan headquarters in Rupert's Land. The sudden death of John Macallum at the Red River Academy very soon after Anderson's arrival, however, prompted the bishop to take up residence at the upper settlement school, effectively making St. John's the new diocesan seat. At a ceremony at the Rapids on December 19, 1849, Anderson consecrated the new church, naming it St. Andrew's after the patron saint of Scotland.

St. Andrew's is a good example of Gothic Revival, the architectural style that was made popular in England in the late eighteenth century. The style appeared in Canada in the 1820s with the construction in 1829 of Notre-Dame de Montréal, designed by the well-known New York architect James O'Donnell. While Notre-Dame represents a major, monumental example of the Gothic Revival style, St. Andrew's was built on a much smaller scale, comparable with a number of stone churches in southern Ontario built in the 1820s and 1830s. The layout of the church is an example of the pre-Tractarian church design. Tractarianism was the name given to the religious principles of the Oxford "High Church" movement of the early to middle nineteenth century. The evangelical movement, with its emphasis upon the sermon over the formal service, an emphasis favoured by the CMS, featured the open hall and gallery, and the centrally located pulpit. The original side location of the altar at St. Andrew's reflected the early emphasis upon the sermon over the service or mass. With the decline of the evangelical influence in Red River after the arrival of Bishop David Anderson in 1849, the altar was moved back to the centre of the church beneath the east window and the pulpit relocated to the north side. Though some changes were made to the interior layout, St. Andrew's remains a fine example of a pre-Tractarian church in western Canada. Repairs and renovations have been carried out at the church over the years, the latest a major restoration carried out in 1995 by the federal and provincial governments in partnership with the parish. In 1972, St. Andrew's was declared of national "historical and "architectural" significance by the Historic Sites and Monuments Board of Canada.

St. Andrew's Church, photographed by H. L. Hime in 1858 (Provincial Archives of Manitoba).

The stone rectory at St. Andrew's built in 1854 and photographed by H. L. Hime in 1858 (Provincial Archives of Manitoba).

The Red River Academy in 1852. Founded by Rev. David Jones, the academy helped educate the children of HBC officers from all over Rupert's Land (Provincial Archives of Manitoba).

When Robert James and his wife first arrived at the Rapids in July of 1846, they found the parsonage house occupied by the chief recorder for the settlement, Adam Thom. Thom had been leased the property by John Smithurst, acting on behalf of the departed William Cockran. James moved temporarily to quarters at the Indian settlement, and a dispute with Thom arose over the occupation of the parsonage. In a letter to George Simpson in 1846, Thom stated that he initially expected to share residence of the parsonage with James. Smithurst, he claimed, had first proposed this scheme, and, while James initially agreed with the arrangement, he later balked and claimed the right to exclusive residence at the Rapids. Moreover, Thom charged that he and his wife had expected to rely on the produce from Cockran's farm for food and therefore had "omitted to provide for ourselves against the winter."[90] James, on the other hand, believed Thom's lease of the property to be automatically cancelled upon the arrival of the incumbent missionary at the Rapids.[91] Animosity developed between the two parties, and Thom characterized his relationship with the James's as "painful." In his letter to Simpson, the recorder described how "Mrs. James' manner and conversation are not such as either to sweeten or to dignify the nauseous pill."[92] As Smithurst realized that purchase of Cockran's mission property (valued at nearly £400) was well beyond James's means, he recommended to the CMS that they buy the land. This the society did, eventually turning over the house and farm to the Rev. James.

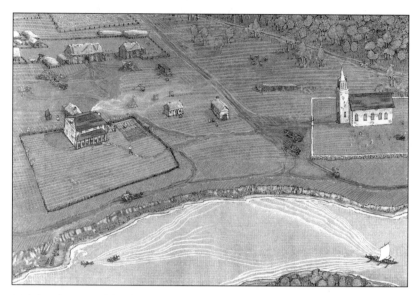

A modern depiction of the mission at St. Andrew's showing River Road and the various buildings of the mission, including the church, rectory, school, and farm buildings (Parks Canada).

Aside from his charge over the parish at the lower settlement, Robert James was also given responsibility for the middle church. According to the missionary, a total of 1,800 people inhabited the two parishes, a congregation that, according to him, presented a challenge that would "fill the hands of any one individual."[93] While pleased with the attendance at Sunday services and at his evening lectures on missionary endeavours in China, James noted that "many of my people still leave the Settlement for Hudson Bay [on the York boat brigades] or go to the hunting grounds."[94] Their absence for a number of months from religious instruction and the acculturative influence of the missionaries allowed the English-speaking Métis to remain removed from the influence of the church. But with the decline of the buffalo hunt after 1850, coupled with a reduction of employment opportunities with the Hudson's Bay Company, local people turned increasingly towards agriculture and animal husbandry for their livelihood. This emerging economy, which in time would separate St. Andrew's from a number of other parishes within the settlement, facilitated the authority of the missionaries among the Métis of the lower settlement.

By 1849, St. Andrew's had evolved from a fledgling mission outpost to a rural church that had made inroads into the lives of the largely Native community at the Rapids. William Cockran was the man most responsible for this development. Possessed of tremendous energy and zeal, he worked tirelessly towards the establishment of an Anglo-Christian ethic in Rupert's Land. Through the promotion of agriculture, education, and Christian morality, the missionary attempted to change Métis customs and lifestyle, and his seventeen-year tenure had a profound influence on the future of this group. The legacy of the fur-trade post, which for years had helped delimit the economic and cultural world of the English-speaking Métis in Rupert's Land, was in decline, the result of a changing Red River economy and the

Duncan McRae, c. 1880. A stonemason and native of Stornoway in the Scottish Hebrides, McRae constructed many of Red River's early limestone buildings, including St. Andrew's Church and Rectory. It was during work on the church that McRae fell from the scaffolding, leaving him partly disabled (Provincial Archives of Manitoba).

influence of the missionaries. Over the ensuing decades, this cultural shift was to play a significant role in the evolution of the community at St. Andrew's.

63

Chapter Four

Church and Company in Red River

In a 1970 article entitled "John West: A Study of the Conflict between Civilization and the Fur Trade," Anglican Church historian Arthur Thompson described the arrival of the missionaries in Rupert's Land as "the herald of advancing civilization and settlement [and] the doom of trapping and hence the fur trade. [They] also represented," he wrote, "the Christian standard of morality which was a rebuke to the free and unfettered life of the voyageur and Indian Trader."[1] This view has traditionally portrayed the history of the Northwest as the clash between civilization and the fur trade, or the civilization-savagery model as described in more recent historiography. Thompson, like W. L. Morton, Marcel Giraud, and George Stanley, viewed Red River society as a community delicately balanced between civilization and barbarism. According to this dichotomy, the fur trade was characterized as an unsophisticated, primitive economic system unchecked by an elaborate legal or social structure. In contrast, the term "civilization" is generally used by these historians to describe a sedentary community that enjoys a more highly diversified economy as well as a relatively sophisticated legal and social organization for the regulation and protection of a mutually interdependent people.[2]

"Evangelizing the Heathen will Militate Against Their Trade"

George Simpson. As HBC governor in Rupert's Land, Simpson often clashed with CMS missionaries, though he shared their view of aboriginal societies (Hudson's Bay Company Archives, Provincial Archives of Manitoba).

The Rev. David Anderson, the first Anglican bishop of Rupert's Land (Provincial Archives of Manitoba).

But such a traditional view of Red River history does not allow for the complexities of a society engaged in a mixed farming and hunting economy. Moreover, the relationship between the Hudson's Bay Company and the Church Missionary Society in Rupert's Land cannot be characterized as thoroughly antagonistic. No doubt the business of Christianizing the Indians and ultimately re-locating them to self-sufficient agricultural communities was, on the face of it, opposed to the goals of the fur trade. In reality, an evolutionary relationship existed between the two concerns, a relationship characterized by periods of conflict and co-operation. This was in part due to the structural similarity of the two organizations. Each had a governing body in London, a supervisor in North America (George Simpson, the Hudson's Bay Company's overseas governor, and, after 1849, David Anderson, as the Bishop of Rupert's Land), and a core of field workers, or fur traders and missionaries. It was at this level, in a community such as Red River or at an isolated fur post, that co-operation was often essential for survival.

The Hudson's Bay Company represented nominal authority in Rupert's Land after 1821, and missionaries entering the region were quickly made aware of the company's influence. Missionaries were dependent on the Hudson's Bay Company for transportation and supplies and, prior to the establishment of a particular mission, for shelter and hospitality. As well, they were forced to rely on the HBC for a multitude of services, as almost all carpenters and tradesmen were in the employ of the company. Fortunately, the company often provided free transportation and accommodation. The host factor usually served the best available food, and the quarters he provided customarily equaled those of the resident officer. A missionary's considerable freight was often transported at no cost and accommodations were found for the holding of chapel service for company employees. A cleric who attempted to alienate the commissioned gentlemen quickly found himself in an uncomfortable position. Gossip, one of the major characteristics of life at a fur-trade post, could quickly and irrevocably destroy a missionary's reputation. The case of the Rev. James Evans, a Methodist missionary at Norway House, serves as perhaps the best example. As Frits Pannekoek has noted, Evans's inability to get along with Chief Factor Donald Ross and others in the fur-trade hierarchy led to his ultimate expulsion from the post in 1846.[3]

While the missionary in Rupert's Land might privately express contempt for the behaviour and morals of the fur trader, he was in fact indebted to the company for its role as an agent of acculturation. Moreover, the missionary was faced with a social structure that included the fur trader. The relationship between a particular postmaster and the Native peoples who frequented his post became a significant consideration for the incoming missionary and for any observer who wished to understand the relationship between postmaster and missionary.[4] Historian Jaye Goossen has labelled this process the triangular nature of the Indian–trader–missionary relationship. If, on one hand, the missionary condemned the role of the secular trader as having a negative impact upon aboriginal society, he was also very aware of previous European contact and used it in his attempts to proselytize to the Indians of Rupert's Land. Conflict between missionaries and traders was often muted by this relationship.

The company, on the other hand, came to rely on the missionaries for the inculcation of regular work habits and the recognition of the sanctity of contracts.[5] In Red River, this dependence went ever further. The company saw the value of missionaries (both Catholic and Anglican) in exercising social control over a society of retired fur traders and their families. As well, the Hudson's Bay Company relied on the agricultural provisions provided by the Red River settlement, and the presence of the missionaries was considered crucial to the communication of proper agricultural techniques. The CMS promoted stability and order in Red River and came to view the company's monopoly as the best guarantee of these. As company and mission discovered the advantages of this relationship, and as each came to recognize that the other was in the country to stay, their relationship gradually improved.[6]

Aside from this realization of permanence, other factors affected the nature of the HBC – CMS relationship in Red River. The character of Red River society was evolving in the 1840s. Changing notions of race and class were being adopted by a growing Victorian, bourgeois elite within the settlement. Retired fur-trade officers, though often critical of missionaries, began to adopt the social values and biases of this group. Concepts of sexual purity, church marriage, and racial superiority were increasingly evident among some of the upper classes of Red River society throughout the 1840s. The influence of the church grew as its values gained greater acceptance within this community.

The Anglican and Catholic Churches, along with the Hudson's Bay Company, shared a common vision of the social structure of Red River society. This view envisioned the clergy, along with the retired and active commissioned gentlemen, as forming the ruling elite within the community and providing guidance for the lower orders. In his attempt to re-create in Red River the social order of the English rural parish, the missionary as parson, teacher, farmer, and lawgiver, enlisted the aid of the local company squirearchy.[7] The disagreements that did occur between church and company usually arose over the establishment of missions outside the Red River settlement. Within the community itself, representatives of the churches, the HBC, and the "principal settlers" sat on the council of Assiniboia, the governing body in the settlement. The members of this elite viewed themselves as the natural secular and religious rulers in a society increasingly fragmented along race and class lines.

By the 1840s, the Anglican missionaries in Red River had become sympathetic to the company, or at least to the kind of social order it represented within society.

When the issue of free trade, or the right to trade outside the monopoly of the HBC, came to a head in 1849, William Cockran, an outspoken critic of the fur trade, risked the ire of his Métis parishioners by siding with the HBC. Cockran's motive was simple. The company represented for him the only logical social and political order in Red River. To deny its monopoly would be to open the doors to an unshackled market economy that would lure Cockran's parishioners away from their riverlot farms and, ultimately, from his pastoral control. In the absence of a sound agricultural economy with secure and nearby markets, the missionary realized that, without the social hierarchy imposed by the company in Red River, the authority of the church would be diminished. The free-trade issue, which is discussed later in this chapter, was a complex affair and represented a turning point in church–company relations within the settlement.

Animosity characterized the early years of the relationship between the Anglican Church and the HBC in Red River. John West succeeded in alienating the gentlemen of the fur trade by publicly criticizing their morals, marriage practices, and treatment of aboriginal peoples. Confrontation with the commissioned gentlemen, whose personal and business interests were opposed by West in his energetic pursuit of evangelical goals, were exacerbated by the latter's intellectual rigidity. For West, the company demonstrated a lack of co-operation. His work, he claimed, "had already excited the fears of some of the chief factors and traders.... They fear that the extension of knowledge among the natives, and locating them in agricultural pursuits ... would operate as an injury to the fur trade."[8] The growing tension between himself and the company, West argued, was due to the fact that "general practice [in the fur trade] is opposed to that solicitude expressed for the moral and religious interests of the Natives and others."[9] In continually preaching against sexual promiscuity, lack of sobriety, and failure to keep the Sabbath, West grew disgusted with the "degeneracy of character" that he found in Rupert's Land. His exhortations won few friends for his cause. By attempting to expand his missionary endeavours beyond the confines of the settlement, he went beyond his role as HBC chaplain to the retired fur traders of Red River. Perceived as a threat by Simpson, the governor described West as "a man of no influence of character, extremely unpopular ... a bustling money making man of the world."[10] Although Simpson was eventually able to have West recalled, the legacy of the missionary's dispute with the company was important for the future development of the Church Missionary Society in Red River. It set the mission slightly apart from the company by claiming an interest divorced from the fur trade. As well, according to John Foster, it reserved for the church in Rupert's Land the right to comment in an appropriate manner on public and private behaviour.[11]

In its minutes of council of the Northern Department for July 5, 1823, the HBC adopted resolutions that seemingly supported missionary activity within its territories. These resolutions instructed chief factors and chief traders to facilitate and assist the work of the CMS, help encourage industry and morality among the Indians, and promote divine services on Sundays.[12] Privately, however, Governor Simpson expressed little sympathy with the missionary cause. Historian E. E. Rich has stated that: "[i]t is difficult, if not impossible, to find in his [Simpson's] vast correspondence any evangelizing impulse, or indeed any genuine religious conviction."[13] Simpson's reasons for his opposition to the expansion of the church outside of Red River were essentially economic. The promotion of Indian settlements and mission schools at fur-trade posts, he argued, would place tremendous strain upon the company's food resources.[14] A sedentary population not engaged in trapping and trading would, in the event of crop failures, come to rely on the meagre supplies of isolated company posts. While a certain level of missionary activity could be permitted in Red River, such practices, Simpson believed, were to be discouraged elsewhere.

With the arrival of David Jones in Red River in 1823, relations improved between the CMS and the company. This improvement was due to a number of reasons. First, the CMS realized that encouraging the policy of extending missions beyond the confines of the settlement would only create tension with the HBC and ultimately impede the progress of its work in Rupert's Land. John West's troubles had been enough to demonstrate to the society the efficacy of maintaining close ties with the company officers. Second, Jones's personality – his apparent humility and ability for compromise – posed less of a threat to the interests of the fur trade. Thirdly, the gradual change of company personnel after the union of 1821 proved effective in improving the relationship between the new missionary and the commissioned officers. For instance, the new governor of Assiniboia, Robert Pelly, possessed definite evangelical sympathies and was generally supportive of the aims of the church in Rupert's Land. As the bitterness of the rivalry between the Hudson's Bay and North West Companies gradually receded after the union of 1821, the monopoly took a less suspicious view of missionary activity, at least in Red River. Church and company reached an accommodation, due primarily to the influence of the new missionaries. As John Foster noted:

> *Jones' qualities of patience and tolerance paid dividends. A workable relationship evolved between the officers and the clergy. It was based on a realistic assessment of the limits of co-operation. A delicate balance was achieved in which neither party demanded more nor gave less than was necessary.*[15]

It was, however, the long ministry of William Cockran, the man whom J. J. Hargrave called the real founder of the Anglican Church in Rupert's Land, that had the farthest-reaching impact upon the association of church and company in Red River.[16] Appointed as assistant chaplain to the HBC in 1825, Cockran was uneasy with his clerical responsibilities to the company. He considered the fur trade to be the greatest impediment to the Christianization of the Indians in the Northwest and was frequently critical of company policy and practice. In his early years in the settlement, Cockran maintained a low profile in his relations with the commissioned gentlemen. By the early 1830s, after his move to the Rapids, the missionary wrote pious and vehement diatribes to the society against those "possessed of an aversion to civilization and Christianity."[17] The fur traders, he charged, "worship no God except profit and pleasure, acknowledge no Saviour; [and] know no Sabbath."[18] He accused the HBC of forcing the Native to aid in their moneymaking schemes. "They never converted a single native," he wrote, "or raised one higher in this life, than the hope of one day starving to death for want of food."[19] Cockran believed that the fur trade impoverished and depopulated the country. He charged the company with deliberately setting out to impede the progress of the settlement through

the exclusion of European immigrants, the preventing [of] any servant
coming to the settlement unless he purchases. The reduction of all country
produce in price while they increase the price of land and reduce the lots
from 10 chains to 6 in breadth, [and] the exclusion of Indians from
coming to the settlement.[20]

The company, according to Cockran, tried to thwart his plans from establishing schools and farms among the Indians at Netley Creek. Their opposition was subtle. "They will do nothing tangible against the word," he wrote, "but they proceed by insinuations and sapping our plans."[21] According to the missionaries, the company opposed church goals because they feared the loss of influence over Native people. Cockran wrote to the society that:

all the discerning among them perceive that sooner or later the evangeliz-
ing of the heathen will militate against their trade and prevent them
gathering filthy lucre by handfuls as they do at present; therefore they have
always considered their principal safety to arise from delays and failures.
Benevolent schemes have always been received with coolness, delayed as
long as possible, and when set on foot treated with such indifference, scorn
and malevolent as to ensure failure.[22]

For Cockran the process of civilizing the Métis population – the "progeny of the adulterer and the whore," as he chose to describe them – was a long and difficult undertaking. "The voyageur's very bones must be broken," he cautioned, "wearisome months must be appointed as his portion, to give him time to remember the transgressions of 30 or 40 years."[23] In a long and strident letter to the secretaries of the society in July of 1833, Cockran described what he labelled as the "pitiful" life of the Red River émigré. He considered the recent English-speaking immigrants from the environment of the company post, those who now comprised the bulk of settlers at St. Andrew's, to be culturally and morally corrupt. The following passage, quoted at length, gives an indication of the missionary's provocative view of fur-trade culture in Rupert's Land:

The Hon. Company's servants seldom continue more than 3 years at the same post, and often only one. In the summer, the whole of their time is occupied in voyaging upon the rivers, carrying out the furs which they had traded in the winter from the Indians; and returning with a new outfit for the trade of the ensuing year. During the summer there are plenty of opportunities for the young voyageur to give vent to his licentious passions; at every post he will find women who will do anything for hire. He has no principles to contend with; he therefore finds it easy to do what is most pleasant to corrupt nature and most popular with his companions. When the young voyageur came [sic] to his winter quarters, he finds he wants many things to fit him for this new existence which he has entered upon. He wants his leather coat, trousers, mittens, duffle socks and shoes, all then must be made and kept in repair. He has no time to do this himself; he applies to an Indian who has got some daughters, or two or three wives; here he is quickly served, he makes a present to the head of the family, they set to work, and make all ready for him, he comes at a certain time for his clothes, brings a little rum, and makes the principal persons of the family merry. He sleeps there, and out of gratitude and courtesy, the old woman puts her daughter to bed with him, or the Indian may give him one of his three wives, who lays under his displeasure; thus the unfortunate voyageur forms his connexion with the Natives, and raises an offspring. He may continue here two or three years, and enjoy the benefit of his helpmate. He goes off in the summer, returns in the autumn, and perhaps find the same young women given to another. This does not distract his mind, he forms another connexion as speedily as possible; by this time he believes that he cannot get on without a woman. The next time he leaves his winter quarters, he perhaps is sent to a post 600 or 1000 miles from all his former wives; he forgets them at once, and serves himself for the time being, with the first that comes to hand; he looks for neither beauty nor virtue; if she is a woman, that is sufficient. The same course is run until old age and grey hairs are upon him; his body emaciated with the fatigues of voyaging, and means too scanty to cast a robe once a year over all his adulterous progeny. His case being desperate, he thinks of making an effort to remedy the errors of 30 or 40 years, by one mighty struggle. Out of his many connexions he finds someone that ranks above the rest. He selects her to be the companion of his old age; collects his multifarious progeny from the ends of the earth, (for he has been every where through all this Continent) and bends his course to Red River, with a worn-out constitution, with small means, with a woman that knows none of the duties of civilized life, with a dispirited family who know nothing but what the heathen have taught them, who have no interest in each other's welfare, to begin life anew, to learn with his heathen family how to discharge his duty to God, his neighbour, and his own soul.[24]

Cockran, like West and Jones before him, directed much of his energies towards condemning the fur-trade practice of country marriages. Prior to 1830, almost all fur traders in the Northwest had entered into liaisons of this kind with Native women.[25] George Simpson, along with the senior officers of the company, had previously attempted to block the introduction of European women into the company's territories, considering them to be fragile, demanding, and useless in forming trade alliances.[26] Simpson's marriage to his cousin Frances in 1830, however, served to reverse marriage trends for at least a small handful of the fur-trade elite in Rupert's Land. Those few company officers who were allowed furloughs to England and Scotland sought out potential marriage partners as a sign of their prominent status within the company hierarchy. The insistence of the clergy in Red River upon church marriages had caused some of these commissioned gentlemen to reconsider their country liaisons and to seize the opportunity to dispose of an "old concern" and acquire a newer, younger and lighter-skinned wife. Their Native wives were "turned off" as it came to be known in fur-trade parlance. George Simpson, for example, left one country wife, Betsy Sinclair, a daughter of Chief Factor William Sinclair and Nahovway, a Cree woman, in the care of Robert Miles, the clerk at Moose Factory. Another Native wife, Margaret Taylor, went to live with Pierre Leblanc, the stonemason responsible for building Lower Fort Garry. Other fur-trade officers followed suit. J. G. McTavish, William Connolly, Roderick MacKenzie, and John Stewart all abandoned their Native wives.

According to Sylvia Van Kirk, "turning off" created much hardship among country wives. Often, these women were no longer accepted into Native or non-Native society and ended up leading lonely and difficult lives.[27]

Many other officers, however, especially those of a lower rank, remained with their aboriginal wives and created enduring family unions that were an integral part of life at the fur post and later at Red River. Upon arriving in the colony, many couples were married according to church rite,

Catherine Truthwaite, the Métis wife of Thomas Truthwaite, who lived on lot 105 in St. Andrew's parish (Thomas Sinclair Collection. Courtesy of the Sinclair family).

despite having lived as man and wife for a number of years. And, as more recent quantitative research by Brian Gallagher has demonstrated, the majority of HBC personnel in Red River continued to marry "daughters of the country" as late as 1870. His data reveals that although a number of company officers in charge of Red River posts before 1845 married European women, this trend reversed itself after that date as senior company personnel in the settlement married Métis women who were, for the most part, the highly acculturated members of the merchant elite.[28] Gallagher's conclusions call into question, not only the accepted view that marriage practices in the fur trade evolved before 1870 according to increasing racial sensibilities (with Indian partners giving way to Métis, and later, European wives), but the notion that racial tension represented an important and even central theme in Red River history before 1870. The endogamous marriage practices of the majority of Red River society were less the result of racial loyalties than they were the product of a hardening class system and the oligarchical rule in the settlement of a merchant-company-clerical elite. For the well-off trader and company gentleman in Red River, the choice of a wife had little to do with her race and everything to do with her family connections.

The introduction of non-Native women into fur-trade life – at least as marriage partners for some senior company officers – and the growing popularity of

Sarah McNab, the Métis wife of trader Andrew McDermot (Thomas Sinclair Collection. Courtesy of the Sinclair family).

church marriages were partly due to the efforts of missionaries such as William Cockran. They urged company people to relinquish their country marriages for unions within the church. Missionary exhortations against fur-trade marriage practices were most vehement when directed toward officers who had retired to Red River. Fur traders settling in a "civilized" society and earning their living by the plow, Cockran believed, were obliged to have their marriage unions sanctioned within the Church of England. If company officers in the settlement continued to marry the increasingly acculturated Métis daughters of Red River merchants and other HBC personnel, they were expected to do so according to the matrimonial rites of the church.

The Foss-Pelly trial of 1850, a complex affair rooted in increasingly Victorian attitudes toward women and their "virtue," as well as in personal animosities among the leaders of Red River society, has frequently been used to demonstrate the growth of racial tension within the settlement. It is not important here to go into the details of the story, as it has been recounted at great length elsewhere.[29] Suffice to say, however, that the trial did help confirm the alliance of church and company within the settlement. The notions of racial superiority inherent within the missionaries' view of Native society were to some degree reflected by a handful of traders and their European wives, who resented the prominent position in local society of Sarah Ballenden, the Métis wife of Red River chief factor John Ballenden. If the attitudes expressed at the trial reinforced the notion among some that a certain moral weakness was innate in women of even partly Indian extraction, the scandal had little effect upon marriage practices within the settlement, although, as Van Kirk has argued, within their social circle, the acculturated Métis daughters of wealthy HBC families studiously endeavoured to disassociate themselves from their Native heritage.[30] More importantly, the scandal seemed to have little impact within the larger population of Red River. The settlement's hunters, merchants, and farmers continued their daily and seasonal activities more than likely unaware, and no doubt uncaring, of the busy-body proclivities of the clergy and company squirearchy.

Although William Cockran often expressed his antipathy toward company officers in Red River, he rarely criticized Governor Simpson. Even in his private correspondence with the CMS, the missionary expressed an almost grudging admiration for the "little emperor." "By economy and prudent management," Cockran wrote, "he has reduced their [the HBC's] expenses to a bagatelle, and made their gains princely."[31] The missionary refused to be over awed by Simpson, or to be co-opted in the same manner that David Jones had been. When Simpson sought to bring the Wesleyan Methodists into Rupert's Land in the early 1840s, Cockran expressed his opposition to the scheme. By aligning himself with the Methodists and their emphasis upon a more itinerant Christianity unencumbered by the trappings of "civilization," Simpson endeavoured to counteract the influence of the CMS. The company, Cockran charged, was hoping to discourage the work of the Church of England. He wrote, "they have brought the Wesleyans into the country at their own expense and place them down at the principal posts."[32] For Cockran, Methodism only reinforced "barbarism" in the country and played into the hands of the fur traders. After his initial meeting with James Evans, he described to the society how

> the doctrine of the Wesleyans [is] 'We will not civilize one family. Rupert's Land is destined by God to remain forever in a state of barbarism. We shall only preach the Gospel to the Indian to comfort him when he is traveling the wood.' This is very charitable indeed! They propose that the body of the Indian should be made over as a legacy for the benefit of the Fur Traders, and his soul made an offering to God.[33]

Cockran protested the presence of the Methodist missionaries. He accused the company of granting facilities to "interlopers," while placing impediments in the path of the CMS. "I am certainly at a loss," he wrote, "how to construe the present conduct of the Governor, my principles are perfectly known to him."[34]

Four Methodist missionaries James Evans, William Mason, Robert Rundle, and George Barnley, were originally invited to Rupert's Land by the Hudson's Bay Company. By 1848, only Mason remained. Evans left after becoming embroiled in a dispute with Donald Ross and his wife at Norway House and being accused of an "unmethodistical and unclerical" intercourse with three Indian women. Barnley departed after quarreling with Chief Factor Robert Miles at Moose Factory and Rundle left the Northwest after having broken his arm. Although Mason remained, he defected to the Church Missionary Society in 1854.[35] Cockran feared the Methodists would attempt to establish themselves at Red River, especially at St. Andrew's.[36] This threat never materialized.

Company attitudes to specific missionaries and missionary activities varied. The particular role of the church in Red River, however, was seen by the HBC to be one of effective social and political control. In this way, the aspirations of church and company, and indeed the very under pinnings of their Anglo-Christian world view, were in fact synonymous. When Simpson wrote to Benjamin Harrison, the secretary of the Church Missionary Society, in 1825, he stated that "few individuals in the country ... conceive that civilization is injurious to the fur trade.... I can with safety assure you that no exertion on our part would be wanting to forward the views of the Society."[37] When overtures were made by the CMS toward establishing agricultural missions outside the colony, though, Simpson grew wary. In attempting to discourage such schemes, he noted to Harrison that "the Gentlemen of the Catholic Mission have conducted themselves with great propriety throughout the year, confining their attention entirely to the object thereof in which they are most zealous."[38] For Simpson, the Roman Catholic mission in Red River under Father Provencher most effectively suited the company's interests both inside and outside the settlement. Itinerant clerics who did not attempt to establish Native agricultural settlements were considered compatible with the more obvious economic goals of the fur trade. The Church Missionary Society and William Cockran, of course, were opposed to the idea of itinerancy:

I am sure [Cockran wrote] that if I set out to convert the heathen by a journeying expedition, I should meet with more wolves and foxes than Indians, consequently I should become a common trapper, and forget the end for which I came into this country.[39]

Cockran's assertion, exaggerated though it may be, points out his strong views regarding the necessity for agricultural settlement among aboriginal peoples as forming the cornerstone of British Christianity.

The shared principles that existed between the Hudson's Bay Company and the Protestant missionaries in Rupert's Land can be explained by their mutual belief in the supremacy of the white man. While disagreements and antagonisms occurred, this basic point was never forgotten. The Rev. James Evans case is a good example. The conflict that occurred between Evans and Chief Factor Donald Ross at Norway House was one of personalities, created by Mrs. Ross and Mrs. Evans vying for leadership of the social hierarchy at the post. It had little to do with any notion that the conflict between the fur trade and "civilization," as represented by the missionary, was inevitable or even predictable.

The Anglican Clergy and Free Trade

After the union of the two competing fur-trade companies in 1821, and the migration of redundant servants to Red River, George Simpson attempted to develop a strategy that would provide a market for the colonists and a livelihood for the new population of resident free-men. Simpson's plan was two-fold and was designed to protect the monopoly of the HBC in Red River and throughout Rupert's Land. The first part involved an attempt to generate economic opportunities that would occupy the energies of the settlers; the second was to fit the colonists into the pattern of trade, transportation, and supply of provisions that would help support the company's extensive trade network. The result was the creation of such enterprises as the Buffalo Wool Company, the Assiniboine Wool Company, a tallow company, a local distillery, the cattle trade, a flax and hemp project, and a succession of experimental farms within the settlement. Most of these projects, however, were failures. The wool and tallow companies eventually folded, the first experimental farm was a failure, and the distillery constructed at Lower Fort Garry was never operated.[40]

With the lack of economic opportunities available to the entrepreneurs of Red River, a limited private trade in furs developed alongside that of the Hudson's Bay Company. During the 1820s and 1830s, relations between the company and the private traders appeared harmonious as the former often found the private trade useful for the conduct and servicing of its own business. A handful of "private adventurers," who were in effect licensed by the company, such as Andrew McDermot, James Sinclair, Norman Kittson, Augustin Nolin, and Narcisse Marion, built up considerable wealth and were considered among the elite of the district. In the 1840s, this harmonious relationship ended. The growing population at Red River, the development of overland American markets, and the inability of a younger generation of Métis to secure economic opportunities within the settlement served to increase the number of free traders operating outside the company's monopoly.[41] Simpson took prompt measures against these entrepreneurs (most notably Norman Kittson and Andrew McDermot). Licenses were revoked and trade goods destined for the free trade were no longer freighted to Rupert's Land aboard company ships. As well, goods were seized and mail was censored. Resentment and open defiance increased among the populace as the HBC invoked measures designed to enforce its outdated monopoly. In 1846, the HBC was able to secure a British military detachment for Red River, the Sixth Regiment of Foot. Ostensibly brought to the colony to thwart the designs of an expansionist American government during the Oregon crisis, the HBC hoped their arrival in the settlement would also help to discourage the continuation of the free trade in furs in the Red River district. Their two-year stay brought tranquillity for the company and economic prosperity to the settlement. The settlers had a ready market for their grain, produce, and meat, and men like McDermot did exceedingly well as a result of the soldiers' purchasing power.[42]

This period of prosperity was short-lived, however. The Sixth Regiment departed Red River in 1848, and once again the company's monopoly was challenged by independent traders. In 1849, Chief Factor John Ballenden arrested Guillaume Sayer, a Métis free trader, on a charge of illegally trafficking in furs. Sayer was tried by the General Quarterly Court of Assiniboia and was found guilty. The jury, however, recommended mercy, and Sayer was set free. The result was a clear victory for the Métis entrepreneurs of the settlement. To the cry of *"La commerce est libre"* from the armed Métis stationed outside the courtroom, the monopoly of the Hudson's Bay Company in Rupert's Land was effectively broken. Red River was no longer subordinate to the company's larger economic strategy; the settlement had now acquired an economic life of its own.[43]

The Anglican Church in Red River played a significant role in the free-trade issue. The alliance between church and company was solidified during this period as the clergy demonstrated their unwillingness to support the economic aspirations of their Métis parishioners. Although critical of the HBC, they could not counsel open rebellion against their rule, afraid that chaos and a loss of social control would result. If the fur trade was thrown open, they believed, the settlers would be reluctant to remain on their small, generally unproductive farms in the lower settlement, preferring to share in the more lucrative opportunities of the private trade. Frits Pannekoek has argued that among the CMS missionaries in Red River only William Cockran was supportive of the aims of the Métis community, but that he chose to stop short of counselling armed revolt.[44] While it was true that Cockran was in disfavour with company officers at Red River and was to an extent ostracized by his clerical peers in the settlement, he could not support the kind of challenge to authority implicit in the free-trade cause. Cockran had traditionally been held in high esteem by the English-speaking Métis community at St. Andrew's. His antipathy toward high church principles and the social elite of Red River society, his style of delivering extemporaneous sermons, and his abilities behind the plow had brought the missionary a good deal of popularity with his congregation at the lower settlement and later at Portage La Prairie. But like other Church of England clergy in Red River, including Cowley, James, and Smithurst, he considered the free-trade crisis a "popish plot." The violent opposition of the French-speaking Métis and some of their English-speaking brethren was, Cockran believed, tantamount to rebellion against the crown.[45] In a letter to Simpson in November of 1849, he commented, "the excitement which was got up by interested persons to answer their own ends is perfectly subsided. All that cunning and malice could do was tried to urge the populace to acts of violence."[46] Threats of violence at St. Andrew's were diffused by Cockran, who still visited the parish regularly, and by the resident minister, Robert James. Despite Cockran's traditional popularity at the Rapids, however, some members of the parish threatened to burn his house after the missionary made speeches in support of Adam Thom, the chief recorder in the settlement and the arch-enemy of the Métis community. But because the movement was described by the clergy as more a plot by the Church of Rome than an expression of anti-company sentiment, the English-speaking Métis community was reluctant to force a confrontation. Cockran, along with the rest of the Anglican clergy in Red River, tried to convince their congregations that a Protestant's soul was in mortal danger if he allied himself for any reason with the French-speaking Métis Catholic faction within the settlement.[47]

Also embroiled in the controversy was the Rev. John Smithurst at the Indian settlement. Originally asked by the company to fulfill the role of chaplain, he refused, preferring instead to continue Cockran's efforts with the new Native mission. During the free-trade crisis, Smithurst steadfastly counselled his parishioners not to join with the cause of the Métis. As a member of the Council of Assiniboia, Smithurst sided with the HBC. In the summer of 1849, he wrote to George Simpson charging that the Indians at his settlement are "threatened with fire and sword if they do not aid the Halfbreed party."[48] While these Native settlers chose not to openly join the free-trade movement, they nonetheless resented Smithurst and his apparent alliance with the company. His position in the colony quickly became untenable. At first, he remained firm in his intention to wait out the storm of protest. To Simpson, he wrote: "I fear that were I to go now it might be regarded by the rebel party as a triumph, and perhaps encourage them in their attempts to get rid of others whom they dislike."[49] Two years later, however, Smithurst left Red River, unable to win back the confidence and respect of the settlement. The free-trade issue highlighted the Anglican clergy's distrust of the Catholic Church. By attempting, largely unsuccessfully, to drive a wedge between the English and French-speaking populations in the settlement, the CMS allied itself with the HBC and, in doing so, risked alienating their own congregations by denying the legitimate economic aspirations of the English-speaking Métis of the lower settlement.

The missionaries' interest in effective social control, and their belief that the Hudson's Bay Company represented the only viable administrative body within the settlement, had been demonstrated by the church's behaviour during the free-trade crisis. Earlier in that same decade, however, a dispute had arisen between the company and the Anglican Church in Red River, which severely strained relations between the two. Known as the "ordination crisis," it involved an attempt by Simpson to weaken the power of the CMS in the settlement. When in 1842 Cockran first expressed his desire to leave the colony for an extended sabbatical, George Simpson suggested to Abraham Cowley and John Roberts, two unordained and newly arrived CMS catechists, that they accompany the Rapids minister to Montreal to receive holy orders.[50] It was Simpson's plan to then have James Evans from the Methodists replace Cockran in the settlement, leaving Smithurst as the lone CMS representative in Red River. Simpson felt that he could more effectively control Evans, who demonstrated a greater willingness to go along with company policies and practices. Adam Thom, the chief recorder for Rupert's Land, argued Simpson's case and expressed his concern that the bishop of Montreal, George Jehosaphat Mountain, was not empowered to ordain Cowley and Roberts as ministers. This duty, he argued, could only be done by either the bishop of London or the archbishop of Canterbury. After heated exchanges between Smithurst and Thom, and extensive deliberations between company lawyers and CMS representatives in London, lasting over two years, a decision was made to have the bishop of Montreal travel to Red River and perform the ordination himself.[51] This the bishop did in 1844, spending a total of seventeen days in the settlement. In the end, Cockran chose not to leave the colony until 1846, and a good deal of animosity resulted, not only between Smithurst and Thom, but between a number of the commissioned gentlemen and the Anglican missionaries in Red River.[52]

In 1850, the Hudson's Bay Company sent Eden Colvile to Red River as the associate governor of Rupert's Land. The free-trade victory of the year before had served to tarnish the image of company control. The appointment of Colvile, it was hoped, would help restore lost prestige. Colvile's immediate problems in the settlement concerned the inept government of Major Cardwell (the head of the Chelsea Pensioners, a regiment of retired soldiers that had replaced the Sixth Regiment of Foot in 1848), racial and religious divisions involving the Métis and Scottish settlers, and the restoration of company power within the colony. He

Eden Colvile. The HBC's deputy governor in Rupert's Land between 1849 and 1852, Colvile took up residence at Lower Fort Garry, where he attempted to re-assert company control in the settlement after the successful Métis challenge to the HBC's trading monopoly (Provincial Archives of Manitoba).

turned out to possess a naturally conciliatory disposition and helped bring a degree of order to the settlement. Colvile's congenial attitude, however, belied a strong distrust of the Anglican missionaries. He was particularly adamant against the expansion of missions outside the settlement. In a letter to the governor and committee in London in July of 1852, Colvile characterized the missions as a "very heavy drain on the limited resources of the country, and under the present circumstances therefore we are not anxious that the number should be increased."[53] He particularly mistrusted William Cockran. The St. Andrew's missionary was the most vocal of the Red River clergy in the support of the expansion of missions, in particular the establishment of a settlement at Portage La Prairie. In a letter to Simpson, Colvile described Cockran as "almost a lunatic, and inclined to be mischievous."[54] When Smithurst decided to leave the country, Colvile wrote Simpson to inform him that Cockran would take over the Indian settlement. "I should be exceedingly glad," he commented, "if we were to lose this latter gentleman also, as he is very troublesome."[55]

Colvile was called upon during his short tenure in Red River to mediate the dispute between the Anglican Church and local Presbyterian settlers. Since the creation of the original Selkirk grant, the Scottish Presbyterians in Red River had been promised a minister of their own denomination. In the face of CMS control, they were forced to make do with Anglican clerics and their high church liturgy for a good number of years, a point of some friction within the community. Led by Alexander Ross, the Presbyterians waged a long campaign to secure their own minister, church, and burial ground in Red River. Colvile dealt extensively with Ross and Bishop David Anderson in attempting to find a solution to the problem, a problem that will be dealt with more extensively in Chapter Six.

The correspondence of a number of other officers gives an indication of company attitudes toward Anglican missionaries in this period. Donald Ross, for many years the chief factor at Norway House and later a resident of St. Andrew's, had very little respect for those who wore the clerical collar. Ross questioned whether the clergy were "loyal subjects for the Company."[56] The HBC, he asserted, was forced to contribute to the welfare of the missions. "Experience has taught us," he wrote to Colvile in

Andrew McDermot, n.d. A successful local trader licensed by the HBC, McDermot was a leader of the commercial elite in Red River (Provincial Archives of Manitoba).

1851, "that to make the Company establishments missionary stations is very detrimental to the interests of the Missions as well as those of the Service."[57] John Black, a chief trader at Upper Fort Garry, and prior to that the clerk at the Lower Fort, resented the superior attitudes of the clergy and their wives. According to Black, Mrs. Robert James, the wife of the incumbent at St. Andrew's, "turns up her nose and talks of the low depraved state of morality in the country generally and among the officers of the Fur Trade in particular."[58] For Simpson, the solution was to publicly concur with the aims of the church, while privately and quietly attempting to discourage and impede their various schemes. He explained to Ross:

> *The missionaries are troublesome people to deal with, though it may not*
> *be to let it be known generally. I think we should endeavour to neutralize*
> *the evil by encouraging all sects indifferently. Then such is the*
> *characteristic humility and charity of missionaries at the present day, as*
> *such as one sect breaks with us, all others will stick by us, and turning*
> *upon the occupant, will fight out battle.*[59]

The period after 1850 saw the continued development of an economy and culture that was increasingly removed from the pervasive influence of the Hudson's Bay Company. The Anglican missionaries who arrived in the settlement after 1840 influenced the evolving social and economic structure of the English-speaking components of the settlement. Missionaries such as James, Cowley, Smithurst, Anderson, and James Hunter, who arrived at St. Andrew's in the early 1850s after serving for a number of years at Cumberland House, did not have the agricultural background and skills of William Cockran and preferred the attitudes and perspectives of the European and Métis elite within Red River society over those of the Métis farmer/hunter class of the lower settlement. By the middle of the century, the Church Missionary Society had established itself as a relatively powerful evangelical body with missions located all over the world. The best of the society's students who trained at Islington College were sent to India. Rupert's Land was considered of marginal interest and was sent only those missionaries generally felt to be unqualified for duty elsewhere.[60] Smithurst and Cowley, for example, were described by their superiors as demonstrating great piety but little else.[61] Bishop Anderson was another unfortunate choice for the settlement. Cultured and punctilious, he displayed the conservatism and pedantry of the lower English gentry.[62] Anderson proved intransigent on a number of ecclesiastical issues and fought a vicious and protracted battle with the Presbyterian Scots in the settlement. Only James Hunter rose above the mediocre. Though he came from humble origins, Hunter possessed a decidedly superior intellect and a more complete education and succeeded in translating the gospels into Cree.

It is evident that the character of the Anglican mission in Red River was undergoing change. In the 1830s, William Cockran shaped his mission around the culture and practice of a society only recently removed from the environment of the trading post. By the 1850s, he was considered by his peers, the company gentlemen, and even his congregation to be inflexible and authoritarian. This change foreshadowed the evolution of the church away from a traditional, agriculturally based frontier-style mission to an institution increasingly concerned with ecclesiastical form, political and social control, and the establishment of a monolithic social hierarchy.

The evolution of clerical attitudes within the settlement played a key role in the Canadian annexationist movement of the 1850s and 1860s. The clergy realized that their interests in the community and throughout the West would be enhanced by either Crown colony status or annexation by Canada. While church and company had arrived at some sort of *rapprochment* by 1850, the clergy realized that with the opening of the West to settlement, their power and influence would accelerate. More importantly, these new settlers would be Protestant and white. New immigrants, primarily agriculturalists and entrepreneurs, would quickly outnumber the Métis and aid the Anglican Church in its battle to defeat the influence of the Catholic Church within the settlement. The decline of the fur trade, the Anglicans believed, would mean the end of a traditional economy in Red River. The mixed economy of farming, freighting, and trading would give way to a purely agricultural community that would see the Protestant residents of Red River more securely tied to the church.

Agitation for a change in Red River began in earnest in 1856.[63] The following year, the British government, as a result of mounting public criticism, convened a committee to look into the affairs of the Hudson's Bay Company and its trade monopoly in Rupert's Land. The committee heard testimony from numerous representatives from the company, church, and settlement. Among those questioned were George Simpson, Bishop David Anderson, Edward Ellice, Dr. John Rae, and Lieutenant-Colonel W. Caldwell, the former governor of Assiniboia. The committee was critical of the company's record in preventing settlement in Rupert's Land and of its treatment of aboriginal peoples. Although the British government wanted to see a change in the Northwest, it was reluctant to aid in the process. As historian Gerald Friesen has commented, the Crown was committed to free trade, colonial self-government, and the protection of Native peoples but attempted to postpone decisions, placing its confidence instead in the Hudson's Bay Company and in the hope that Canada would eventually take the problem off its hands.[64] The Hudson's Bay Company's exclusive right to trade, a right originally granted to the company in 1670 and re-affirmed in 1821, was allowed to lapse in 1859. It was only the sovereignty of the Crown and some vague appeal to the Charter of 1670 that allowed the HBC to effectively govern in Rupert's Land. The 1860s would see the development of interest groups determined to bring about some change of order in the West.

The Corbett case of 1863 is illustrative of the changes occurring within Red River society in this period. The Reverend Griffith Owen Corbett, a member of the Anglican Colonial and Church Society and the incumbent at the English-speaking Métis parish of Headingly, was accused by the company of having tried to induce an abortion in a member of his congregation whom he had allegedly made pregnant. According to Frits Pannekoek, this scandal effectively alienated the English-speaking Métis community from the Hudson's Bay Company.[65] Corbett was a vociferous critic of company rule in the Northwest. He campaigned vigorously for Crown colony status for Red River and attempted to have the Métis community view itself as more English than mixed-blood.[66] His arrest was viewed with suspicion by the Métis, who effectively organized a jailbreak for the accused minister. In Pannekoek's view the case implied that the Métis openly announced their opposition to the rule of the HBC in favour of the newly arrived Canadian and Protestant annexationists. His theory proposes that the turmoil that followed – the resistance of 1869-70 – was in fact a civil war. The racial and religious tensions between the whites, the Métis, and the English-speaking Métis in Red River, Pannekoek argues, precipitated a sectarian and racial conflict that had its roots deep in Red River's past. Further, he maintains, this conflict was exacerbated by the Protestant missionaries, who used the English Métis to defeat Catholic power in the settlement.

But, as has been pointed out more recently, such an analysis does not allow for the more subtle social and political dynamics operating within the community. Gerald Friesen maintains that the problems that beset Red River were not unique. "As life in any village will reveal," he argues, "the Red River Settlement was not alone in being united and divided by neighbourhood loyalties, kinship networks, and other social obligations."[68] By the 1860s, the settlement was opening up to the markets and influences of the United States and Canada. Red River was no longer an isolated enclave of Métis and European settlers and fur traders removed from the aspirations and intentions of Canadian politicians and entrepreneurs. Though the Anglican Church helped shape the development of Protestant Red River, it could not be held responsible for the promotion of a racial "war" within that society. Such a view would suggest a degree of influence the church did not have. The scandals of the 1850s and 1860s illustrate the social

Lower Fort Garry, c. 1875 (Provincial Archives of British Columbia).

tensions within the elite of Red River but do not necessarily shed light upon the evolution of that society as an organic whole. The Métis groups in Red River, though they differed in origins, language and religion, were nevertheless united by a common tradition based on the hunt and the fur trade. While the Protestant clergy were no doubt interested in defeating the power of the Catholic Church in Red River, it does not necessarily follow that their Métis parishioners were willing to engage their French-speaking brethren in a do-or-die struggle for ascendancy.

By 1869, the Anglican Church had adjusted to the coming order in Red River. Realizing that the HBC could no longer effectively rule both the settlement and the vast hinterland of the Northwest, the church since the mid-1850s had pursued its subtle campaign for Canadian rule in Rupert's Land. The company as sole representative of authority in the territory had long represented a mechanism for the social and political control the church considered necessary for the introduction of Christian values. The clergy realized, however, that the economy of the fur trade could never create a truly sedentary population of farmers and entrepreneurs either in Red River or throughout the West. In their view, only settlement and market agriculture in the Anglo-British tradition could fashion the kind of pastoral village society that they had initially conceived for Red River when they first arrived in the settlement in 1820.

Chapter Five

The Mission and the Community

"By a Union of Effort We Effect a Great Deal"

In the very early years after their migration to Red River, the English-and French-speaking Métis were confronted with the fundamental problem of defining the colony's relationship with the fur trade, as well as with the missionaries who arrived in the colony less than a decade after its founding. The Selkirk period had left a record of uncertainty and confusion. The Battle of Seven Oaks, the emergence of the Métis as the "New Nation," and the monopoly of the Hudson's Bay Company after 1821, contributed to this ambiguity. Andrew Bulger, representing the Selkirk estate as governor of the colony, had clashed with Chief Factor John Clarke, the company's senior resident officer in Red River.[1] With Selkirk's death, and the appointment of Chief Factor Donald MacKenzie as governor in 1824, the colony was more clearly linked to the fortunes of the fur trade. Finally, in 1834, the Selkirk estate – the huge Assiniboia land grant – reverted to the company, completing the HBC's domination over the organization and future of the settlement.[2] The uncertainty of the situation resulted in a lack of confidence in the governing structure of the young colony. Governor Simpson, writing to Andrew Colvile, described the circumstances in Red River:

Take the Colony all in all, and it is certainly an extraordinary place, the Great folks would cut each other's throats if they could with safety; there is nothing like a social feeling among them and the best friends today are the bitterest enemies tomorrow. Among the lower orders it is much the same, they have a certain feeling of pride, independence and equality among them which is subversive of good order in Society: they are opposed to each other in little factions and every man in the Colony looks to his arms along for safety and protection.[3]

Thomas Sinclair, a Métis settler in St. Andrew's, n.d. (Thomas Sinclair Collection. Courtesy of the Sinclair family).

It was the Métis challenge in Red River to help establish the social institutions that would resolve the difficulties that faced the population. Although the traditions of the trading post remained strong, they had to fit comfortably into a new set of customs and norms that were to be partly determined by the company and the churches.

The financial means of the Métis families who migrated to the lower settlement after 1826 varied. The retired company officers who were British-born, along with their Native wives and children, usually possessed sufficient savings to establish a credible farming operation on their land grant. Others were not so fortunate. Many Native-born heads of families lacked the capital necessary to begin farming and ended up living off the charity of relatives and the church. As well, an Orkney or Scottish-born male possessed other natural advantages – greater familiarity with the English language, the structure and working of local government, and the rudimentary techniques of agriculture.[4] Those former company servants who had spent their natural lives in the trading-post environment knew little of farming. The kind of agriculture that existed in the fur trade, especially in the early period at some bayside factories, functioned at a minimal level and was intended only to augment the supply of overseas provisions.

Letitia, a Métis woman of the lower settlement, photographed by H. L. Hime in 1858 (Provincial Archives of Manitoba).

The Métis began arriving in larger numbers in Red River after 1823, and many of the English-speaking families took up land grants north of the Selkirk lots on the west side of the Red beyond Point Douglas. At Frog Plain, and, by the end of the decade, at the Grand Rapids, these settlers established small riverlot farms, the latter settlement forming the nucleus of William Cockran's mission at the lower settlement. Statistics from Cockran's school roll in 1830 provide a racial breakdown of people at the Rapids. Ninety-six children, both male and female, were registered at the Grand Rapids School that year. Forty percent of the fathers were listed as Orkney, while thirty nine percent were listed as Métis. There were also eight "English" fathers (retired company officers), four Indian fathers, two Canadians, one American, and one Norwegian in the parish.[5] Of the mothers listed by Cockran, sixty two percent were Indian, while thirty five percent were Métis.[6] Five years later, in 1835, in his "State of Religion" report to the CMS, Cockran listed 102 families in the Grand Rapids parish with only forty-three headed by European-born (Orkney, Scottish, and English) males.[7] In his comments to the secretaries of the CMS in London, Cockran described the Métis heads of families and their offspring as being too easily pulled by the "immorality" of their Native heritage. As for those European-born males who had settled at the Rapids, the missionary believed them to have led "licentious" and "intemperate" lives. The transgressions of thirty or forty years, he remarked, could not be overcome

93

Thomas Norquay, n.d. A Métis born in the Red River settlement in 1843, Norquay married Elizabeth Miller and lived on lot 181 in St. Andrew's (Thomas Sinclair Collection. Courtesy of the Sinclair family).

overnight.[8] Cockran argued that the traders' "conscience must be quickened" through long years of patient prayer and devotion.[9]

While the missionary promoted agriculture as the means to salvation, the Métis families at the Rapids engaged in a mixed economy of farming, hunting, fishing, and trapping for the company. It was a regimen necessary for survival. Settlers were reluctant to expand their farms in the absence of significant external markets. Although the company purchased grain from the colonists, it was not enough to create a healthy agricultural economy. Without cash, the settler was unable to purchase the European goods necessary for life in the settlement. Red River had no small-scale manufacturing and was dependent upon the yearly HBC shipment from England for much of its clothing, manufactured goods, certain foodstuffs, seed, and tools. Consequently, settlers at the Rapids were forced to diversify their interests in order to earn a living, usually adjusting their activities on a seasonal basis. In this way, the traditions of the fur post survived amid the realities of a country where, for most, participation in a variety of activities was an essential fact of life. Rather than indicating some inherent strain within the Métis community between "civilization" and the "traditions of the chase," as the missionaries believed (and which came to be echoed in traditional historiography), the mixed economy of the settlement was an accepted and natural economic response. It was only the church and those settlers not part of the fur-trade tradition who felt that this particular economic lifestyle posed a threat to the survival of the community.

In their attempts to establish an Anglo-Christian agricultural settlement in the lower parishes, Cockran and Jones grew frustrated with what they felt was a lack of response to the teachings of the church. Cockran referred to his parishioners

John McKay, an English-speaking Métis of the Red River settlement. Photographed by H. L. Hime in 1858 (Provincial Archives of Manitoba).

Annie McDermot, the Métis daughter of trader Andrew McDermot, who married A.G.B. Bannatyne in 1851(Thomas Sinclair Collection. Courtesy of the Sinclair family).

as "principally composed of the seed of the adulterer and the whore,"[10] while Jones judged the people at the Rapids to be "excessively ignorant."[11] The English-speaking Métis, according to the church, lacked an evangelical zeal. The expectation by the missionaries that their message would create a "quickened" religious response throughout the community proved erroneous, as many of the Métis families at the Rapids were largely apathetic toward Christian admonitions, at least in the period before 1850. "The people seem ... drowsy at the time of service, apparently unacquainted with the prize that was now put into their heads," wrote Cockran in his journal in 1829.[12] Half-empty churches greeted the missionaries during the season between May and October when the young men were working the company boat brigades that operated between Red River, Norway House, York Factory, and the English River district. While the retired British-born heads of families in the community were, to a degree, influenced by church sanctions, the response of their mixed-blood families was varied and uneven.[13] Economic factors, the tradition of the fur-trade post, the pattern of kinship networks, and the new experiences in the settlement all contributed to shaping the attitudes of the new community at the Rapids.

The nature of family life in the settlement evolved after the initial period of consolidation. Kinship ties originating in the trading-post environment continued to play an important role within the community. Those who had established their small riverlot farms at the Rapids in the early years were quick to assist the families that came later, a practice that derived from the lack of economic opportunity in Red River. Unable to establish themselves as British gentlemen farmers, English-speaking Métis families employed traditional kinship methods to provide a mechanism for mutual community support.[14] William Cockran commented upon this behaviour in a letter to the secretaries:

If I find any in want, the first time I meet anyone who has been successful, I tell the tale of pity, and then will say, we must not let this or that man starve.... He or she will say I will give so and so, and ... thus by a union of effort we effect a great deal.[15]

Although the missionaries in Red River were critical of much of the behaviour of their Métis parishioners, they nevertheless documented changes in personal habits and family life within the community. To a limited degree, social custom did change in the direction encouraged by the missionary. Cockran, though of course a much-biased observer, noted the decline of "unrestrained sensuality," "whoring," and "seducing [of] each other's women."[16] By 1838, the clergyman could boast to the society that his congregation was "regular and attentive and generally speaking endeavour to lead a Christian life."[17] Cockran's success at the Rapids was not simply the result of the influence of the gospel. The missionary's personal style had much to do with this process. Stubbornly aggressive, anti-company, and at odds with his elitist colleagues at the Forks, he gained a reputation as being unpretentious and straightforward. By promoting and practising a kind of agrarian, muscular Christianity, Cockran enjoyed a good deal of popularity with his congregation at the Rapids. His physical abilities and stature were respected by many. One non-believer admitted to Cockran that, "I am afraid of you, but not of God. You have a strong arm if you grow properly angry you could break my bones."[18] If the missionary's homespun style gained him a measure of respect within the community, it did little to endear him to the increasingly affected elite at Red River. Arriving at one of Mrs. Simpson's dinner parties at Lower Fort Garry perched atop a cow, Cockran was viewed by this class with a degree of bemused contempt. The missionary's low social background was ridiculed by the gentlemen of the fur trade. Describing one of Cockran's sermons at the Rapids, Donald Ross commented to James Hargrave that the missionary spun "out his long yarns as usual murdering the King's English most unmercifully in the flights of pulpit eloquence."[19] Cockran's unpopularity with the nabobs of Red River only increased his acceptance at the Rapids and in no small way helped promote the CMS at that settlement.

Going to church in Rupert's Land, c. 1875 (Provincial Archives of Manitoba).

The rearing of children in the Rapids community was one area of family life that came under scrutiny by the missionaries. Attitudes toward children tended to reflect the influences of both the trading-post tradition and the settlement. Anglican missionaries often condemned Native males for treating their wives as little more than beasts of burden, while at the same time allowing their children a virtual free reign. Family practices in Rupert's Land represented the antithesis of Victorian custom. In nineteenth-century England, women (or at least those of the upper class) were considered virtuous and delicate creatures, while children were viewed as simply unrestrained little people much in need of discipline. In his journal, Cockran moralized upon the state of family life in the settlement:

> *The greatest part of the children here seem to be altogether their own*
> *masters – do every day what is most agreeable; eat when they please, waste*
> *what they please, sleep when, where and how they please ... from their*
> *infancy they go astray, and because their parents neglect to use the rod ...*
> *they are never brought back. It is viewed as cruel and tyrannical to*
> *chastise children.... I am sorry to say, that many of the parents of my*
> *congregation follow this method with their families ... there are only a*
> *few, a very few, who will command their children.*[20]

The extent to which the Métis children of British-born fathers at the Rapids were taken from the old environment of the trading post and exposed to "civilizing" influences depended upon the initiative of individual fathers.[21] Many of their sons, especially when they grew older, aspired to assimilate into their father's world. The case of James Ross, the son of Red River patriarch Alexander Ross serves as an example.[22] Alexander Ross was one of the leading principal settlers within the Red River community. Married to an Indian woman, he was determined that his mixed-blood offspring be exposed to all the civilizing

James Ross, English Métis leader in the Red River settlement, c. 1860 (Provincial Archives of Manitoba).

benefits the settlement had to offer. James Ross was such an outstanding pupil of Bishop Anderson's at the Red River Academy that he was sent to further his education at the University of Toronto in 1853, where he won a number of scholarships and prizes. In the resistance of 1869-70, while a supporter of the Canadian cause, Ross participated in Louis Riel's provisional government in the hopes of avoiding the bloodshed of a war between "brothers and kindred."[23] Criticized by both sides, he suffered the ignobility of being passed over for a position in the administration of Governor Archibald in favour of the newly arriving Canadians. While Ross's dual racial heritage did not preclude his membership in the social and political elite of old Red River in the years before 1870, after this date, he was excluded from participation in the new Anglo-Protestant order that had begun to transform the West.

In their move from the fur-trade post to the settlement at the Rapids, Métis families were ultimately selective in their adaptation to new customs and practices. Behaviour that had earlier proven disruptive was for the most part dispensed with, while functional and enjoyable practices were maintained, even in the face of heavy censure from the church. This, in part, explains the often contradictory nature of Cockran's observations of the English-speaking Métis community in his parish. The missionary alternately criticized and praised the behaviour of his parishioners, who adopted some customs from the British example but maintained others derived from their Native heritage. Such an accommodation was not without purpose. Family life, marriage practices, child-rearing, and, most importantly, economic activity reflected the particular adaptation of mixed-blood culture to the physical, economic, and social realities of Red River society.

A strong and vibrant community life developed in the early years at the Rapids. Kinship bonds established in the days of the fur-trade post were strengthened, helping to facilitate social and community interaction. Cooperative activities in farming, hunting, and building were common, and families increasingly sought each other's company for such social events as weddings and baptisms.[24] Cockran disapproved of much of this behaviour. He cautioned his parishioners against holding dances and parties at weddings and noted in his journal that these celebrations, lasting two or three days, might involve upwards of one hundred people.[25] What particularly disturbed the missionary was that the guests were often away from their farms for an extended period of time, an absence that Cockran viewed as reflective of a general indifference to agriculture in the community.[26] Despite the missionary's opinion, however, social and communal ties played a major role in the regular performance of daily duties within the parish.

If traditional kinship networks helped to minimize social conflict within the parish (at least among those with little material wealth), they did less to hide a hierarchical structure in Red River that was based largely upon social standing and material wealth. At the top of the hierarchy were the principal settlers.[27] Made up primarily of Scottish-born former HBC officers who had retired with their mixed-blood families to Red River, these individuals possessed considerable material wealth (as well as management experience and literacy skills) from their days in the fur trade. This gave them the capital to invest in the land and implements needed to run a moderately successful farm at the Rapids. It also placed them on a par with the highest class in Red River, the company squirearchy. If widowed or single, the principal settlers became eligible to marry the few available European women in the settlement, unions that unquestionably raised the status of retired fur traders. Retired officers such as Andrew Linklater, James Sutherland, and Donald Gunn settled with their mixed-blood families near the Rapids in the first decade after the union of the two competing fur companies. In Red River's developing social structure, the principal settlers aspired to be British "gentlemen." To accomplish this goal, however, their families' Native heritage had to be downplayed. Education was considered the key in gaining their children's entry into Red River's upper class. To have their mixed-blood offspring achieve a station in life comparable to their own was considered by these former traders to be of paramount importance.[28]

Who were the principal settlers and former company *engagés* who settled at the Rapids? James Sutherland, for example, was a principal settler who claimed lots 96 and 97 on the west side of the river in the lower part of the parish.[29] Sutherland was originally from Ronaldsay in the Orkney Islands and joined the Hudson's Bay Company in 1797. He served for many years at Cumberland House, and, in 1821, he was made chief factor in charge of the Swan River district.[30] Sutherland retired to the settlement in 1827. His long-time country marriage to Jane Flett, a Native woman, was sanctioned by the Anglican clergy in 1828, and she eventually bore a total of seven children.[31] By 1835, Sutherland could boast twenty-five acres under cultivation, making him one of the most successful farmers in the district.[32] According to the 1835 Red River census, Sutherland owned eighteen head of cattle, five horses, and three carts – material assets that put him among the elite of landowners at the Rapids.[33] Characteristically, he placed considerable emphasis upon the education of his Métis children.[34] His daughter, Sally, was once described by John West as "one of the best informed and most improved half-caste" women he had seen.[35] While Sutherland shared many of the attitudes of his race and class, it seems he remained faithful to his Native wife, Jane. Writing to his brother in 1838, he commented on the changing nature of marriage practices in the settlement:

> *We have now here some rich old fellows that have acquired large fortunes in the service, have got married to European females and cut a dash, have introduced a system of extravagance into the place that is followed by all that can afford it.*[36]

101

Sutherland, like Alexander Ross, was considered one of Red River's original "patriarchs." He died in 1844 at the age of sixty-seven. In contrast, William Spence, a Métis former labourer with the HBC, moved to Red River in 1823 at the age of 17.[37] Later, with his wife Anne and five children, he settled on a portion of lot 94 at the Rapids.[38] According to census data, Spence did not appear to engage in any type of farming.[39] He had no land under cultivation, except for perhaps a small garden plot, and did not own any farm implements. His possession of two head of cattle suggests that he might have freighted or participated in the annual buffalo hunt. As well, he could have tripped with the company, perhaps working on the Red River-York Factory boat brigades. Spence's children attended Cockran's school at the Rapids.

In 1835, James Sutherland had the greatest number of acres under cultivation at the Rapids. William Spence, on the other hand, was one of about five or six landowners in the parish who chose not to till the soil at all. By 1840, Spence, while increasing his livestock, had cultivated only a little over one acre.[40] This varying commitment to agriculture suggests that economic life within the parish was never homogeneous; in fact, it was the economic gulf between the principal settlers and the rest of the population that helped polarize society within the lower settlement. Historian Irene Spry has argued that there were two fundamental divisions within Red River, both of them economic. The first was between the former officers of the HBC and their mixed-blood families, and those residents who at one time worked as company tripmen and labourers. This division in many instances paralleled the second: the gulf between those in Red River who were primarily farmers and those who were primarily hunters.[41] Economic standing within the community dictated social status and one's role in the political process, as well as access to superior education. In turn, education helped perpetuate, if not enhance, class divisions with the settlement. So while the acculturated sons and daughters of former company officers shared a racial heritage with the larger Métis community, they nonetheless enjoyed a level of status and opportunity in keeping with their superior economic position.

It is useful then to view the social hierarchy at St. Andrew's within the context of class relations. Such a model presumes the vertical ordering of classes and the existence of superior and inferior social and economic status that remains largely permanent and that sees little cross-over between groups. There must be a degree of consciousness within each class, though this consciousness may fluctuate between benign awareness and militant solidarity. Moreover, a class-based society is marked by the social isolation of particular classes and the lack of closer contacts between individuals at different levels. In traditional Marxist theory, classes are defined by their relationship to the means of production (the purchase and sale of labour), as well as by their role in the social organization of labour. Although a class analysis is traditionally applied to the forces of production operating within a mature capitalist society, a comparable model might also be applied to pre-industrial agrarian societies, or to dynamic cultures in the process of blending a variety of economic strategies.[42] All societies exhibit elements of stratification based upon individual functions and skills, kinship ties, or material wealth, and agrarian and mixed resource-based communities can also demonstrate the varying relationship of individuals to the means of production. With the collapse of the HBC monopoly in the 1840s, the Métis of Red River became increasingly involved in the buffalo robe trade, a process that historian Gerhard Ens has described as "proto-industrial" and as the beginning of the transformation of Métis strategies away from what he has called the traditional peasant economy of Red River.[43]

However, employing European models to describe the economy in Red River as "peasant" (outside of perhaps the Scottish Kildonan settlers who pursued an almost exclusive farming livelihood) mislabels the complexity of economic activity within the settlement. The Métis were in fact involved in a variety of economic strategies, including hunting, fishing, freighting, and other contract work, as well as agriculture and animal husbandry. Though clergymen such as William Cockran tended to view their Métis parishioners as peasants, or at least wished to see them so within a rural English tradition, the reality of nineteenth-century life in Red River – a poor climate, isolation from potential agricultural markets, and the need to exploit a variety of resources – belied these European views of an idyllic peasant-based agricultural society. Ens's use of the term "traditional" to describe Métis life in Red River prior to the 1840s would suggest a long period of adaptation. However, the Métis only began arriving in Red River in any numbers by the 1820s, and the economy of the settlement over the next generation was never static; it constantly evolved and adapted to new circumstances in the decades before mid-century. [44] But as the economy of St. Andrew's evolved throughout the 1830s and 1840s, the parish tended to become an increasingly class-divided society with the existence of superior and inferior social status based upon economic choices. While gentlemen farmers and buffalo hunters and tripmen might be seen as occupying opposite ends of this hierarchy, the economic elite of the settlement also contained a number of successful freighters who had accumulated significant wealth through their economic activities, though there were fewer of these types of individuals at St. Andrew's than there were in some of the French-speaking parishes.

Census records for the parish indicate that, between 1831 and 1849, there appeared to be very little change in the wealth of individual settlers, suggesting a strong degree of permanence within each class. [45] In terms of agricultural holdings, those farmers who were "poor" in 1831 tended to remain so throughout the historic period. Despite the economic separation of groups in St. Andrew's, these differences were mitigated to an extent by racial and kinship ties. Though one might be hesitant to claim the existence of class-consciousness within the parish, there was certainly a degree of class-awareness. The hierarchical traditions of the fur trade – the separation of officers and servants – helped maintain a sense of group identity among those who later retired to the parish. As tripman and hunters rarely rose in the company's service, there was little belief within this group that any real economic opportunity existed – the type of belief that might moderate one's awareness of their position in the economic hierarchy. In the history of the community at St. Andrew's, it was the free-trade crisis of the 1840s that best illustrated this awareness. The expressed opposition of Métis to the HBC monopoly during this period demonstrated shared concerns based upon mutual economic interests. The presence of the church at St. Andrew's, however, served to promote the bonds of community within the parish. The performance of marriages, baptisms, funerals and other liturgical duties, helped regulate the community and strengthen existing kinship ties. The church provided a mechanism for community action, such as the raising of money and materials for the construction of the church building itself, or the management of parish affairs. It also served as a focal point for social life within the community. As a gathering place within the settlement, the Sunday and Tuesday services or Wednesday evening prayer meetings provided an opportunity for social interaction.[46] This interaction helped blur social and economic divisions within the parish through the promotion of a wider sense of community.

Efforts by the local clergy to build community solidarity could not hide the fact that, by the 1840s, the economic situation in the lower community had begun to deteriorate. The years of relative prosperity that followed the flood of 1826 soon gave way to a period of drought, early frosts, and crop failure. The situation was made worse by diseases such as scarlet fever, which ravaged the settlement at various times during the decade.[47] Their impact in the community is evident in the parish burial records. In 1846, for instance, the records show that at St. Andrew's many deaths occurred in children under two years of age.[48] While infant deaths were quite common for the whole of the historic period, random sampling from later decades (1864, 1870, and 1884) show that infant mortality reached a peak in the lower community during the 1840s.[49]

Yet, St. Andrew's was not alone in experiencing problems during this period as crop failures throughout the settlement, coupled with declining wage labour opportunities with the HBC, threatened the economic livelihood of Red River's Métis population.[50] During the previous decade, the people of the Rapids settlement enjoyed a mixed economy that more or less satisfied their material and community needs, while effectively meeting the economic demands of the settlement. However, the great buffalo herds that had once been in close proximity to Red River had now moved further west, and, after 1840, many in Red River either travelled great distances from the settlement in pursuit of the new buffalo robe trade (and to eventually establish wintering or *hivernant* communities on the plains) or came to rely more heavily upon agriculture. At the same time, the HBC attempted to restrict the number of Métis working on a seasonal basis with the company, especially those who were also engaged in free trade.[51] Turning to agriculture, the population as St. Andrew's soon discovered that the continuing practice of subdividing riverlots among offspring had resulted in overcrowding and unprofitable farmsteads. In 1854, William Cockran recognized the problem and led a group of settlers to new lots at Portage La Prairie on the Assiniboine River. Not all, however, were willing to abandon their friends, families, and churches along the Red River, and opportunities diminished for the younger generation of St. Andrew's settlers.

By the middle of the century, changing racial sensibilities, particularly among the Anglican clergy of the lower settlement, posed another challenge to the English Métis of St. Andrew's. Though highly critical of Métis lifestyles, William Cockran endeavoured to build a sense of community among his parishioners. The Archdeacon's successors, however, exhibited little sympathy with his attempts to establish a viable agricultural settlement at the Rapids, and missionaries such as Robert James viewed their new Métis parishioners with suspicion.[52] On his journey from York Factory to Red River, James commented that:

> *The men who brought us to Red River were nearly all members of my own future congregation at the Rapids.... Only one or two showed any regard for us, others robbed our scanty provisions and generally they acted without affection. The first two days they were all intoxicated and this with their subsequent conduct induced us to regard them as nearly all "heathens."*[53]

The departure of Bishop Anderson, the death of William Cockran in 1865, and the arrival of Bishop Machray that same year, signalled the end of the old Anglican mission in Red River. The new church, preoccupied with making Red River "British" awaited the imminent arrival of Ontarian farmers and entrepreneurs to the West. The greater affluence these groups were bound to bring to the country would increase the wealth and prestige of the Anglican Church and succeed in removing the community from the traditional influences of the fur trade.

Red River's economic problems were further aggravated by the severe drought that occurred throughout the 1860s.[54] As well, grasshoppers infested the settlement and a scarlet fever outbreak in 1864 carried off a large number of the population.[55] The settlement's crops were destroyed each year between 1862 and 1865 and again in 1868.[56] The latter year also witnessed the absence of small game near the settlement, the failure of the buffalo hunt (an almost regular occurrence by this date), and the collapse of the fisheries. The settlement sought relief in the form of food and clothing from Canada. At St. Andrew's, the Rev. J. P. Gardiner organized relief committees to gather and distribute badly needed seed wheat, foodstuffs, and clothing.[57] The settlement's economic woes helped precipitate an increase in the calls for the annexation of Red River to Canada.

Earlier, in 1857, Captain William Kennedy, a resident of St. Andrew's and an embittered ex-employee of the Hudson's Bay Company, organized meetings throughout the parish to agitate for political change. He succeeded in interesting not only a number of leading Kildonan and St. Andrew's settlers, but also James Hunter, the incumbent at St. Andrew's Church.[58] In a letter dated April 8, 1857, Hunter described to the Church Missionary Society the general discontent that existed with the company's administration in the settlement. "The fact is," he wrote, "the people are tired of the present government and are anxious for any change that will open up the country to colonization....

Captain William Kennedy, n.d. Kennedy, the son of Chief Factor Alexander Kennedy and his Cree wife, Aggathas, opposed the HBC monopoly in Rupert's Land and favoured Canadian annexation. In 1866, the onetime arctic explorer built a large stone house (known today as Kennedy House) on the Red River adjacent to St. Andrew's Church (Provincial Archives of Manitoba).

[The] people have suffered so long from the company that they are now determined to make a great struggle for emancipation."[59] By 1869, a land rush was imminent. Settlers and surveyors arriving from Ontario proceeded to stake out claims that implicitly challenged the traditions, assumptions, and geography of the old colony.

The Anglican clergy preached the benefits of the coming Protestant-Canadian order in Red River to the English-speaking Métis of the lower parishes. Disaffected and disenchanted after years of unpopular company rule, the Métis had endured failed harvests, a depletion of wild game in the region, as well as disease. Some now expressed cautious optimism regarding their future in a Canadian Red River. However, like James Sinclair, many of St. Andrew's Métis population were sympathetic with Louis Riel's attempts to establish a provisional government to help avoid bloodshed in the transition from Hudson's Bay Company rule. As a result, the local Anglican clergy, who opposed Riel and believed the resistance to be the

Donald Gunn, n.d. Farmer, schoolmaster, and author, Gunn lived at St. Andrew's on lot 109. A petty court justice and foreman of the jury in the Sayer trial of 1849, Gunn was also a delegate to Riel's 1869 council and member of the provincial legislature between 1871 and 1876 (Provincial Archives of Manitoba).

result of a "popish plot" orchestrated to increase Roman Catholic influence in Red River, lost some of their authority among those English Métis concerned with land rights within the settlement.[60] The antipathy was mutual. Robert Machray, the new Anglican Bishop, had little confidence that the "new" West could be built upon a group whom he considered poor and ignorant. For Machray, the energies of the church would best be devoted towards preparations for its new parishioners, the white, Anglo-Protestant Canadian farmers and entrepreneurs from Ontario.[61] And while Bishop Machray privately opposed Riel's provisional government, labelling it a "perfect abomination" in a letter to Sir John Young, [62] he publicly counselled moderation. At St. Andrew's, Rev. J. P. Gardiner, a vociferous critic of Riel and the Métis, later urged caution after receiving a threat on his life. Gardiner refused to organize his parishioners at St. Andrew's or to collect arms to recapture the Upper Fort, which was controlled by Riel and his supporters.[63] Initially, at least, support for the provisional government existed among the people of the lower settlement. In a letter to Thomas Bunn, Donald Gunn suggested that it was "advisable to respond to the call made by our French fellow colonists," and at a meeting held at St. Andrew's Church on February 12, 1870, Thomas Sinclair and Edward Hay were elected as parish delegates to Riel's provisional government.[64]

It is clear that the population at St. Andrew's vacillated over the course of the ten-month protest. On the one hand, they hoped to fulfill an important role in the settlement after its annexation to Canada. To an extent, they listened to the counsel of their clergy and some of the principal settlers and mistrusted Riel, critical of the Métis leader's refusal to admit constitutional authority into the territory. Many in the parish, while sympathetic to the goals of the Resistance, nevertheless opposed the tactics of Riel and his followers. In February of 1870, a large group of armed men from the lower settlement, encouraged by Canadian party leader John Christian Schultz, prepared to march on Riel at the Upper Fort to force the release of prisoners taken by the Métis leader. The poorly led counter-insurrection never materialized, however. Riel released the prisoners on his own accord, thus removing the objective of the march, and the men quietly dispersed. Frits Pannekoek has suggested that it was the lack of firm leadership among the English Métis of Red River, or from the Anglican Church and the retired fur-trade elite, that prevented open opposition to Riel and the eruption of sectarian violence among the Métis groups in Red River.[65] But if they were divided by language and religion, the Métis in the settlement remained essentially united, not only by their shared experiences of life in Red River, but by a common heritage forged in the days of the buffalo hunt and the fur trade. As John Tait, a resident of St. Andrew's, so eloquently said at a public meeting in the parish in 1869: "[The French-speaking Métis] were born and brought up among us, ate with us, slept with us, hunted with us, traded with us, and are our own flesh and blood.... Gentlemen, I for one cannot fight them. I will not imbrue my hands with their blood."[66]

What is less clear in the events surrounding the Resistance of 1869-70 is the degree to which differences in attitude toward Canadian annexation among St. Andrew's families paralleled economic inequalities within the parish. Historian D. N. Sprague has maintained that because the Resistance represented a quest for property rights on behalf of the unofficial owners of riverlot properties, those English-speaking Métis who were secure in their title and status were inclined to support the Canadian party in Red River, while the persons who took up arms on the side of the insurgents were likely to be hunters and tripmen without title.[67] In this sense, then, the internal tensions generated by the Resistance represented more a struggle between Red River's economic classes than it did racial strife. Ultimately, the English-speaking settlers who supported annexation and the mixed-bloods' loss of "corporate" rights in 1869-70 – largely those who were land-secure – unwittingly believed they could maintain their status in the face of the Protestant, Ontarian immigration that was to come after 1870.[68]

In anticipation of the arrival of the railway in Manitoba, lots in St. Andrew's and other parishes in Red River were bought up by speculators hoping to turn a quick profit when land-hungry immigrants began arriving in the new province. As early as 1871, it was decided to extend a rail line from Fort William through the village of Selkirk and northwest to the Lake Manitoba Narrows. Geological and engineering considerations dictated that the line cross the Red River at Selkirk. The banks were more stable at this point, and the area was less prone to the flooding that frequently occurred at Winnipeg. In 1883, a Selkirk spur to the Pembina Branch connected the town with Winnipeg and the American border. A line had also been constructed eastward from Selkirk to meet up with a section of the main CPR line out of the Lakehead. While Selkirk had long lobbied with the federal government to become the railway depot in Manitoba, it was decided in 1881 to build the main line south, closer to the forty-ninth parallel. Accordingly, the CPR chose to have its line cross the Red River at Winnipeg and proceeded to construct its railway engine houses, roundhouses, and, most importantly, a bridge at that location. Eventually, in 1907, the line running west from the Manitoba-Ontario border was straightened, and Selkirk and the former east side of St. Andrew's parish were left off the main line altogether.

In the years following the Resistance, those Métis who remained in St. Andrew's hoped to play a major role in the opening of the settlement to Canada. In 1870, the population of the province was about 12,000, of whom approximately half were French-speaking Métis, a third English-speaking Métis, and less than one-sixth European or Canadian by origin.[69] During the next decade, British and Canadian immigration to the new province continued at a moderate enough pace that the influence of the old English Métis families (at least those who had a secure land base within the community) remained somewhat stable. In the latter part of the 1870s, however, immigration took a dramatic upswing. Although John Norquay, a Métis from St. Andrew's, became Manitoba premier in 1878, his administration was powerless to stop an assault on the established Métis power base. The traditional mixed-blood alliance in Red River was crumbling. In the electoral re-organization of 1879, the English-speaking Métis were left in control of only one seat in the twenty-four seat legislature – Norquay's riding at St. Andrew's. They were soon swamped by the flood of immigration to the province after 1883. By 1886, the population of Manitoba had increased dramatically to 109,000.[70] According to census reports, the Métis, both French-and English-speaking, now accounted for only seven percent of this population.

Where the Métis had traditionally viewed themselves as a separate "New Nation," those English-speaking Métis that remained at St. Andrew's after 1870 increasingly reflected an Anglo-Protestant world view. The influence in the community before 1850 of the old mixed-blood families and the white patriarchs such as Alexander Ross and James Sutherland, along with a commonality of language and religion with the incoming settlers, led the English Métis to believe that they could exercise some power and influence in the new province. Ultimately, they were mistaken. And while the French-speaking Métis took pride in their Native roots, many of their English-speaking counterparts sought to purge themselves of their aboriginal heritage, choosing instead to be viewed as Anglo-Protestants settling the frontier. This view has subsequently tended to permeate the community and in some ways has influenced the way it has viewed its own history.[71] In 1948, for example, when a provincial government plaque commemorating the career of Premier John Norquay mentioned that he was a "Halfbreed," his descendants threatened legal action and commissioned a genealogy "proving" him to be of English and Welsh lineage, this despite the fact that their illustrious ancestor was widely known to be Métis and had once declared his pride in his aboriginal heritage.[72] For those at St. Andrew's who had grown uneasy with their Native heritage in the face of marginalization by non-Native immigrants, it had become sadly necessary to try and place themselves solidly within the "civilizing" tradition of post-1870 settlement in western Canada. "Triumph over adversity" in the Whig tradition had become as much the creed of many of the old families of the lower community as it was for Canadian immigrants and their descendants on the prairies.

St. Andrew's and the Built Environment

In the nineteenth century, St. Andrew's parish reflected the collective character of its Native origins. A commonality of language, religion, family ties, and economic strategies was characteristic of life within the parish, as were the unique building customs of its European and mixed-blood residents – customs that reflected both

111

the certainties of climate and geography and the realities of social and economic divisions within the community. Architecture can reveal a great deal about how members of a community lived and interacted with their environment. It also provides a physical clue as to how the community was organized and stratified; it can identify both the elite and the underclass and show how each lived. Those forms of architecture that often survive from an earlier period, such as the stone churches and houses that dot the river edge in St. Andrew's, as opposed to those that have not survived, such as the tents and log houses of aboriginal and Métis peoples, can often influence our view of the past and bias what we might consider typical of life in the settlement. The stylistic origins of the whole range of architectural types, as well as the methods and materials that were employed and the adaptation of building to the local environment, can provide clues to what it would have been like to live in St. Andrew's a century and a half ago.

The history of building and architectural style in St. Andrew's, and throughout Red River, prior to 1870 reflected the realities of climate and technology in the region, as well as the availability of building materials. From the bark-covered lodges of the Ojibwa who travelled throughout the parish to the wood and stone houses and public buildings of the fur traders, missionaries, merchants, farmers, and hunters who occupied the district after 1829, the form and function of settlement architecture demonstrated a practical response to the environment of the pre-industrial West. Building materials, construction technologies, and weather all figured into the building styles that evolved in the settlement. Although often derivative of earlier architectural forms – western Ojibwa lodges, for instance, were largely patterned after their antecedents of the Lake Superior region, and the large limestone houses of the parish mimicked the manor houses of eighteenth-century Scotland – these styles evolved into vernacular forms that were in many ways unique to the colony that originated at the Forks of the Red and Assiniboine.

Aboriginal peoples, primarily Cree and Ojibwa, were seasonal inhabitants of St. Andrew's parish throughout the nineteenth century, and their dwellings, both before and after contact with Europeans, reflected a practical response to environmental factors within the region as well as an adaptative exploitation of available resources. While some of the Ojibwa peoples who had migrated to the

112

Ojibwa conical bark lodges called *wigwassikanikag* on the banks of the Red River in the lower settlement. Photgraphed by H. L. Hime in 1858 (Provincial Archives of Manitoba).

Red River region in the late eighteenth century camped and travelled within the settlement, others settled along with Cree peoples within St. Peter's parish at the northern end of the settlement. By the 1840s, many of these "Christian" Indians (as they were known within Red River) had constructed log houses there under the direction of Church of England clergy. Those who moved throughout the settlement and the adjacent plains and woodlands on a seasonal basis engaged in such activities as buffalo hunting, fur trading, maple sugaring, and the supply of provisions and country-made articles to local settlers and to HBC personnel at Lower Fort Garry.[73] Residing for brief periods of time in and around the settlement, the Ojibwa of the Red River area employed a style of lodge construction that differed from the hide-covered tipis of traditional plains groups. Examples of this form of lodge construction show up in the early nineteenth-century paintings of Peter Rindisbacher and the 1850s photographs of H. L. Hime. Called *cabandawan*, these domed-shaped structures were formed by saplings driven into the ground in a circular or elliptical pattern and then bent over and bound together at the top. Large sheets of water-resistant birch rind were then used to cover the frame and woven rush mats were often laid around the base of the lodge.[74] Several layers of bark could be separated with moss for insulation during the winter months. The entrance to the lodge was usually covered with a flap of hide or matting, and a hole in the top allowed smoke to escape. Although most of these structures housed only one family, some of the larger elliptical-shaped lodges might be inhabited by several families. The Ojibwa also used conical-shaped shelters called *wigwassikanikag,* which were described in 1804 by Peter Grant of the North West Company and consisted of:

> *slender long poles, erected in the form of a cone and covered with the rind of the birch tree. The general diameter of the base is about fifteen feet, the fire place exactly in the middle, and the remainder of the area, with the exception of a small place for the hearth, is carefully covered with the branches of the pine or cedar tree, over which some bear skins and old blankets are spread, for sitting and sleeping. A small aperture is left in which a bear skin is hung in lieu of a door, and a space is left open at the top, which answers the purpose of window and chimney.*[75]

A variety of other structures were used by aboriginal peoples in the St. Andrew's and Red River district, including the temporary fir-bough lean-to favoured by hunters in wooded areas during the winter months, and ceremonial structures that included the sweatlodge, a domed-shaped shelter with willow branches and buffalo-hide cover, the cylindrical shaking-tent, and the large *midewiwin* ceremonial structures of the Lake Winnipeg area.

The style of log construction that became common in the Red River area in the nineteenth century derived from the architectural styles of the fur trade brought to the West by traders from New France. Known variously as *"poteaux sur sole"* or *"pièce sur pièce,"* and later as the "Hudson Bay Style" or more commonly as "Red River frame," this particular style evolved from the *"maison en columbage"* of New France, popular in that colony between about 1680 and the late eighteenth century. Its European ancestor was the medieval half-timbered houses found throughout France that employed closely spaced wooden timbers on a sill plate, the intervening spaces being filled with stone rubble and mortar. In New France, the rubble

A view of the settlement along the west bank of the Red River looking south from St. Andrew's Rectory, 1858 (Provincial Archives of Manitoba).

infill was often replaced by horizontal timbers that were mortised into the evenly spaced upright posts using a tongue-and-groove method.[76] When *voyageurs* and traders from the French colony began their first incursions into the territories west of Lake Superior in the early eighteenth century, they brought this architectural form with them. Log construction and local materials were employed in almost all building projects from this period and characterized the form and style of the residences, stores, and warehouses that remained an enduring feature of fort architecture in the early days of the fur trade.

Despite the end of the French regime in Canada in 1759, traders from Montreal continued to ply the lakes and rivers of the prairie and parkland, constructing their fur-trade posts in the home territories of the aboriginal peoples of what is now Manitoba and Saskatchewan. Organized into the North West Company later in the century, and headquartered in Montreal, the wooden *"columbage"* style of building was quickly consolidated by the peripatetic representatives of that fur-trading company. With the union of the North West and Hudson's Bay

Companies in 1821, this style of log construction was used by fur traders at their posts from Labrador to Vancouver Island.

When the Kildonan and Métis settlers arrived at the forks of the Red and Assiniboine rivers, they quickly adopted the construction style and technique that had become prevalent throughout the fur trade. The Red River frame style came to characterize the bulk of construction in the various parishes of the colony, including St. Andrew's. The use of log construction in Red River, as opposed to the relatively small number of later stone houses and churches, provides an interesting illustration of socio-economic differences in the colony. Red River frame tended to be the building style of choice among the settlement's lower and middle orders and represented an affordable and functional adaptation to the environment for farmers, hunters, and traders (and those who pursued some combination of these activities). Stone houses, on the other hand, were costlier and more labour-intensive and were generally built by the wealthier members of Red River society such as the retired chief factors of the Hudson's Bay Company or the small elite of entrepreneurs who resided in the settlement. As St. Andrew's was home to a small elite of well-to-do retired traders, the parish boasted a number of these substantial structures. Their builders, keenly aware of their privileged position in local society, constructed stone houses and churches as monuments to their wealth and prosperity, and a handful of these stone buildings, such as Kennedy House, Twin Oaks, Hay House, and St. Andrew's Church and Rectory remain in the parish today.[77]

Red River Frame architecture, though simple in design and layout and devoid of stylistic embellishment, was nonetheless ideally suited to the environment of southern Manitoba. The four walls of the structure were formed by long vertical uprights, spaced from one to one-and-a-half metres apart and joined by shorter horizontal logs. The squared vertical members were connected by mortise-and-tenon joints to a sill plate that rested upon a fieldstone foundation and to a top plate horizontal log. Tongues were then cut into the ends of the shorter horizontal logs that would form the wall, and these were slid into grooves that had been chiselled into the vertical posts. In this manner, the horizontal logs were built up to form a sturdy wall. Spaces between the logs were filled with mud and thatch, while hay or split shingles were used for the roof. Roof styles were usually of the

Unidentified family with their two-storey Red River frame home in St. Andrew's, c. 1890 (Thomas Sinclair Collection. Courtesy of the Sinclair family).

plain gabled design, but occasionally a hip roof with dormer windows could be seen on the houses of the better-off residents of Red River. Few nails were used in the construction of a Red River frame house or outbuilding as the use of tenoned logs and wooden pegs allowed for the expansion and contraction of the wood according to the extremes of temperature that characterized the climate of the valley.[78] This style of construction also facilitated some variation in size among Red River buildings. Although most houses were small, a few larger structures, such as the Grey Nun's convent built in 1846 near the forks, or the John Inkster house constructed in 1853, were quite large by comparison. Vertical posts spaced at regular intervals also allowed for the enlargement of an original structure. The short horizontal logs could be removed and, unlike a structure composed of single continuous logs, an addition could easily be made.

Red River frame was used for more than just house construction in the settlement and was the preferred method of building for barns and other farm outbuildings as well as for many of the early churches and schools in St. Andrew's and throughout Red River. Barns, granaries, byres, and storage buildings were an essential part of most parish riverlot farms. Of generally rougher construction than many of the houses in the colony, these buildings were constructed hastily and often with materials from other structures. Local settlers often moved their farm outbuildings, disassembling a structure piece by piece for reassembly at some new location. Of the more significant building types in the settlement in the period before 1870 were the handful of wind-and-water mills that dotted the parish. Constructed for the most part in the Red River frame style, these mills were used to grind the grain supplied by local farmers. Many of the early paintings and sketches of the settlement depict wind-and-water mills, and travellers to Red River often remarked upon them. Unfortunately, none of these uniquely constructed mills remain.

Public buildings such as churches and schools were an important part of community life in the parish, and greater care was usually taken in their construction. The first church built in Red River was the Roman Catholic church of St. Boniface, begun in 1818 on the east side of the river at the forks by the Oblate fathers Provencher and Dumoulin. St. John's, constructed two years later on the west side of the river by John West of the Anglican Church Missionary Society, was the first Protestant mission in the West. Both these buildings employed Red River frame construction and were characterized by small wooden bell towers and steeples. Wood remained the primary building material for subsequent churches and schools within the settlement until the 1840s, when many Red River churches were rebuilt with limestone. The first church at St. Andrew's (or the Grand Rapids as it was initially called) was built in 1832 with stout oak logs and was pulled down seventeen years later, in 1849, for the much larger stone edifice that still stands north of Winnipeg along River Road.

Lower Fort Garry, constructed by the HBC on the west bank of the Red River north of the rapids in the early 1830s, fulfilled a major role in the economy and society of St. Andrew's parish, and the variety of construction styles employed by the company there, including wood, stone, and rubble construction, represented a number of fur-trade building traditions. While larger stone buildings such as the Warehouse, the Big House, and the Saleshop/Fur Loft, which were built in the 1830s, are still standing, many of the later buildings used by the

Buildings of the "industrial complex" at Lower Fort Garry, 1858 (Provincial Archives of Manitoba).

company in and around the lower fort were built with logs, and few of these buildings have survived. The buildings of the industrial area near the creek, such as the distillery-brewery, the malt barn, the "red store," and other smaller buildings were constructed of log and set upon fieldstone foundations. Similarly, the buildings associated with the HBC farm located just beyond the fort's north wall were also of log construction, for example, the stableman's house, cattle byres, and barns. The original farm manager's house and forge were also built of logs in the Red River frame style. A number of rubble-fill, or columbage-style buildings are also present at Lower Fort Garry and include the Men's House, the annex to the Big House, a stable that no longer stands, and possibly the malt barn that was located south of the fort near the creek. The essential design of these particular buildings was similar to Red River frame, but rather than employing logs as horizontal members, loose stone and mortar was placed between the regularly spaced wooden uprights. The exterior wall was then lathed and stuccoed. All the rubble-filled buildings at the fort were erected in a twenty-year period between 1840 and the 1860. Rubble-fill (or *"columbage pierroté"*) was a Canadien design and building technique that derived from the half-timbered houses of medieval France. Although no documentation exists that might prove the case, it is likely that they were built by Montreal stonemason Belonie Gibeault, who worked for the Hudson's Bay Company in the Lower Red River district throughout the period.

Unlike other forms of construction in the prairie West before 1870, Red River frame was an accessible building technique that required few specialized skills. For this reason, most frame buildings in the parish and the surrounding area were assembled by the owner himself with the help of two or three neighbours. The labour-intensive part of the operation involved the cutting of logs for the posts, sills, and horizontal members, the planing of the rough timbers, and the cutting of tongues in the horizontal pieces, as well as the grooves in the upright posts that received them. Once this work was complete, the actual building could be assembled in a few days by a crew of two or three men. Chinking the logs with mud and thatch, constructing the interior partitions, and making the wood floor and clay fireplace might take another week or so. The wood necessary for the construction of log structures was abundant in the parish before 1840 when the Red River; and the small creeks that flowed into it, were bordered by thick stands of poplar, maple, elm, and oak. As settlement expanded at St. Andrew's, the demand for wood increased and local residents were forced to travel greater distances in order to collect the large logs that were required for fuel and construction purposes. Wooding sites preferred by local settlers included "the pines" east of the Red in the Bird's Hill area and along the shores of Lake Winnipeg. Large oak logs were favoured for the construction of the exterior framing of a log building, and pine was used for the interior flooring. Pine and sometimes cedar were used to make roofing shingles, and poplar was employed in the construction of interior partitions. Finishing materials, such as hay for thatch and mud for chinking the cracks in the logs, the making of roughcast plaster, and the construction of fireplaces, were available along the banks of the river. Lime for whitewashing was obtained by burning limestone from riverbank deposits in specially dug pits. Tools used in the construction of Red River frame buildings were rudimentary. Chisels, simple planes, axes, and adzes were the only implements required, and, as these were frequently in short supply, they were often loaned out by local settlers to their neighbours. While some of these tools were handmade within the settlement, others were purchased from the nearby Hudson's Bay Company stores at Lower Fort.

In keeping with the design simplicity of most Red River architecture, the interior of a typical house in the parish was fairly basic. Partitioned into one, two, or three rooms by interior walls of poplar wood, lath work and plaster, these cottages presented a comfortable, if unpretentious, accommodation. One contemporary account described the interior of a typical home:

Inside is but a single room, well whitewashed ... and exceptionally tidy; a bed occupies one corner, a sort of couch another, a rung ladder leads up to loose boards overhead which form an attic, a trap door in the middle of the room opens to a small hole in the ground where milk and butter are kept cool; from the beam is suspended a hammock, used as a cradle for the baby, shelves singularly hung hold a scanty stock of plates, knives and forks; two windows on either side, covered with mosquito netting, admit the light, and a modicum of air; chests and boxes supply the place of seats with here and there a keg by way of an easy-chair. An open fireplace of whitewashed clay gives sign of cheer and warmth in the long winter.[79]

Larger log houses had a second story, a greater number of rooms heated by Carron stoves rather than a central fireplace, a better quality of furniture (including pieces ordered from England) and perhaps even area carpets to cover the bare wood floors. Summer kitchens often adjoined the main house or were located close by.

The extremes of climate in the Red River valley, especially the long, cold winters, presented serious problems for the residents of St. Andrew's parish. The style of construction used by the settlers, however, helped to alleviate some of these difficulties. Wood walls were able to "breathe" and provided reasonably good insulation against the elements. Logs were chinked with a combination of mud and straw, or sometimes buffalo hair, a mixture that could expand and contract with the temperature and helped to insulate the structure. Some larger log buildings were also sided with weatherboard, which gave them further protection against the cold, and in other instances roughcast, or stucco, was applied to exterior wood surfaces. Interior walls might be panelled with wood, or covered with a lime plaster that was manufactured in the parish. Describing homes in the Red River settlement, Alexander Ross noted that "the generality of the people use thatch roofs, which are light, watertight, and durable." As straw is a good insulator, and later prairie farmers often banked their houses with straw to ward off the cold, Red River frame houses were probably reasonably warm in winter. Although oak and occasionally cedar shingles were used, cedar was hard to come by in Red River and oak warped in the summer heat and had to be replaced every twelve to fifteen years. The small number of windows and doors in the average home served to keep out the summer heat and the winter cold. Window glass was imported from England and was often packed in barrels of molasses in order to survive the rough journey aboard the York boats that travelled between Hudson Bay and the settlement. Cellars were usually dug and were accessed through a trap door in the floor, and while a handful of homes in the parish might have had full basements – which provided further insulation against the cold – most had only partial cellars that served as a cold storage area in summer for vegetables, meat and dairy products. Despite these protections against the winter cold, surviving the elements in Red River required a great deal of energy from area settlers. Buffalo robes and thick wool blanket bed covers could be found in almost every St. Andrew's home in the nineteenth century. Fireplaces and stoves were used to heat the homes, and though some of the more affluent in the settlement used stone to construct their fireplaces, most log homes had fireplaces comprised of a frame of willow or poplar branches mudded with a mixture of clay, water, and straw that was kneaded into a paste and baked hard by the fire in the hearth. Metal stoves were also popular and had to be imported from Britain or, later, from the United States. Stoves made by the Carron Company of Scotland were shipped in pieces to York Factory, where they were assembled and fired and then shipped south to the Red River settlement. Stoves were usually centrally located inside the home, either in the front hallway of the larger structures, or against an interior partition. When the temperature reached minus twenty or thirty Celsius, as it often did in the settlement during the depths of winter, the stoves and fireplaces were kept constantly burning. Gathering wood for fuel was an essential part of life in the parish. Each fall, residents had to travel some distance to the various wooding sites on Lake Winnipeg or east of the Red River, where two or three days were needed to chop and stack the wood for transport back to the settlement. The firewood was hauled home on oxen-pulled sleds or on Red River carts. A large quantity of wood was needed to heat the average home through the winter months, and settlers were often forced to return to "the pines" one or more times during winter to replenish their depleted supplies.

While St. Andrew's settlers lived a somewhat precarious existence in the initial decades after the founding of the parish (a fact reflected in the rudimentary style of their architecture), by the mid-nineteenth century and the growth of a commercial and ecclesiastical elite within the parish, the nature of construction began to change. For a number of the area's more prominent citizens, or at least those who considered themselves the elite of the settlement, the style, size, and architectural sophistication of their residences, churches, and forts provided outward signs of their privileged position within local society. The creation of a "little Britain in the wilderness," a goal close to the hearts of the "aristocracy" of Red River (active and retired Hudson's Bay Company chief factors and chief traders, the Anglican clergy, and the major Métis and European traders and entrepreneurs), was partly reflected in the scale, materials, and design of their homes and public buildings.[80] The design of these larger buildings drew heavily upon the architectural traditions of the fur trade and its French and Scottish ancestries. In the West, the nature of architectural design and the choice of building materials reflected the ethnic origins of a Euro-Canadian fur-trade tradition as represented by the Scots and Orcadians of the HBC and the Canadiens, Scots, and Métis of the North West Company. It was the manor houses of Scotland and the stone cottages of old Quebec that provided the basic design for similar buildings in Red River. The design of the typical manor house in eighteenth-century Scotland was characterized by a symmetrical plan and facade, where windows were regularly spaced about a central door. The "laird's house," or the kind of house built by small Scottish landowners, was characterized by its modest size, symmetrical design, and hipped roof and was widely adopted throughout Britain by clergymen, merchants, and master craftsmen. As many of these types of people formed the bulk of early immigration to western Canada, the "laird's house" design was brought to Red River. The simplicity of the early external design and facade was continued in the interior, where a central hallway and staircase divided the ground floor into two main rooms. Bedrooms were located on the second floor, while a third-floor attic was usually used for storage. Large fireplaces might be located at either end of the building.[81]

Stone construction in St. Andrew's and throughout Red River in the nineteenth century also derived from the building traditions of Quebec, which, in turn, had evolved from the centuries-old traditions of Norman architecture. Though variations on a basic design existed throughout the different regions of Quebec, domestic structures were usually characterized by a common oblong shape, steep-pitched roofs,

Shown here in an 1858 photograph by H. L. Hime, the "Big House" at Lower Fort Garry was constructed in the early 1830s by Lower Canadian stonemason Pierre Leblanc and was considered one of the finest buildings in Rupert's Land (Provincial Archives of Manitoba).

low white-washed walls, and small dormer windows. The construction of stone buildings in Red River – whether of Scottish or French design – was usually carried out by skilled stonemasons, and the ethnicity of the individual mason had much to do with the ultimate form and layout of a particular structure. Thus, the Big House at Lower Fort Garry, constructed by Pierre LeBlanc from Quebec, mimics the symmetrical fenestration, sweeping balcony, and pavilion or bellcast-style hipped roof that was common to the stone houses of French Canada.[82] Conversely, the large stone Warehouse, built at the lower fort in the late 1830s, or the Rectory at St. Andrew's, built in the 1850s, both constructed under the direction of Scottish stonemason Duncan McRae, reflect the simple manor house design of the laird's house.

Stone construction was used for more than the Hudson's Bay Company forts or the houses of the elite in Red River and also characterized public buildings in the colony, such as the numerous stone churches that were built after 1830. These included St. Boniface Cathedral and the Anglican churches of St. Andrew's, St. Paul's, St. John's, St. Peter's, and St. Clement's, as well as Kildonan Presbyterian north of the Forks and the Little Britain Presbyterian church constructed in 1874 on lots 123

St. John's Anglican Church, Red River, 1858 (Provincial Archives of Manitoba).

and 124 near Lower Fort Garry in St. Andrew's parish. At St. Boniface, Bishop Provencher's first log church was replaced by a large stone cathedral designed by Jérome Demers, a colleague of Thomas Baillairgé, the great Québécois church architect. The church was destroyed by a fire in 1860 and a second stone cathedral was constructed under the direction of Mgr. Taché. This second cathedral was influenced by the neo-classical style, which marked the detailing of the pilasters and pillars of the cupola and verandah, the pediments of the dormers, the rounded windows of the porch, and the regularity of the fenestration. It was replaced by a larger cathedral in 1908, which burned in a spectacular fire in 1968.

Most Anglican churches in Red River in the nineteenth century were characterized by the Gothic Revival style. Pointed windows and doorways were employed in a simple, box-like form of cut limestone that did not differ substantially from the wood churches that marked the early years of the settlement. The first stone Anglican church in the settlement, the Upper Church (consecrated as St. John's Cathedral in 1853 by Bishop David Anderson) was erected north of the Forks in 1834 under the direction of the Rev. David Jones. St. John's was not built in the Gothic Revival style, having rounded or arched

St. Paul's Anglican Church, Red River, 1858 (Provincial Archives of Manitoba).

windows. It was constructed by the stonemason Pierre LeBlanc, who had directed much of the early building at Lower Fort Garry. Foundation problems and a severe flood in 1852 led to the demolition of the first stone St. John's Church and to its replacement by a larger structure, begun in 1862. (The present church dates from 1926.) Later stone churches (e.g., the Middle Church or St. Paul's built in the 1840s, and St. Andrew's completed in 1849) were long rectangular buildings with a high tower and belfry and Gothic Revival detailing in the windows and crenellated towers. The Hebridean mason, Duncan McRae, supervised the building of these two churches, along with a number of other church buildings in Red River, including St. Peter's, the later St. John's Church, and Kildonan Presbyterian. This latter building was patterned after the traditional Scottish Kirk but integrated a number of Gothic Revival details in its construction. Without the large east window that characterized most Anglican churches in the settlement, it was, according to one Red River historian, "plain, even to severity." (For a discussion of the architecture of St. Andrew's Church, see above pp. 58-62)

The limestone used in the construction of houses, churches and fort buildings in St. Andrew's was quarried from areas along the riverbank. Many of the richer areas of limestone in the lower settlement were located along the lower Red River

The rectory at St. Peter's Dynevor, c. 1880 (Provincial Archives of Manitoba).

where large outcroppings of the easily worked stone punctuated the forested riverbank between Lower Fort Garry and Netley Marsh. Other sources of limestone occurred at Stony Mountain and along the shores of Lake Winnipeg. Quarrying the stone was an arduous, time-consuming, and expensive task. Describing the quarrying operations for the stone used in the building of St. Andrew's Church, Rev. William Cockran wrote in 1845:

> *The rock is covered with gravel and clay to the depth of 8 feet which has to be wheeled off before it can be worked. And after all our expense and labour, there is only one strata about 3 feet thick above water.... The second strata is under water everytime the North wind blows, consequently we shall be able to work it occasionally.... The rock must be blasted with powder which [costs] 1/6 per lb., and our wages and other implements are also expensive from the high cost of Iron and Steel.[83]*

Limestone was often quarried in the spring and then transported to the building site, where it was worked, or shaped, by the masons. Stone from the riverbank was obtained with the use of a windlass that lifted the rough-cut slabs

127

Kildonan Presbyterian Church, 1858 (Provincial Archives of Manitoba).

Miss Davis's School, St. Andrew's Parish, c.1880. A fashionable school for the daughters of HBC officers, it was founded in the late 1850s by Matilda Davis, herself the daughter of a company officer. Davis, assisted by an English governess, provided "a solid English education, with French, Music, Drawing, Dancing, [as well as] Plain & Ornamental Needle-Work," in short, the kind of training required by acculturated young Métis women to ensure their suitability as marriage partners in Red River society (Provincial Archives of Manitoba).

onto Red River carts that were pulled by oxen to the top of the bank and transported to the building site. Here limestone was also burned in deep pits to produce the slake lime that would be used as mortar. After working the stone and producing the mortar, the masons began the painstaking task of setting the limestone blocks. Depending upon available labour, this was a slow process; the walls at Lower Fort Garry took almost ten years to build. While much of the actual construction of a stone wall or building employed either rough-cut or partially worked stone blocks, some of the more decorative features such as the smoothly shaped stone lintels and arches of the parish churches were far more labour-intensive.

Today, the area along River Road in old St. Andrew's parish boasts many fine examples of the stone-built architectural tradition of Red River. St. Andrew's Church and Rectory, Twin Oaks, the former Miss Davis's School (all three national historic sites), along with Little Britain Church, Kennedy House (built by William Kennedy at the rapids in 1866) Hay House, the remains of Scott house, and the stone buildings of Lower Fort Garry, all stand as stone symbols and reminders of life in the parish in the nineteenth century. However, it is the hundreds of log buildings of the parish's early settlers – the houses, barns, and outbuildings of those Red River farmers, hunters, and tripmen who settled the riverlots of the lower settlement, almost all of which have disappeared – that better describe parish life in the decades after its founding. Today, it is the names of Kennedy, Davis, Cockran, and Scott that survive in St. Andrew's, at least through association with their extant stone houses. The memories of such individuals as Andrew and Margaret Spence, who inhabited lot number thirteen, or the family of John and Elizabeth Tait on lot fifty-six, have faded, however, as their nineteenth-century log houses disappeared, and the old riverlots became increasingly obscured by modern development in the parish. Sadly, with them went many of the tangible reminders of an early mixed Métis and European community in Manitoba's past.

Chapter Six

St. Andrew's and the Agricultural Economy

"The Multiplicity

of their Pursuits"

Historians have traditionally character-ized agriculture in Red River, including St. Andrew's, as primitive, essentially subsistence in nature, and incapable of freeing the economy of the colony from the constraints of the fur trade. As far back as Alexander Ross, writers have labelled farming in the settlement before 1870 to be largely subsistence-based and almost always subservient to the hunt and such economic pursuits as freight-ing, hunting, and the trade in furs.[1] In his book, *The Red River Settlement*, first published in 1856, Ross described the Métis population of the settlement as living a "ragged life which habit has made familiar to them.... The multiplicity of their pursuits," he argued, "oftener lost the advantage of all than accomplish one."[2] According to the explorer Henry Youle Hind, who arrived in Red River in 1857, "no one can fail to be struck with the indifference to the future which seems habitually to characterize the people, especially the French portion of the population, [which shows] itself in their unfinished dwellings [and] neglected farms."[3] Writing in the 1940s, the ethnologist Marcel Giraud described the "natural inclination" of the Métis toward buffalo-hunting, an "inclination," which Giraud maintained created a "struggle between two incompatible environments" within the colony.[4] The notion of tension between the hunt and the farm is a theme later picked up by historian W. L. Morton. He argued that the dominance within Red

River of a buffalo-hunting economy served to effectively discourage the development of a purely agricultural community before 1870. The two economies, he contended, acted as a "fatal check" upon each other, depressing returns in a limited local market.[5] Like Morton, George Stanley believed the economic behaviour of Red River's aboriginal population to be irrational, improvident, and largely non-adaptive.[6] In short, Giraud, Stanley, and Morton considered the settlement's Métis to be the nomadic "misfits" of the pre-1870 West.

More recently, geographer Barry Kaye and historian Leland Clarke have put forward the notion that the two economies of Red River were more complementary than competitive.[7] They maintained that, in times of agricultural scarcity, the returns from the hunt and the fisheries went a long way toward feeding the settlement's population. Likewise, when the buffalo hunt failed or returns were meagre, the hunters relied almost exclusively upon agricultural foodstuffs produced in the settlement. While both Kaye and Clarke believed that the distinction drawn between farmers and hunters should not be over-emphasized, they generally conceded that, compared to the larger mixed-blood population, the Kildonan Scots agriculturalists represented the most "progressive" element within Red River society. In much of Red River historiography, the Métis have been considered part of a primitive and subsistence economy, while the Europeans located at the upper settlement (or the parishes of St. John's and Kildonan) represented the potential for the introduction of stable agriculture in the West. The colony failed, according to these perspectives, because of its reliance upon a mixed or "hybrid" economy in the decades prior to Manitoba's entry into Confederation.[8] In his analysis of economic life in the Red River settlement Gerhard Ens contends that the proto-industrialization of the Métis economy in Red River after 1840 and the growth of the buffalo robe trade led to the gradual abandonment of "peasant" agriculture in the French-speaking Métis parishes of Red River. Conversely, the Métis of St. Andrew's, less inclined to participate in this new commerce (which removed participants from the colony for long periods of time), continued a "peasant," subsistence-based farming economy oriented towards household consumption. Ens suggests that neither economic strategy successfully prepared the French-and English-speaking Métis for the development of commercial farming and the emergence of a new economic order in the West after 1870.[9]

Settler's horse and cart, Red River, c. 1870. Painted by W.G.R. Hind (National Archives of Canada).

The history of St. Andrew's parish before 1870 suggests that (in a community characterized by scarce resources and a primitive technology) the mixed economy of this predominantly English-speaking Métis parish was well adapted to the limited economic opportunities offered by Red River in the nineteenth century. With their combination of small-scale agriculture, hunting, and freighting for the Hudson's Bay Company, along with other commercial pursuits, the settlers at St. Andrew's demonstrated a flexible economic strategy that was superior to that of their Scottish neighbours at the upper settlement. Faced with few markets for their farm produce, a harsh climate and the limited availability of up-to-date agricultural techniques and technology, the Selkirk settlers were ill-equipped to establish a stable agricultural economy in Red River.[10] St. Andrew's settlers, on the other hand, maintained a mixed economic base as a deliberate and practical solution to the greatest challenge that faced the settlement, that of scarcity. Hunting wild game, fishing, working as wage labourers for the HBC, milling, gathering wild fruit, or participating in the private trade in furs allowed Métis families to overcome the fragility of agriculture in Red River, especially in the early years of the colony. Census data and other records suggest that, as traditional economic opportunities declined in Red River, participation in agriculture at St. Andrew's increased over the second half of the century. This increased commitment represented a rational adaptive response to the changing circumstances that were occurring in Red River in the1840s, a decade that saw diminished opportunities for the Métis with the HBC, new restrictions on free trade, and the decline of the traditional buffalo hunt. The notion that a subsistence economy characterized Red River in the half-century before 1870 can also be challenged. Evidence from St. Andrew's suggests that an active commercial economy existed within the parish, distinguished by such activities as the buying and selling of land, the sale of wage labour, and the exchange of goods and services. Moreover, through commercial and financial links with the fur trade, the economy of the parish was tied to international commodity capitalism.

Before 1870, Red River was essentially a riparian settlement. This developmental pattern was the result of a variety of factors that effectively served to restrict habitation to the long narrow lots bordering the Red and Assiniboine. The rivers and their tributaries facilitated transportation, and their banks provided the timber necessary for both fuel and shelter. Only near the river's edge was the land considered viable for cultivation, the rivers and creeks providing the main source of water for the settlement as well as fish to supplement the local diet.

The pattern of land use at St. Andrew's and throughout the colony, derived from the infield and outfield system found in Scotland and brought to Red River by the Selkirk settlers.[11] The colonist's home, assorted outbuildings, and small kitchen garden were located near the river's edge. Behind the farmstead was situated the infield or the small fenced and cultivated "parks" where the farmer grew his cereal and garden crops. Beyond the infield, and occupying the rest of the two-mile lot, stretched the larger outfield. While some settlers submitted the outfield to the occasional cropping, most used these unfenced areas to graze their livestock. As well, each settler possessed a "haying privilege" on the two miles of land located adjacent to his particular lot. Beyond the haying privilege, colonists in Red River possessed equal rights to the hay and timber of what became known as "the common."[12]

The majority of crops grown in St. Andrew's and throughout much of Red River were field crops, primarily wheat, barley, and potatoes. Wheat accounted for about 65 percent of the total cultivated acreage. Seeding in the colony generally took place between the last week of April and the third week of May.[13] Depending upon weather conditions, and for many the timing of the fall buffalo

A modern depiction of a typical St. Andrew's riverlot farm in the mid-nineteenth century. In the usual layout, the house and associated kitchen garden were located nearest to the river, while barns and stables were situated immediately behind. The rest of the long narrow lot was occupied with fenced field crops of wheat, oats, and barley. Hay was also grown on the riverlot and at the "hay privilege" (Parks Canada).

hunt, harvesting of the wheat crop could occur any time between mid-August and mid-September. In the early years of the colony, seed wheat was brought from England and the United States.[14] The most common variety of wheat in Red River before 1850 was Prairie du Chien, although other strains such as Black Sea became popular in later decades. An early maturing wheat, Prairie du Chien was a soft grain suitable for grinding in the wind and water mills located in the parish. Barley was the second most common grain crop in Red River and was used for brewing, bread-making, barley broth (at least among the inhabitants of the English-speaking parishes), and as livestock feed. The most consistent crop in Red River, however, was the potato, grown both as a field crop and in gardens. In the years when the grain crop failed, especially in the early days of the colony, potatoes (along with fish and pemmican) provided much of the basic sustenance for the inhabitants of Red River. The potato was generally able to survive such common calamities as early frosts, periodic flooding, and insects. Oats were also sown as field crops, although the quantity never rivalled that of wheat, barley, and potatoes. Oats did not do well in the hot, dry summers of Red River, preferring a climate that was both cool and wet.

Aside from cereal crops, St. Andrew's farmers grew vegetables in the small gardens located adjacent to their riverfront houses. These included carrots, cabbages, cauliflower, celery, onions, turnips, beets, and peas. Crops indigenous to North America also played a small role in Red River agriculture, including Indian corn and squash.[15] There were few attempts by local farmers to introduce fruit cultivation into the settlement. Most settlers simply gathered the wild berries of the plains.

While it is relatively easy to locate information concerning cultivation patterns and the types of crops grown in Red River as a whole, it is more difficult to ascertain the specific crop preferences of settlers in St. Andrew's parish in the nineteenth century. However, by identifying households in the parish and then linking this information with Red River census data, the average amount of acreage under cultivation in the parish can be determined, at least in general terms. Similar types of data can also be obtained in relation to livestock, farm implements, barns, sheds, and carts, and, these along with more impressionistic findings, are useful in coming to some conclusions regarding the level of agricultural activity in St. Andrew's parish and how it might have changed over time. The data can also be used to assess the distinctiveness of agricultural activity at St. Andrew's vis-à-vis the settlement as a whole. When this information is coupled with a variety of other documentary sources, a picture emerges of the evolving economy of St. Andrew's parish in the nineteenth century.

Remarkably complete, the various Red River censuses give a detailed breakdown of demographic elements in the settlement during its formative years. Although enumerators recorded the names of only the heads of households, they documented a large number of variables for each, including sex, religion, birthplace, married and unmarried males and females living in the household, sons over and under the age of sixteen, daughters over and under the age of fifteen, as well as male and female servants. Each census also included a breakdown per household of the number of houses, barns, stables, agricultural implements (ploughs and harrows), livestock (horses, cattle, sheep, oxen, and swine), boats, carts, and acreage under cultivation. The Red River censuses failed to assign parish affiliation before 1870. Lower Settlement,[16] Cree Settlement, Saulteaux Settlement, and Grantown were the only geographical designations made by HBC enumerators prior to 1849, when the designations "Protestant Settlement" and "Catholic Settlement" were added. Table 2 of D. N. Sprague and R. P. Frye's *The Genealogy of the First Métis Nation,* entitled "Family Size, Personal Property, and Geographical Location of Landowners, 1835," uses HBC files or "memoranda" concerning land grants in the colony to establish parish affiliation for the 1835 census return. When George Taylor surveyed Red River parishes in 1835 for the company, he prepared memoranda that reflected existing occupancy. The HBC entered Taylor's field notes into account books indicating whether individual land grants had been made via purchase from the company or as a prior grant from Lord Selkirk. The listing of male heads of families affiliated with St. Andrew's identified in Table 2 of *The Genealogy of the First Métis Nation* was augmented with data from other documentary sources, including the parish registry of births, deaths, and marriages, CMS journals, Red River settler accounts found in HBC records, and the general locational clues provided in the 1835 census. These same documentation sources, coupled with the parish affiliations of settlers provided in the first provincial census of 1870, were used to identify St. Andrew's heads of households who were enumerated (without parish affiliation) in the 1849 census.[17]

According to the 1835 census, there were 559 households in the Red River settlement, cultivating an average of 5.7 acres. At St. Andrew's in 1835, ninety-seven farmers were cultivating a total of 568 acres, for an average per settler of just under 5.8 acres of cropped land. Of course, many settlers in the parish had little or no land under cultivation. Seventeen households in St. Andrew's recorded no cultivated acreage, while nineteen farmers had over ten acres of ploughed land in 1835, and a few of the wealthier inhabitants such as James Sutherland, James Whitway, and Andrew Setter reported in excess of fifteen acres of cultivated land in the parish. What is of note is that the average amount of cultivated land at St. Andrew's in 1835 is almost identical to the overall average for Red River in the same year. While cultivated acreage was far from evenly distributed throughout the colony (Scottish settlers near the Forks ploughed more land than did the Métis inhabitants of Grantown), and the handful of households in the parish who cultivated over fifteen acres skew the average somewhat, it is evident that in the 1830s St. Andrew's settlers were representative of the overall level of agricultural activity in Red River, at least in terms of ploughed land.

By 1849, the amount of cultivated land in the parish, when compared with the totals for the settlement as a whole, had increased. That year, 185 households in St. Andrew's cultivated a total of 1,558 acres, for a mean average acreage per settler of 8.4 acres. According to the 1849 census, there was a total of 6,392 cultivated acres in Red River distributed among 1,052 households, an average acreage per household of only 6.1 acres, or 2.3 acres per household less than the amount of land being cultivated at St. Andrew's. Although the ratio of population density and cultivated acreage between St. Andrew's and the whole of the Red River settlement was fairly equitable in 1835, the figures have changed by 1849. With less than eighteen percent of the total number of households in Red River, the parish possessed twenty-four percent of the cultivated land in the settlement. Clearly, where St. Andrew's had been relatively typical of cultivation patterns in the early years of the Red River colony, by 1849, the parish was one of the stronger agricultural areas of the settlement. Again, it is instructive to look at the distribution of cultivated acreage within the parish itself. According to census data, the percentage of those in St. Andrew's who had no cultivated land remained the same in 1835 and 1849. However, the percentage of farmers who cultivated between ten and twenty acres increased from nineteen percent to thirty six percent during this same period. Thus, the amount of agricultural activity in the parish (at least as can be determined by comparing acreage under cultivation) increased on a per household average in the years between the censuses of 1835 and 1849.

Although census records provide data on the extent of cultivation in St. Andrew's before 1849, they contain no information on the distribution of specific crops within the parish. From private journals such as the Samuel Taylor diary, missionary journals, and correspondence, and from entries found in HBC Red River settlers' accounts, however, it is possible to comment generally on the types of crops cultivated at St. Andrew's. Like elsewhere in Red River, wheat formed the largest single cereal crop in the parish. Generally, the wheat grown at the Rapids in this early period was Prairie du Chien, which was sown in spring. While a few farmers experimented with winter wheat planted in the fall, the initiative proved a failure.[18] Barley amounted to perhaps twenty five percent of the total amount of grain grown in the parish and was favoured because it required a relatively short growing season.[19] Sown in late May or early June, the barley crop in the parish was generally ready for harvesting some time in late July or early August. Potatoes also had a short growing season and were counted on when grain yields were low or failed altogether. In his correspondence with Church Missionary Society officials in London, William Cockran frequently noted the importance of the potato crop in the parish. Though generally planted as field crops in rows, they often grew "wild" close to the riverbanks.[20] According to Henry Youle Hind, potatoes grown in the settlement were a "round and white skinned variety like those known in Canada as the 'English White'."[21] By the 1860s, a yield of 300 bushels per acre was not uncommon among the parish's better farmers.[22] Oats were far less popular at St. Andrew's. While it is difficult to assess the extent of their cultivation in the parish, it is instructive that oats are never mentioned in the Taylor diary. A wide variety of garden vegetables were grown at St. Andrew's in the small plots adjacent to the settlers' houses. Again, there is little specific information in regard to the extent of vegetable cultivation in the parish, or which vegetables were preferred over others. Each riverlot likely contained a vegetable garden, even those lots that did not support grain farming.

Farm homes, windmills, and cultivated acreage in the middle settlement. Photographed by H. L. Hime in 1858 (Provincial Archives of Manitoba).

Census data reveal that the period of greatest increase in the per capita rate of cultivated acreage at St. Andrew's occurred between 1843 and 1849. Prior to this date, increases were marginal, no doubt the result of poor weather, grasshoppers, and substandard seed and tools, as well the attractiveness of other commercially viable activities in the settlement. Declining commercial opportunities within the settlement after 1840, combined with the increase in the market for agricultural produce, helped to expand farming activity in the parish after 1843. At first glance, the increase in cultivated acreage during this period seems puzzling in light of the considerable documentation that indicates that the 1840s was a decade of drought, early frosts, and partial or complete crop failures. In 1846, Alexander Christie, the governor of Assiniboia, reported that the year's grain crop was a complete failure,[23] while Marcel Giraud, in his study *Le Métis Canadien*, noted a similar result for 1847.[24] Apparently, some farmers in the parish attempted to offset low yields by increasing cultivation, hoping to salvage at least enough grain to survive the winter. As well, the presence at Lower Fort Garry between 1846 and 1848 of the Sixth Regiment of Foot, sent to Red River to help suppress the free-trade movement, served to stimulate local agricultural activity. A rise in demand for flour, fresh meat, and vegetables to feed the troops helped increase cultivation by providing farmers with a ready market for their produce.

Animal husbandry was an important part of Red River agriculture in the nineteenth century. Domestic livestock provided much of the fresh meat, dairy products, and transportation necessary for day-to-day life in the colony. Farmers in Red River raised cattle, pigs, horses, sheep, oxen, and poultry, albeit with indifferent success as much of the livestock was of a generally inferior quality, and little effort was expended to improve the stock. Cattle formed the largest part of the livestock population, accounting for approximately one third of all domesticated animals in the settlement.[25] Cattle were first introduced to Red River in 1822 with little initial success.[26] Later, superior breeds were brought in with hopes of improving the herds, but, because of poor breeding techniques and periodic hay shortages, the quality of Red River cattle remained low. Despite these problems there were almost 4,000 head in the settlement by 1849.[27] Sheep were first brought to Red River in 1833 in hopes of creating a wool industry that would provide an export trade for the colony. Despite numerous obstacles, 250 sheep were brought to Red River that year, and, over the next decade, the colony enjoyed a modest sheep boom. By 1849, however, numbers were on the decline as severe winter temperatures, indifferent breeding, and wolves took their toll on the colony's sheep population.[28] Pigs and poultry, although comprising a significant portion of the total livestock in Red River, were seldom mentioned in the English records and were generally taken for granted by local farmers.[29] Very little bacon or ham was cured by the English-speaking farmers in Red River, and pork never achieved the popularity of beef or pemmican. Oxen were used in the settlement as draught animals, pulling the farmers' ploughs, sleds, and carts, or the carts of freighters. Many settlers kept a pair of oxen, and, by 1849, there were over 2,000 of these animals in Red River.[30] Although horses were also used as draught animals, most were kept by local inhabitants for riding or driving. The first horses in Red River came from the American southwest, but later the HBC brought in a few English stallions and mares to help upgrade the local stock. The better-bred horses in the settlement were reserved for such activities as the drive to church by sleigh or carriole, visiting, hunting, or running races on the plains or on the river ice in wintertime. Not surprisingly, the Métis parishes in Red River maintained a greater number of horses than did the European parts of the settlement.

Though the quality of Red River livestock before 1870 was generally poor, a small but significant trade in cattle, oxen, and sheep operated between Red River and the frontier regions of the American Midwest.[31] Initially, livestock herds were brought into the colony from the south, but as the size of herds increased in Red River, farmers began supplying a limited number of livestock to new farm settlements, mission stations, and developing urban centres in Minnesota.[32]

At St. Andrew's, the raising of domestic animals was a significant part of the local economy as farmers maintained cattle, sheep, horses, pigs, and oxen. During the summer months, cattle were put out to graze on the unfenced riverlots. In winter, the small herds were stabled and fed on the hay collected between July and October. The severe winters took their toll on livestock in the parish. Frequent shortages of hay severely depleted the local cattle population, and the animals that did make it through the long cold winters were often weak, emaciated, and susceptible to disease. In the spring of 1859, Samuel Taylor of St. Andrew's reported that "a great many cattle [are] dying for want of something to eat."[33] Shortages often forced settlers in St. Andrew's to travel great distances to secure wild hay, and some chose to winter their cattle at these distant locations. One such favoured location was Netley Creek near Lake Winnipeg, where lower settlement farmers could usually find an abundance of hay during the late summer and early fall.

Census records indicate that the number of cattle per household in St. Andrew's declined between 1835 and 1849, as did the per household total for the whole of the Red River settlement. In 1835, St. Andrew's residents could claim thirty two percent of the total cattle population in the settlement. This percentage remained unchanged fourteen years later in 1849. In 1835, almost all parish landowners had cattle – only two residents were listed as having none – and approximately ten percent of the respondents claimed larger herds of over twenty head. James Whitway, for example, had twenty-four head of cattle, John Slater, twenty head, and Andrew Setter, thirty-seven. By 1849, the percentage of those in the parish owning twenty or more cattle had decreased to seven percent, which might explain at least part of the per household decline in cattle ownership in the parish between 1835 and 1849. In the early period, the high percentage of large cattle owners distorted the average. Thus, the figure for 1849 might be more representative of the average farmer in the parish. Cows and calves made up a greater part of cattle herds at St. Andrew's in 1835 and 1849. Few farmers had bulls, and most relied on the services of the Hudson's Bay Company, which periodically brought bulls into the parish from Lower and Upper Fort Garry. Oxen served as draught animals for the farmers and freighters at St. Andrew's and were used for ploughing, harrowing, and pulling Red River carts. They were also raised for sale to the HBC, which after 1858 began to use oxen in their development of an overland transportation system between Red River and St. Paul.

Oxen steadily increased in number in Red River, multiplying more than threefold between 1835 and 1856. At St. Andrew's, few settlers kept more than five of these animals, with most having one or two. Samuel Taylor notes that oxen were loaned from farmer to farmer and were often used by parish residents to haul the larger loads of firewood that came from as far away as the shore of Lake Winnipeg.[34] In 1835, St. Andrew's settlers had an average of less than one horse per landowner, a rate almost identical with the settlement as a whole. Few in the parish had more than two horses, while half had none at all. Fourteen years later, the average throughout all of Red River had increased to almost two horses per household, while the St. Andrew's figure rose to only 1.5, indicative, perhaps, of a shift in the parish away from buffalo hunting to sedentary agriculture in the period before 1850. The number of pigs in the Red River settlement fluctuated widely between 1835 and 1849. From over 3,000 in 1835, the numbers had declined to just over 1,500 by 1849. At St. Andrew's, the per-household average declined as well from almost five in 1835 to just under two in 1849. This reduction was due primarily to the harsh Red River climate, as severe winters took their toll on the local swine population. In 1856, Alexander Ross noted that the number of pigs had declined by one third in a single season. Left to scavenge on their own for the better part of the year, swine were fed during the winter months with surplus potatoes. In 1835, most farmers in the parish owned a few pigs, with some having as many as twelve or thirteen. By 1849, however, roughly half of the households are listed as having no pigs, and only a very small handful had more than ten. The decline could also have been due to the fact that pork was not a preferred meat among the inhabitants of St. Andrew's and the English settlement. Consequently, little interest was shown in increasing the parish's swine population after 1840. The number of sheep owned by farmers in St. Andrew's rose dramatically between 1835 and 1843. By 1849, however, the number of sheep in the parish had declined by more than half from an average of about seven to just over one per household. Ownership of sheep in St. Andrew's tended to be concentrated amongst a small handful of successful farmers. Most settlers in the parish kept no sheep at all by 1849, while eight landowners had thirty or more that same year. As has been indicated by W. L. Morton and Barry Kaye, the vast majority of sheep in Red River were to be found in the parishes of St. John's, St. Paul's, and St. Andrew's.[35] Although sheep were quite numerous in Red River in the early years of the colony, wolves, cold winters, and summer prairie fires helped deplete the flocks after 1843.[36] With the demise of the Assiniboine Wool Company and the colony's failure to export locally spun woolen goods, sheep declined as an important domestic animal in St. Andrew's and throughout Red River.

The number of agricultural implements in St. Andrew's can also serve as a useful tool for measuring the level of farming activity in the parish. For much of the nineteenth century, the agricultural implements available to local farmers tended to be simple, limited in number, and made largely within the settlement from local timber. For the limited cultivation that was carried out in the parish, a plough, harrow, spade, scythe or sickle, hand rake, and cart were the essential tools of the St. Andrew's farmer, who did most things by hand. The difficulty in procuring more technologically advanced agricultural equipment from Britain or the United States helped restrict the amount of cultivation, especially in the early years of the settlement. Red River farmers used wooden ploughs shod with iron until steel ploughs were eventually brought into the settlement from St. Peter's on the American frontier. Spring seeding at St. Andrew's was done by hand (potatoes, for instance, were planted with the use of a spade), and a horse- or ox-drawn harrow was used to work down the soil and cover the seed.[37] In the fall, grain was reaped with a sickle, though the scythe was in use by the 1840s and 1850s. Threshing the harvested grain took place during all seasons of the year and was accomplished with the use of a flail, usually on the ice floor of a barn.[38] The threshed grain was then taken to one of the seven wind or water mills that operated in the parish between 1825 and 1870. In the early years of the colony, before mills were constructed, settlers were forced to grind much of their grain in simple hand mills called "querns." A quern consisted of two flat stones, the upper stone attached to a handle that was used to turn the stone over the wheat. Hand mills produced a course and not entirely white flour.[39] Those settlers who owned and operated mills in the parish ground their neighbours' wheat and barley in exchange for cash or barter, thus representing one aspect of the commercial economy that operated in St. Andrew's before 1870.

The number of farm implements in use in St. Andrew's increased between 1835 and 1849, though the per household average remained relatively fixed in this period. While, in 1849, a few settlers such as George Setter had two ploughs and two harrows, and Phillip Kennedy had two ploughs and three harrows, most farmers had only one of each. Even though the amount of cultivated acreage in the parish had increased from 1835 to 1849, only one of each implement was actually needed to break the ground, plant the seed, and harvest the resulting crop.

The number of farm buildings (barns and stables) is also a useful indicator of agricultural activity in the parish. The 1835 census records that St. Andrew's farmers owned approximately the same number of outbuildings on their riverlots as did other Red River landowners. By 1849, these figures had changed with householders in St. Andrew's having an average of one barn or stable on their property, while other settlement residents maintained an average of less than one farm building per household.

Red River census data reflect a number of trends in agricultural activity at St. Andrew's between 1835 and 1849. By 1849, the parish had surpassed the rest of the settlement as a whole in cultivated acreage, farm implements, outbuildings, and some livestock. Once representative of the mixed economy (with little emphasis on agriculture) that characterized the Red River settlement, the economy of St. Andrew's was changing by 1849. Farming had become more important by this date and complemented the involvement by local settlers in many of the other economic activities that traditionally prevailed in Red River before 1870.

As 1849 represented the last complete census in Red River before the creation of the province in 1870 (other than an incomplete census for the year 1856) information regarding agriculture in St. Andrew's after mid-century can be found in a variety of other documentary and descriptive sources such as private journals, newspapers, published accounts, and church and HBC records. By 1850, a decade of hot dry summers that had plagued St. Andrew's and Red River farmers throughout the 1840s had ended. In 1852, a major flood inundated the upper settlement and overflowing creeks threatened crops in St. Andrew's and the lower parishes. According to Marcel Giraud, the years 1855, 1856, and 1857 were also excessively damp, restricting crop yields and affecting the nourishment of livestock.[40] Grasshoppers visited the settlement in 1857 necessitating the importation of grain by the HBC from the United States and Canada.[41]

According to Samuel Taylor, 1860 was a bountiful year for crops in St. Andrew's, perhaps the best that most residents could remember.[42] The following year, however, the heavy spring rains returned, delaying the sowing of wheat until late in May. The HBC was forced to advance quantities of seed grain to destitute farmers in the settlement. The summer of 1862 marked the beginning of a decade of drought and locusts. "Dry, dry," wrote Taylor in 1863, "the weather was never seen, people say, so long without rain, it thunders often and yet no rain."[43] The drought caused crop yields to decline in the parish, and this resulted in the closing of a number of water-powered grist mills.[44] The next year, 1864, was even worse and as the settlement newspaper, *The Nor'Wester*, commented:

> *The oldest inhabitant does not remember a summer of such extraordinary, long continued heat as we have experienced this year.... One day of sultry, scorching, hot weather follows another.... The case will readily be believed when we say that the thermometers have indicated 87 to 90, 97 and even 100 degrees in the shade!*[45]

By the 1860s, land use patterns at St. Andrew's had begun to change. On the lands traditionally reserved for the "hay privilege" many farmers were cultivating "park lots," which were small plots of land ranging in size from two to eight acres. While some were used for pasturing livestock, other fenced plots were used to cultivate wheat, oats, barley, potatoes, and other vegetables. The creation of park lots after 1860 helped reduce the growing congestion caused by the subdivision of the old riverlot farms in St. Andrew's. Farming techniques also changed after 1860. Some local settlers began to experiment with crop rotation and began employing manure as a fertilizer. Earlier, travellers such as H. Y. Hind had remarked on how Red River farmers simply piled their manure near their barn or stable.

A farm along the Red River, lower settlement, c. 1870 (Provincial Archives of Manitoba).

"Sometimes," he wrote, "it is thrown into the river, or heaped in such a position that it may be swept away by spring freshets."[46] A few years later, however, Samuel Taylor described how he helped his neighbour John Flett "to spread dung on his land."[47] The practice became increasingly more common in the parish throughout the 1860s.

According to *The Nor'Wester*, the major change in animal husbandry in the settlement after 1860 was the rapid decline of sheep raising, an activity that the paper described as having "nearly gone out of fashion altogether."[48] As well, drought conditions resulted in the deterioration of other livestock in the settlement due primarily to the inadequate supply of hay for feed. The continuation of inferior breeding techniques and the report of disease among cattle in 1868 further weakened the stock at St. Andrew's.

The creation of the province of Manitoba in 1870 had an important effect upon agricultural development and settlement patterns in Red River. In 1877, the federal government added a two-mile extension to the boundaries of the old parish riverlots. These new lots were roughly "squared" by surveyors, and the ends of the long narrow lots were made to fit with the new rectangular land survey. The continuing redivision of riverlots among extended families after 1870 created a situation where farms in the settlement were no longer productive in the market-oriented, wheat economy taking shape under the national policy of the federal government. Hoping to attract Euro-Canadian settlement into the community at St. Andrew's, the Anglican Church expressed its desire to see a reform of traditional settlement patterns.[49] With the crumbling of the old mixed-blood alliance in Red River as a result of the machinations of the church and the new provincial government, many of the old English-speaking Métis families who did not assimilate into the new community (some of whom could trace their residency in the parish as far back as the 1820s) left St. Andrew's, displaced by the new group of Anglo-Ontarian farmers and entrepreneurs who descended upon Manitoba after 1880.

After 1850, agriculture had become an increasingly important part of the mixed economy of St. Andrew's parish, a trend that had begun a decade earlier with the decline of large-scale hunting activities and the reduction in wage labour opportunities on the HBC's boat and cart brigades. It is important to underscore the commercial character of this economy, and the degree to which an exchange of goods and services continued within the community. To conclude that farmers in the parish practised a purely subsistence, or peasant style of agriculture is misleading. Though outside markets were limited, the Hudson's Bay Company purchased settlers' produce to help provision its fur brigades and posts throughout the Northwest. Before 1841, the company operated two farms in Red River; the first lasted from 1831 to 1836, the second, located at the Forks, from 1836 to 1841. For a variety of reasons, both farming operations failed. From 1841 until 1857, when it established a third farm at Lower Fort Garry, the HBC relied on the country produce it was able to secure from local settlers. This included meat, dairy products, vegetables, and, most importantly, wheat. Lower Fort Garry, located in St. Andrew's, served as one of the company's principal trans-shipment posts, as well as the supply depot for the York boat brigades, and later the schooners that sailed between Red River and Norway House. An important commodity shipped from the lower fort to posts throughout Rupert's Land was hard-tack biscuit. After 1847, the major source of biscuit was the bakehouse facility located within the North West Bastion at Lower Fort Garry. The flour used to produce the sizable quantity of biscuit required each year by the company was purchased from local farmers. Between 1847 and 1857, the amount of biscuit shipped from Red River to the interior averaged approximately thirty-three hundredweight a year.[50] An equal amount of the yeastless bread was also distributed by the HBC throughout the Red River district.[51] As well as biscuit, the bakehouse at Lower Fort Garry produced bread for consumption by local company officers and servants. The Sixth Regiment of Foot, stationed at the lower fort between 1846 and 1848, consumed approximately 150 pounds of bread each day, along with an equal quantity of meat.[52] With this rate of consumption, the Hudson's Bay Company at Lower Fort Garry represented a significant commercial market for farmers in St. Andrew's parish, at least after 1847.

Within the settlement itself, items such as grain, potatoes, vegetables, and live-stock were bartered or sold, as was farm labour. Non-agricultural foodstuffs such as pemmican, wild game, and fish were also exchanged by local residents. Whitefish from the fishery at Grand Marais on the east shore of Lake Winnipeg were sold by local settlers and represented an important marketable commodity in St. Andrew's.[53] In his diary Samuel Taylor frequently noted purchases of pickerel, sturgeon, goldeye, and catfish, either for cash or in exchange for products or services.[54]

The limited trade in livestock between Red River and American settlements south of the border represented another commercial market for settlers in St. Andrew's. As Barry Kaye has noted, the export of cattle and sheep that began in the late 1830s developed quickly into a thriving livestock trade.[55] In 1840, Red River Governor Duncan Finlayson promised the St. Peter's cattle market three to four hundred head annually.[56] By 1854, George Simpson of the HBC described the livestock trade as "considerable," as local settlers exported cattle and imported horses from the American Midwest. While the number of cattle involved in the trade probably never exceeded a few hundred a year, the American livestock market no doubt represented a viable commercial outlet for the owners of domestic livestock in St. Andrew's.[57]

The development of various crafts represented another commercial aspect of the parish economy. A limited service sector existed in the community, with some settlers finding seasonal employment as woodcutters, sawyers, carpenters, coopers, and blacksmiths, and as part-time labourers for the HBC at Lower Fort Garry. (Samuel Taylor, for instance, was a stonemason and helped construct many of the stone buildings in Red River.) The milling of grain was an important activity in the parish, and millers such as John Tait, John Gunn, Donald Gunn, and Thomas Sinclair contracted with local farmers and the HBC to grind their grain in privately owned wind and water mills.

Métis farm in the Red River area, 1882 (Glenbow Archives).

In addition to farming, a number of the Métis of St. Andrew's traditionally participated in the spring and fall buffalo hunts, voyaged to York Factory, manned the cart brigades that travelled west to the Saskatchewan, or traded in furs outside the company's monopoly. By the mid-1840s, however, the great buffalo herds had moved further away from the settlement, and returns from the hunt diminished. Freighting contracts with the company also declined in this period. Moreover, the lack of opportunities for some mixed-bloods to rise above the level of apprentice postmaster with the company's permanent service meant that alternative sources of income had to be found. As James Sutherland of St. Andrew's commented to his brother in Scotland:

> *I could get him [Sutherland's son] in the Cos. service, but Halfbreeds as they are called [have] no chance there nor are respected whatever their abilities may be, by a parcel of upstart Scotchmen, who now hold the power and control in the concern.*[58]

For the second generation of St. Andrew's settlers, the private trade in furs represented one alternative within the mixed economy of the parish. In the 1830s, the HBC licensed a number of free traders to help it compete with American traders who operated just over the border at Pembina. By the mid-1840s, however, the HBC had decided that these independents posed a threat to its monopoly, and the company moved to curtail their activities. The arrival of troops in Red River in 1846 helped the HBC reassert control in the settlement, if only for a brief period.

Faced with these growing restrictions on the traditional economies of Red River, the residents at St. Andrew's turned increasingly toward agriculture and wage labour between 1843 and 1849 in order to earn a living. Many in the parish developed an appropriate and adaptive economic strategy to deal with the peculiarities of climate, geography, technology, and commercial markets that existed in the Red River colony. This strategy – a mixed-economy in which agriculture had a prominent role – helped families exploit the available resources of the rivers and plains and was an expedient, if not profitable, tactic for life in a restrictive economy. No tension existed between the hunt and the farm at St. Andrew's, except in the minds of the clergy and the Anglo-historians who wrote about life in Red River. Nor did non-agricultural activities present a "fatal check" on the colony's transition to a large-scale farming economy before 1870. A study of the economy of Red River reveals that the Métis of St. Andrew's were neither "improvident" nor "irrational" in their economic behaviour. In fact, these labels might better describe the activities of the Kildonan Scots community who pursued an exclusive but limited agricultural economy in Red River, even in the face of the recurrent crop failures that characterized the early years of the colony. In this respect, it could be argued that the settlers at St. Andrew's represented the most "progressive" element in nineteenth-century Red River.

Chapter Seven

Anglican Mission to Rural Church

"*The Most*

populous Parish

on the Red River"

Like the changing structure of community life within the parish, by mid-century, the Anglican Church at St. Andrew's had evolved from its roots as a mission outpost. The 1850s were a pivotal decade for the church, not only in the lower settlement, but throughout all of Protestant Red River. The appointment of David Anderson as first bishop of Rupert's Land in 1849 and the departure of William Cockran from the Rapids signalled a new Episcopalian influence within the settlement. Where early missionaries such as Cockran had to an extent remained independent from the old "blues," or the members of Red River's social and economic hierarchy, the more recently arrived clergy and their wives now sought entry into this privileged class. The decline of the buffalo hunt and the changing economic structure within the settlement was reflected in the move away from the earlier traditions of the fur trade.

At the opening of the decade, the future of the CMS in Red River looked bright. The new stone church at St. Andrew's had just been consecrated, and plans were being made for the construction of a stone rectory. The society was contemplating the expansion of its operations outside the settlement, and the Rev. David Anderson, a graduate of St. Bee's College in Cumberland and the former vicar of All Saints' Church in Derby, had recently arrived in the colony with his children and spinster sister. Although the creation of an Anglican bishopric in Rupert's Land was welcomed by the local clergy, David Anderson was perhaps a poor choice for the position. Short of stature, with balding head, he has been described by one author as possessed of "affectations of dress and habit ... weak-willed ... [and] ... unable to discipline his contentious and divided clergy."[1] Anderson, who was greatly influenced by the opinions of his sister, found himself unable to deal with the large community of Métis in the settlement and preferred to operate almost exclusively within the political and social elite at the Forks.[2] The shift in emphasis by the church in Red River away from its Métis constituents helped create a greater wedge between that community and the Anglican Church in the settlement.

Robert James, who had first arrived in Red River in 1846, continued as the local curate at St. Andrew's until 1851. It is evident by this date that James's role in the community appeared to have involved the administrative duties of a large rural parish rather than actual missionary work. Writing to the society in 1851 he stated, "The Society knows the nature of my work so well that they will not expect to hear of heathenism being overturned where it does not exist."[3] He added that, "I have not been privileged to baptize a single Heathen this year, though I have had many close conversations with them."[4] In the summer of 1851, Robert James, his wife in poor health, decided to return to England.

With James's departure, the Rev. James Hunter was appointed on a temporary basis at St. Andrew's. Hunter and his wife were better educated than previous missionaries in Rupert's Land. Arriving at York Factory in 1844, Hunter was sent to Cumberland House, where he served for seven years. At this northern Saskatchewan posting, the missionary worked extensively upon the translation into Cree of a number of religious texts, including the gospels of Matthew, Mark, and John, and the Book of Common Prayer. His wife died there in 1847, and some eight months later Hunter married Jean Ross, the daughter of Norway House Chief Factor Donald Ross. Jean Ross had lived her whole life in the country except for a few years of schooling in Scotland. She was fluent in Cree and helped her husband in his translations. It has been stated in a few publications that, as Jean Ross was Métis, Hunter's marriage to her demonstrated that he was without the "racialist predilections of many of his colleagues."[5] In fact, Jean Ross was white. Her mother Mary McBeath, who married Chief Factor Donald Ross in 1820 was the daughter of an original Selkirk settler.[6] The perception of Jean Ross as being of mixed European and Native blood has come from a misinterpretation of a letter from Letitia Hargrave to her mother in which she remarks that because of Hunter's marriage "everyone was appalled and his brethren in this country were much annoyed.... There must be something far, far wrong with him."[7] Letitia was "appalled," it has been assumed, because Hunter did not marry a white woman. In reality, tongues

Rev. James Hunter and wife Jean Ross, n.d. (Provincial Archives of Manitoba).

wagged over the fact that the minister waited only eight months between the death of his first wife and his marriage to Jean Ross. Such an indiscretion, according to fur-trade gossips, showed little respect on Hunter's part for proper mourning practices. No doubt, James Hunter himself decided to remarry because he felt it would help further his missionary endeavours in the Northwest. He commented to the society that:

> Situated as I am in the midst of the wilderness surrounded only by Indians, and having no one to superintend my household, or to take charge of the Establishment when called to make missionary Tours, it at once became necessary to take the step which I have adopted [i.e., marriage] or return to England with my little boy who is only 3 years of age.

Hunter remained at St. Andrew's for a period of eight months, returning to Cumberland House on June 6, 1852.

In October of 1852, William West Kirkby, newly arrived from England to take over what T.C.B. Boon calls the "Model" school at St. Andrew's, found himself

Rev. William West Kirkby, c. 1875
(Provincial Archives of Manitoba).

the minister in charge in the parish after Hunter's departure.[8] Kirkby was not yet priested and waited until January of 1856 before receiving Holy Orders from Bishop Anderson. In fact, Kirkby's tenure as senior curate at St. Andrew's lasted only one month. For the next three years, the parish was administered by a succession of Anglican ministers including the Rev. Thomas Cochrane, the son of William Cockran (the change in spelling was a family arrangement), the Rev. G. O. Corbett from the Colonial and Continental Church Society (CCCS), and William Cockran himself, who had been superintending the Indian mission at St. Peter's since the departure of John Smithurst in 1851. Kirkby served as schoolmaster at St. Andrew's between 1852 and 1859.

With the completion of the new stone church at the Rapids in 1849, attention was focussed upon the need for a new dwelling house for the resident minister. In the summer of 1849, James wrote to the CMS complaining about the dilapidated condition of the old wooden parsonage at the Rapids. Removing some interior plastering, he noted the "rotten state of the logs of which the walls are built."[9] James's proposal for a new stone structure was not acted upon by the society until 1851. James left shortly thereafter, and his interim replacement, James Hunter, attempted to initiate construction by having mason Duncan McRae begin the quarrying of limestone for the house. The great flood of 1852, which inundated almost all of the upper settlement, further delayed the project, and Bishop David Anderson was forced to live in the old wood parsonage at St. Andrew's until the flood waters had retreated at his residence at Bishop's Court near the Forks. With his appointment to St. Andrew's in October of 1853, William Cockran took over superintendency of the building project at the Rapids. The house was finally completed in December of 1854.[10]

During Cockran's short second tenure at St. Andrew's (he was also responsible for the Indian mission during this period), the elder missionary constructed the "Orphan Asylum" or "Indian House" as it came to be known. Cockran commented upon the need for such a building in a letter to the CMS, dated December 6, 1853:

> *It has been thought by men of Christian sympathy and benevolence that in the present state of the Country an Orphan Asylum would be of considerable benefit to relieve and preserve certain unfortunate children who may have lost the protection and support of their natural parents – which is of frequent occurrence among the Indians owing to their particular habits.*[11]

Work on the home began in the spring of 1854, and, according to Cockran's plan, he hoped to admit ten male and ten female orphans by September or October of that year. Later that summer, Cockran noted in his correspondence the desire by the bishop in Red River to have the home admit not only orphans but the children of those Natives who wished to turn over their children to the care of the church. Cockran wrote to the society that:

> *Our Bishop has thought it advisable to change the name [Orphan Asylum] to the Indian House, for the following reasons. Several Indians give up their children to baptism and to be trained ... when children are thus given up we have no proper place to receive them [and] we are obliged to lodge them with some Christian Family or permit them to continue with their parents. Should the latter be permitted they are sure to follow their example and remain heathen.*[12]

By the end of 1854, the house remained unfinished, though five Native boys were already in residence there.[13] William Cockran moved into the newly completed stone parsonage in December of 1854, while Kirkby moved his quarters to the Indian House when it was finally opened in the late winter of 1854-55.[14]

During the 1850s, as the St. Andrew's mission expanded, the Anglican Church in Red River became embroiled in a heated dispute with the settlement's

Presbyterian population. The Red River Presbyterians were for the most part the children of the original Selkirk settlers, or the offspring of retiring Scottish fur traders who had arrived in the colony after 1821. The dispute with the Presbyterian population went as far back as the Selkirk period, and the Scottish earl's failure to send a minister of that faith to the inhabitants of Red River. For the next forty years, the Presbyterians lobbied strenuously with the HBC for their own minister. Under the leadership of Alexander Ross, numerous petitions were sent to Governor George Simpson in an attempt to obtain redress for their claims. One such petition, organized by Ross, Robert Logan, and James Sinclair in the 1840s, contained thirty signatures, and, though it complimented William Cockran on his "Christian charity" and desire to accommodate the particular liturgical desires of the Presbyterians, the petition also charged that some of Cockran's "fellow labourers in this vineyard have not shown the same spirit of charity and forbearance towards us."[15] Finally, in 1851, a Presbyterian minister from Scotland, John Black, was secured for the congregation in Red River. Eden Colvile offered land at Frog Plain, as well as the sum of £150 toward the building of their own church. The withdrawal of the Presbyterians from the upper, middle and lower Anglican churches substantially decreased the number of communicants within these parishes.[16] While these defections reduced the ability of parishes such as St. Andrew's to raise money within the community, it did allow the CMS Anglicans to return to a more Episcopalian style of service within their respective churches.

Shortly after the arrival of John Black, a new dispute between the two groups arose. Bishop Anderson decided to consecrate St. John's Church in the upper settlement, as well as the graveyard where some four hundred Presbyterians were buried. The bishop's action meant that the Presbyterians who wished to bury their dead in the St. John's churchyard (a concession they had been given in lieu of their contributions to the church prior to 1851) would be forced to submit to an Episcopalian burial rite, a rite to which they strongly objected. The Hudson's Bay Company was quickly brought into the debate, with both sides petitioning Colvile to provide a solution to the problem. Colvile asked Anderson if he would be willing to consecrate the cemetery at St. Andrew's, where there were no Presbyterian claims, rather than the one at St. John's. He also suggested that the Anglican Church might build a new cathedral, unencumbered by previous

Presbyterian claims.[17] Anderson stubbornly refused to back down and pressed on with his intention to consecrate the churchyard at St. John's. A heated exchange of letters between Colvile and Anderson throughout November of 1851 outlines the problem in great detail. Colvile, like the other local company gentlemen, grew exasperated with Anderson's behaviour during the dispute. Donald Ross, who by this time inhabited the cottage outside the walls of Lower Fort Garry, wrote to Simpson that the bishop was as "obstinate as a mule and for all his meekness and learning is very deficient in charity and common sense."[18] In the same letter, the retired chief factor noted that James Hunter (stationed that year at St. Andrew's) had refused to sign Anderson's petition against the Presbyterian claims, the only Anglican clergyman to do so.[19] Hunter claimed that, having only recently arrived in the settlement from Cumberland, he was "unqualified" to make an informed judgment in such a case. Relations were noticeably cool between Hunter and Anderson after this particular incident. Eden Colvile eventually referred the matter to the London committee, who placed the burial yard under company control. This solution was viewed by the community as a very clear putdown of the bishop and ultimately helped lower his prestige in Red River.[20]

Within a few years of the dispute, however, relations between the two Protestant churches in Red River had gradually improved. By the early 1860s, ecumenical prayer meetings were being held throughout the community, and the Presbyterian minister John Black had established a courteous relationship with local Anglican curates such as James Hunter.[21] By the 1870s, the Presbyterian population of St. Andrew's parish was on the increase. According to the Rev. J. P. Gardiner, who was stationed at St. Andrew's between 1865 and 1872, these people lived mainly in the northern, or lower end, of the parish. They "have long taken a strong objection to the Bishop's plans," Gardiner wrote to the society in London, "and will not contribute anything to the Church funds."[22] But with Bishop Machray's decision to return to the more traditional Anglican high church liturgy after 1865, and his termination of ecumenical prayer meetings in the settlement, relations between the Presbyterian and Anglican churches deteriorated.

An event that occurred at St. Andrew's Church in 1850 had important ramifications for the whole Anglican missionary movement in the Northwest. That year, the lower church witnessed the ordination of the Métis catechist Henry

Rev. Henry Budd, ordained at St. Andrew's Church in 1850 as the first Native Anglican missionary in Rupert's Land (Provincial Archives of Manitoba).

Budd, the first to be ordained in Rupert's Land under the Church Missionary Society's "Native Church Policy."[23] First drafted by Henry Venn, the secretary to the Church Missionary Society between 1842 and 1872, the Native Church Policy provided the guiding principal of the CMS during the second half of the nineteenth century.[24] Every European missionary sent to the field was instructed to create an indigenous Native clergy supported by a self-governing, self-supporting, and self-propagating Native church. It was hoped by the society that this system would allow the non-Native missionary to then move on to some new outpost, leaving behind an established and well-regulated missionary station in the hands of a Native pastor. Henry Budd had originally been a pupil of John West at the upper settlement and had been singled out by West as the best student enrolled in that first school at St. John's. Budd's ordination was quickly followed by those of James Settee, J. A. MacKay, and Henry Cochrane, as well as four other Métis clergymen. In 1840, Budd was sent as a schoolteacher to Cumberland House and helped found the Anglican mission at The Pas. James Settee was first sent to the Churchill River district in northern Saskatchewan, and, after his ordination in 1854, he travelled for many years in the country between the Saskatchewan and Qu'Appelle Rivers. John Alexander MacKay was ordained in 1862 and worked at York Factory, The Pas, and at the Stanley Mission in northern Saskatchewan. Henry Cochrane, originally from St. Peter's mission on the lower Red River, was ordained in 1858 and worked at CMS missions ranging from northwestern Ontario to northern Manitoba.[25]

Venn's Native Church Policy enjoyed some success in the Northwest in the years prior to 1870, as Native catechists proved competent in bridging the gap between the European, Christian traditions of the CMS and aboriginal cultures in Rupert's Land, especially those in the more northern parts of the territory.

Ultimately, however, the policy failed. The inherent racial intolerance of many of the CMS missionaries never allowed the Métis catechists the kind of freedom and influence necessary to establish a viable Native ministry in the Northwest. Missionaries such as Budd, Settee, and the others who followed were rarely given work above the level of schoolteacher or assistant chaplain. With the economic decline of Native societies in the Northwest after 1870, the conditions that might have allowed the blossoming of a Native Church community in the West disappeared. While Venn's policy proved more successful in India and West Africa, in Canada, it could not overcome the Church Missionary Society's inability to understand or respect Native culture.[26]

In the fall of 1855, James Hunter returned as the resident missionary at St. Andrew's. His appointment to one of the more established parishes in the Northwest indicated that Hunter was rewarded for his long work at Cumberland House and for his success in translating religious tracts into Cree. William West Kirkby fulfilled the role of schoolteacher in the parish and assisted Hunter in his ministerial duties. During Hunter's tenure in the parish, the mission at St. Andrew's took on an air of almost solid Victorian respectability, as evidenced by the photographs left behind by H. L. Hime, who travelled to Red River and the Saskatchewan country with explorer Henry Youle Hind in 1858. His photographs are the very first of the mission (and among the first to be taken in western Canada) and depict solid stone structures situated on a virtually treeless and cheerless plain. Hind described the church at St. Andrew's as "a new and very substantial structure of stone well buttressed and very conveniently and neatly furnished: all its interior arrangements are attractive and substantial."[27]

Upon his arrival at St. Andrew's, Hunter undertook alterations to both the furnishing and layout of the church's interior. One of his first improvements was to secure a pipe organ that he had viewed while in London the year before.[28] The CMS parent committee was successful in obtaining the organ for Hunter the following year, and the missionary wrote back that, "it is up in the gallery of the Rapids Church, and is a great assistance in conducting the singing."[29] In 1857, Hunter undertook a number of renovations to the interior of the church as part of the mission's move away from an evangelical style of worship. Writing to John Smithurst, who had left Red River for Upper Canada some six years previous, he stated:

[At] St. Andrew's Church I have had the red screen removed and the Pulpit and Reading Desk put in the corners, I am making a private vestry behind the Communion table by putting up a handsome screen before the window, thus we shall have ample place for the Communion rails, and a convenient vestry without going up and down stairs as in the old arrangement.... Last year I improved the tower which is now almost completed.[30]

Hunter also brought out a "time piece" for the church and remarked to his former colleague, "You can therefore imagine that Saint Andrew's is improving."[31]

H. Y. Hind in his journal also described the parsonage at St. Andrew's. The structure, he wrote, "is 50 feet by 30 feet and two stories high. The walls are of limestone, 2 feet, 8 inches thick, and the rooms are lofty and capacious. In its internal arrangements," the explorer noted, "it leaves nothing to be desired."[32] When he first moved into the house in 1855, Hunter did not share Hind's enthusiasm. "Our new house is very cold this winter," he wrote to the Rev. Chapman that same year. "The House is very roughly furnished," he continued, "especially the plastering and the carpenters' work, and I am very sorry that I was not here to superintend the work when it was building [sic]."[33] The "Indian Home" at St. Andrew's, in which the Rev. Kirkby resided, was also described by Hind: "The Rev. W. W. Kirkby's house [he wrote] is roomy and comfortable, but its architectural points are far from being attractive."[34] The schoolhouse, built in 1853, was "constructed of wood [and] admirably arranged."[35] Describing the school, Hind remarked that, "I saw 60 children pursuing their studies, under the instruction of Mr. Meyhew, [hired as a second school-teacher by Kirkby and Hunter] lately from Dublin, with a decorum and attention not often to be surpassed in the primary schools of this or the European continent."[36]

In his *Narrative of the Canadian Red River Exploring Expedition of 1857,* Hind has also left us with a general description of the parish at St. Andrew's. "It is the most populous parish on the Red River, and the Church of England element is very largely in excess of the Roman Catholic, there being two hundred and six Protestant and eight Roman Catholic families."[37] According to Hind, the parish boasted a congregation of approximately 1,200 people, over double the size of St. John's at 500, and four times the size of St. Paul's (Middlechurch), which had roughly 300 members. The average attendance at worship, he stated, is "about 500," and the number of communicants he claimed to be about 207.[38] Hind, in his *Narrative*, also gives the respective salaries of the various CMS missionaries stationed in Red River. Bishop Anderson received a yearly income of £700, made up of £300 from the HBC and £400 that came from "funded property." Hunter at St. Andrew's is next on the salary scale at £250 a year, all of which was contributed by the Church Missionary Society. The rest of the CMS clergy in Red River, including, at that time, Cockran, Cowley, Chapman, and Kirkby, all received £200 yearly. Other Anglican missionaries in the settlement, such as Thomas Cochrane and W. H. Taylor, who represented the Society for the Propagation of the Gospel, were paid £100 and £200 respectively. The Presbyterian minister, John Black, while receiving a yearly grant of £50 from the HBC, was the only Protestant minister in Red River who at that time lived off the contributions of his congregation, a stipend of about £100 per year.[39]

James Hunter served at St. Andrew's for ten years between 1855 and 1865. During that period, both the parish and the settlement of Red River underwent major changes. In the lower settlement, Hunter encouraged the displacement of Native traditions by promoting Anglo-Christian values in an agricultural context. Well respected in Red River by both the people and the other Protestant clergy, Hunter also had the support of the Hudson's Bay Company.[40] His duties at St. Andrew's were extensive, as the parish was one of the largest and most populous in the settlement. "It gives us much occupation," he wrote to Venn in 1856, "to visit the continuous Houses along the banks of the River." Hunter considered Kirkby a valuable helper in this task and described him as "useful in assisting me with the duties of this large parish."[41] Part of Hunter's success at St. Andrew's was a result of his considerable abilities behind the pulpit, as well as his apparent flexibility in liturgical matters. During the dispute between Anderson and the Red River Presbyterians, Adam Thom remarked to George Simpson that, "Mr. Hunter cant be made to wear the Episcopal collar on any terms.... [He feels] that the essentials of Christianity are more important than its trappings." Moreover, Thom adds, "Mr. Hunter commits the inevitable enormity [sic] of preaching better than his neighbours."[42]

Hunter was also a strong temperance advocate at St. Andrew's. The movement to ban alcohol was in full swing in England by the middle of the nineteenth century, and the Red River missionaries felt that drinking was a major reason why Native peoples had moved slowly "along the path to Christian civilization."[43] The St. Andrew's Temperance Society was formed by Hunter on March 25, 1857. It was never a major movement within the parish, but in 1861 Hunter remarked that:

> [a] marked change for the better is coming over the Parish, nothing like the usual quantity of liquor has been sold and drank at this season; and many were in Church today who usually spent the day in dissipation and drunkenness. The introduction of the temperance cause has done much good in this parish.[44]

A year later, he noted to the society that at temperance meetings held in the schoolhouse, "We never had larger gatherings with more attentive audiences ... although we taxed their patience I fear." He commended his parishioners when he remarked that, "However ... dull and uninteresting we may be, they never allow any sign of impatience or weariness to escape them."[45] He concluded by stating that he felt temperance would become "a permanent institution in the land."[46] Others in Red River were not so sure. Rev. John Black commented to his brother in 1862 that the St. Andrew's Society experienced a good deal of apathy and "backsliding" among parish tipplers.[47] Sir George Simpson told Hunter that while he sympathized with the missionary's campaign, he believed it unrealistic to expect that liquor could be kept out of the country. In a letter to David Anderson, Simpson wrote:

> The Company's officers will most willingly support you as far as precept.... In the present state of the country, however, when spirits are so largely induced from the United States for the purpose of opposing the Company in their trade, it is hopeless to attempt the establishment of rules and regulations for the protection of the use of spirituous liquors.[48]

In 1857, Hunter and Kirkby became peripherally involved in the Canadian annexationist movement. As discussed in Chapter IV, Hunter, like most of the Protestant clergy in Red River, maintained a cordial relationship with company officers in the settlement. Nonetheless, he and his colleagues gave William Kennedy (who was actively circulating a petition throughout the settlement in support of Canadian annexation) their warm if indirect support. Hunter believed that "our missionaries will never prosper under the Company's rule," and he looked toward Canada to provide an influx of Anglo-Protestant settlers into the colony.[49] That same year, Hunter proposed to the society that he undertake a journey to the Mackenzie District to explore the possibility of establishing a mission in that region. "If we delay another year," he wrote, "the Mackenzie River will be in the hands of the [Catholic] Priests, and we shall have lost the golden opportunity."[50] The HBC remained cool to the idea of setting up an Anglican mission in the north. Eden Colvile, writing to George Simpson, felt that "however well fitted Church of England Clergymen may be for Red River, they would never, with our limited means of transport answer for MacKenzie River or Athabaska."[51] Eventually Hunter, travelling on the HBC brigades from Norway House, made it as far as Fort Simpson, remaining in that district until the summer of 1859, when he returned to St. Andrew's. In his report to the society and to the bishop, Hunter recommended the establishment of missions at Fort Simpson, Good Hope, Laird, and Rae. In 1859, William West Kirkby, recently ordained, was dispatched from St. Andrew's to the Mackenzie district and ordered to establish CMS missions in that region. Kirkby remained for almost twenty years in the north and was eventually made an archdeacon in 1876.

With his return to Red River, Hunter settled once again into the day-to-day duties of the parish. These included twice-weekly services, prayer meetings, meetings of the St. Andrew's Temperance Society, visiting the sick, and officiating at marriages, baptisms, and funerals. A description of the St. Andrew's mission in the *Proceedings of the Church Missionary Society* states, "The ministerial duties of [this] station are altogether of a pastoral character."[52] *The Nor'Wester,* Red River's first newspaper, published an account of the parish in June of 1860:

The parish contains a population of about 1200 under the sole charge of the Ven. Archdeacon Hunter, M.A.... The Church ... is about 90 feet long and 46 feet broad, having a tower containing a peal of three bells ... communicants number about 200. There are two Scripture-readers in this parish - Mr. Andrew Setter and Mr. Peter Corrigal. Every Saturday evening a large class meets in St. Andrew's schoolroom for the practice of vocal music under the direction of Mr. John Hudson.[53]

In 1858, with the opening of the Hudson's Bay Company's southern supply route through St. Paul, Hunter inquired about the possibility of bringing in his yearly indent of supplies from England via this new route rather than through York Factory. At the time, however, the company was merely experimenting with the southern supply route, and the bulk of its yearly indent still came through York for a number of years after 1858. With the loss of the HBC supply ship, the *Kitty,* in Hudson Strait in 1860, Hunter redoubled his efforts to have the company send the mission supplies through New York. In June of 1860, he wrote to the secretaries of the CMS: "The Steamboats are running regularly on the Red River... could not all of my mission supplies be sent this way early in Spring.... I think you will find on inquiring that the freight to St. Paul will be less than to York Factory."[54] The society began employing the new route in the early 1860s. For a few brief years, it was shut down because of the wars with the Dakota in the United States, which made the journey from St. Paul to Red River far too dangerous. In 1864, Hunter informed London that, with the end of hostilities, he would "advise that the mission Supplies be again sent that way.[55]

A few years after the departure of Rev. Kirkby to the Mackenzie district, Hunter was joined at St. Andrew's by Rev. John Mackay, a recently ordained minister sent to Red River by the society.[56] Mackay assisted Hunter in the carrying out of his ministerial duties, as well as serving as the local schoolmaster. Hunter and Mackay actively conducted baptisms among the people of the parish, and in 1855 Hunter, along with Kirkby and Hillyer, baptized a total of sixty-nine parishioners, most of them children. Nine years later, in 1864, Hunter had raised that figure to eighty-four. While the increase does not seem to be overly dramatic, it does show one of the largest increases for any parish in Protestant Red River for the same period.[57] Moreover, St. Andrew's had experienced an overall decline in attendance with the creation of St. Clement's Mapleton in 1857. The new parish was carved from the lower part of St. Andrew's when it was felt the growing population at the Rapids made it difficult for the incumbent missionary to meet the spiritual needs of the lower settlement. It was decided to build a new church at Mapleton north of Lower Fort Garry, and David Anderson donated £100 towards its construction. Stonemason Samuel Taylor, formerly from Moose Factory, was hired to supervise the building project. On December 1, 1861, the new church was consecrated by Bishop Anderson and James Hunter. While St. Clement's could never claim a congregation as large as St. Andrew's, it was regularly attended by company personnel at Lower Fort Garry, and in 1870 by the men of the Quebec Rifles, who had been sent to Red River to help quell the Resistance.

In 1863, James Hunter was appointed by David Anderson to investigate the charges against the Rev. G. O. Corbett of the Colonial and Continental Church Society and the resident pastor at Headingly parish. (The Corbett case is discussed in greater detail in Chapter 4.) Hunter concluded that the Headingly missionary was in fact guilty of helping a young Métis girl to procure an abortion. As Corbett, who was strongly anti-company, had a large and loyal following throughout the settlement, feelings ran high against James Hunter. A great deal of gossip and innuendo circulated throughout the community during 1863 and 1864. Hunter was upset by the talk and described to CMS Secretary Venn in December of 1864 how he had been "wounded in the house of my friends."[58] In a libel suit against a local parshioner, John Tait, who was particularly vocal in his criticism of the St. Andrew's missionary, Hunter was awarded £100 in damages. After the trial, he observed that Tait was now considered "a despised man and an outcast in the settlement."[59] While Hunter believed that "not the slightest stain remains on my character," he was left embittered by the whole experience. "All who know Red River and have lived in it," he wrote to Venn, "know how addicted it is to gossip and scandal.[60] On another occasion, he wrote, "Let a man of the finest character come to this country and he has no guarantee that he will escape the venom of slanderous tongues."[61] At St. Andrew's, some of the parishioners rallied around the embattled missionary. In a letter to Hunter, they expressed "their sincere and heartfelt sympathy" over the whole affair. It read in part:

It is with feelings of deep regret that we have ... learnt that certain malicious reports have been ... circulating which no person in his right mind could believe to be true: reports calculated to weaken and destroy your usefulness ... and to injure your private and public character.[62]

Unfortunately for Hunter, the scandal all but destroyed his chances at being named to succeed David Anderson as bishop of Rupert's Land. Hunter felt that he possessed sufficient education for the position, and with his over twenty years of work in the North American missions, thought he deserved the appointment. In lobbying for the job with the society, Hunter wrote, "Now I will not be so modest as to pretend that both the Clergy and the Laity here did not fully expect that I should succeed the Bishop."[63] (Anderson was scheduled to leave in May of 1865.) He then went on to include "testimonials" from many of the local clergy, including Kirkby, J. P. Gardiner, and Abraham Cowley. By this time, however, word had reached London regarding Hunter's troubles in the settlement. The missionary realized that he had little chance to succeed Anderson, for in a letter to Venn in early 1865 he posed the question:

Is Archdeacon Hunter to be the Bishop of Rupert's Land? The answer is an empathic 'No, there is something against it,' mentioned with 'bated breath' 'as being private'. Now if this is circulated from mouth to mouth [in London] ... I leave you to draw your own conclusion what must be the damaging effect against my character of such remarks made in this mysterious way.[64]

Hunter accused Anderson of spreading gossip about him in his letters to the society. "Not for a moment," he states, "will I permit the Bishop to cast the slightest stain on my character."[65] Two months later he wrote:

It would have been [for Anderson]... a wiser and more judicious course... to have allowed the tittle tattle and scandal of Red River, for which it is alas! too famous, to have remained in its grave, rather than have given it the slightest shadow of any weight by resuscitating and transferring it across the Atlantic.[66]

Considering that Anderson was the one who appointed Hunter to the Corbett investigation, and that he agreed with Hunter's conclusions regarding the Headingly minister's guilt, it is not surprising that Hunter expressed anger at Anderson's subsequent reproach. No doubt the animosity between the two Red River clergymen had its origin in the Presbyterian problem and Hunter's refusal to sign Anderson's petition some fourteen years earlier. In late 1864, Hunter, tired of the gossip and scandal and disappointed over not receiving the position as bishop, decided to leave Red River. Pleading that his wife's health was in a "precarious state," he left for England in the spring of 1865.[67] Despite the

Archbishop Robert Machray, c. 1895. The Bishop of Rupert's Land from 1865 to his death in 1904, Machray attempted to eradicate evangelical influences within the local Anglican Church. Although publicly neutral in the events of 1869-70, Machray privately opposed Riel's Provisional Government and supported Canadian intervention (Provincial Archives of Manitoba).

last year of Hunter's ministry at St. Andrew's, he had enjoyed a successful tenure at the mission, leaving the church upon a relatively solid footing within the lower community.

Bishop David Anderson, who had left Red River shortly before Hunter, was succeeded by the Rev. Robert Machray. Machray proved to be unlike Anderson and some of the other clergy in Red River. An academic, Machray was far more Episcopalian than his predecessor and was determined to eradicate the Presbyterian influence within the Anglican Church. Although Anderson had fought a long battle with the Presbyterians, he had allowed joint prayer meetings and other Presbyterian traditions to become a part of the church in the settlement. Machray immediately ordered an end to prayer meetings and the holding of baptisms and marriages in private homes. (In the period from 1830 to 1850, William Cockran had rarely baptized anyone actually inside a church.) Moreover, Machray attempted to reinstitute weekly communion, rather than the four or five times a year it was then being offered. The latter tradition had remained a holdover from the days before the Kildonan Scots had received their own minister.

The Rev. Joseph Phelps Gardiner, Hunter's successor at St. Andrew's, opposed the bishop's plan to move the settlement away from its evangelical traditions. Gardiner was the product of a strongly evangelical background and had instituted a program of popular lectures and prayer meetings in the parish. Machray's demand for his resignation was refused by the minister and the two remained on less-than-friendly terms until the latter's departure in 1872.

In his report to the CMS Committee in 1867, Gardiner described his work in the lower parish. He reported 163 Church of England families at St. Andrew's and a total of 230 communicants. Services were held Sundays and Wednesday evenings and at Christmas, New Year's, Good Friday, Ascension Day, and a special celebration at harvest time. Services were also held at Parks Creek and Little Britain, Gardiner stated, as well as in the "open air."[68] Sunday schools operated in the parish, with Gardiner superintending a total of eleven part-time teachers. Gardiner's evangelical style is evident in the program of "select readings," "secular lectures," and "missionary prayer meetings," held at St. Andrew's, as well as the fact that communion was given only twelve times in the year.[69] Evidently, Gardiner has resisted Machray's plan to bring back weekly communions.

The St. Andrew's minister maintained a low profile during the turbulent events of 1869-70. A Committee for Public Safety was formed in the parish, and it recommended that a company of volunteers be organized. Those in the parish who opposed Riel were supporters of John Shultz's Canadian party.[70] Gardiner counselled moderation to this group, especially after receiving a threat on his life from the insurgents. Bishop Machray, on the other hand, while appearing to remain publicly neutral, was privately urging the Red River clergy to incite their congregations against Riel. Gardiner and Cowley were reluctant to involve the church in the struggle, arguing that Church Missionary Society regulations cautioned against a missionary's involvement in political matters.[71] Machray dismissed their arguments, stating that in this particular case CMS rules did not apply. However, if the Anglican clergy in Red River disagreed among themselves over tactics, they all agreed that the Resistance represented a threat to their dominant position in Red River society. "There is little doubt," Gardiner wrote in is annual letter to the society in November of 1870, "that the instigation of rebellion was intended to make this a Roman Catholic colony."[72] Despite the fact

St. Andrew's Church, 1860, by Nanton Marble (Provincial Archives of Manitoba).

that the Anglican clergyman attributed far too much influence in Red River to the organized churches, the St. Andrew's minister, like his colleagues, believed that the power and influence of the Church of England in Rupert's Land could only be enhanced with the influx of Anglo-Protestant settlement that would soon follow annexation by Canada.[73]

Following the Resistance, Gardiner continued his opposition to Machray's plan to make the Red River missions self-supporting. The missionary argued that the lower parish should remain the "representative" station of the Church Missionary Society in Rupert's Land.[74] He reasoned that the eventual arrival of the railroad in the West, and the CPR's initial plan to cross the Red River at Selkirk, meant that a land rush would result in the parish. The Society for the Propagation of the Gospel had made overtures to the CMS to assume control of St. Andrew's. Gardiner felt that the parish's strategic location in Red River increased its value to the society. Moreover, he felt that it should serve as the headquarters for a general superintendent to oversee missions throughout the territory.[75] Gardiner refrained from recommending himself for the position, however, and in 1872, citing poor health, he left Red River.

Gardiner's successor at St. Andrew's was Abraham Cowley who remained at the parish for approximately one year. Cowley was a veteran CMS missionary in Rupert's Land and had founded the mission at Partridge Crop (Fairford) in 1842.[76] Since 1854, he had been in charge of the Indian settlement and eight years later was given the temporary responsibility for both St. Andrew's and St. Peter's. The elderly missionary found his new task onerous. His wife, Arabella, took the unprecedented step of writing directly to the society to complain about the "crushing weight that has been placed upon the Archdeacon's shoulders."[77] She chided the secretaries for their "want of thought and consideration ... and your unaccountable dilatoriness to fill the vacancy [at the Rapids]."[78]

In late May of 1873, his replacement, the Rev. John Grisdale, arrived in the settlement. Grisdale was considerably more Episcopalian in orientation than Gardiner and supported Bishop Machray's plan for self-support in Red River.[79] The young missionary became a favourite of Machray's, and, in 1874, he was offered the "Chair of Systematic Theology" at St. John's Collegiate school in Winnipeg.[80] Cowley reluctantly took over duties once more at the parish until

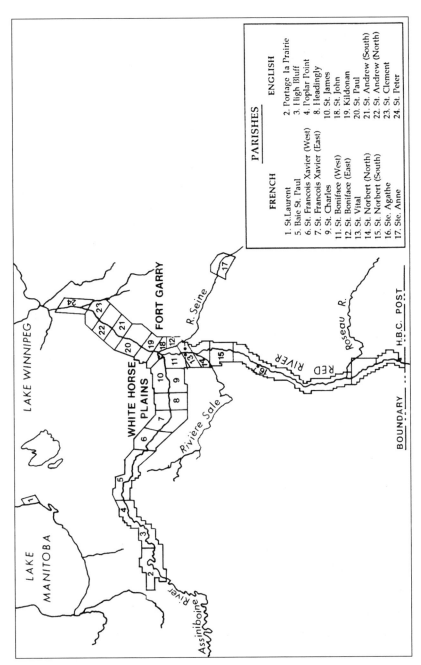

The Red River Settlement in 1870.

PARISHES

FRENCH

1. St. Laurent
5. Baie St. Paul
6. St. Francois Xavier (West)
7. St. Francois Xavier (East)
9. St. Charles
11. St. Boniface (West)
12. St. Boniface (East)
13. St. Vital
14. St. Norbert (North)
15. St. Norbert (South)
16. Ste. Agathe
17. Ste. Anne

ENGLISH

2. Portage la Prairie
3. High Bluff
4. Poplar Point
8. Headingly
10. St. James
18. St. John
19. Kildonan
20. St. Paul
21. St. Andrew (South)
22. St. Andrew (North)
23. St. Clement
24. St. Peter

the appointment of the Rev. Richard Young in May of 1875. While Young admitted that his first impressions of the parish were "most pleasing," he was forced to modify his opinion after "nearer acquaintance."[81] Young provided an interesting description of his Métis congregation at St. Andrew's. In a letter to the CMS secretary, he wrote:

> For almost half an hour before services the outside of the Church presents
> a very animated and interesting scene. Groups of men and women gather
> at the approaches of the Church and in the Churchyard, their dark
> countenances and long raven black hair speaking strongly of their Indian
> origin. The men with gay coloured sashes round their waists and often
> tastefully decorated moccasins. The women are soberly dressed, usually in
> black and their black shawls covering the head and shoulders.[82]

As well as campaigning for self-support for the Red River missions, Young was also actively involved in the "Church of England Temperance Society" at St. Andrew's. He considered drinking the greatest evil in the community and criticized the behaviour of his congregation at weddings and other social events. Young was particularly critical of political life at St. Andrew's. "The parish," he wrote to the society in 1878, "has only just emerged from the ... demoralizing influence of the elections to the local legislature. The drinking ... and bribery which has characterized politics here; the absence of great party principles, all tend to lower the political tone in this country."[83] Though critical of politics in Red River, Young was proud that the newly elected premier, John Norquay, was a parishioner at St. Andrew's. Norquay's education at the hands of the CMS, Young believed, had laid the "ground work for his prosperity."[84] A strong Victorian Episcopalian, Young formed the Church Missionary Juvenile Association and attempted to raise money for "liberated African children."[85] As well, he fitted up an old store in the parish as a Christian reading room and circulated such Victorian periodicals as *The British Work Man* and *Cottage and Artisan*. Young felt his attempts to "civilize" the inhabitants of the parish were successful. In 1881, he reported "quiet steady progress" in his work at the lower settlement. In 1883, William Bompas, the bishop of Athabaska, invited Richard Young to visit the Peace River district and report upon the possibility of splitting the huge Athabaska diocese. Young returned to Red River in the fall of 1884 and on October 18th was consecrated bishop of the new smaller diocese of Athabaska. Bompas became the Bishop of the newly created MacKenzie River diocese.[87]

Throughout the 1880s, the Church Missionary Society slowly disengaged itself from support of the Anglican parishes in Red River. The Rev. A. L. Fortin, who replaced Young in 1884, was serving as minister at St. Andrew's when the Church Missionary Society formally ended its sixty-year association with the mission in 1887.

During William Cockran's long tenure at the Rapids, education had been a cornerstone of the Church Missionary Society's program of evangelization in the parish. In those early years, the missionary established a school of industry that taught such activities as spinning, weaving, and farming. When Robert James replaced Cockran in 1847, he deplored the lack of formal education at the mission. In a letter to the CMS, James wrote:

The schools are in a disheartening state ... the settlers are indifferent toward Education. Instead of hailing their educational privileges as a boon, they need plying with reasons why their children should be instructed rather than ignorant. I think the schools were the worst feature amongst the mission operations. The children were not only ignorant but rude and little removed from those I have seen in the Wigwam.[88]

James, determined to reverse this decline at the Rapids, introduced an educational program that placed greater emphasis upon academics, including a heavy dose of catechism and religious instruction. Kirkby and Hunter continued this program after 1852. The curriculum included bible studies, arithmetic, geometry, spelling, music, grammar, history, and geography.[89]

In 1853, the original log schoolroom at the Rapids was replaced with a new and larger wood building.[90] (This building actually stood until 1946.) In an attempt to relieve the CMS of the financial burden for the school, parents were charged a tuition of fifteen shillings per annum, with a third child admitted free. Those parents who wanted their children to be taught Euclidean algebra were charged an extra £1 (presumably to cover the cost of the textbook). In addition, each family was asked to provide a cord of wood to heat the school in the wintertime. William West Kirkby served as the superintendent of schools in the parish between 1852 and 1858. There were four church schools in the district, including buildings at St. Andrew's, Parks Creek, Mapleton, and Little Britain. As well, Miss Davis's school, built in 1858 about a mile above the church, served as a private school for the daughters of Hudson's Bay Company officers in Rupert's Land. Kirkby's four schools were attended by a total of 186 pupils. Approximately sixty-four students attended at St. Andrew's, ranging in age from 6 to 18.[91] Caleb Mayhew taught at the Rapids along with Kirkby, while John Norquay, James Corrigal, and Charles Hillyer served as teachers at the other normal schools in the parish. In 1854, Kirkby pronounced the state of education in the parish to be decidedly superior to that of previous years:

> My earnest desire [he wrote] is to impart to every child in both the Day and Sunday school a full and saving knowledge of the gospel plan of salvation, an intelligent acquaintance with the word of God, and to foster in their minds an enlightened attachment to the services of our beloved Church. As a correct knowledge of Scripture, Geography (Physical and Historical), Jewish Sects, Manners and customs of eastern nations, and the government and public worship of the Jews, is indispensable to the proper understanding of the sacred volume.[92]

After Kirkby's departure from the parish, George Kennedy took over the school at St. Andrew's. According to *The Nor'Wester*, it was an "excellent school, and is furnished with all the recent fittings and apparatus adopted in the training schools in England."[93]

The plagues of grasshoppers that infested the settlement throughout the 1860s and impacted agricultural productivity caused a decline in school attendance. Crop failures created a great deal of poverty throughout Red River, and many families could no longer afford the price of tuition. Though fees were waived in many cases, attendance did not pick up again until after the 1870 Resistance.[94] Beginning in 1867, the CMS gradually cut their funding to parish schools in Red River, and, in 1871, they completely withdrew their support for education in the settlement. That same year, the first legislature of the new province of Manitoba passed an Act to Establish a system of Public Education in Manitoba.[95] Organized along the lines of the separate school system in Quebec, half of the electoral divisions became Protestant school districts while the other half became Catholic.[96] In fact, the Act helped perpetuate the educational scheme of Red River. Schools, either Protestant or Catholic, could be established by local initiative and be administered by local trustees under the control of the department of education.[97] With the influx of settlers to the lower parishes after 1873, the school at St. Andrew's flourished.[98] That same year, Matilda Davis, the tutor at the parish's private girls' school died and was replaced for a time by Abraham Cowley's wife, Arabella. In June of 1877, the school was moved to the parsonage at St. Andrew's, and Young and his family were forced to live for a time in the home of a parishioner. A year later, the school's eleven girls were transferred to a new building in Winnipeg.[99]

For over forty years, the Church Missionary Society had controlled education at the Rapids. The close association between church and school had long been a feature of education in Red River, where the missionary was usually the only educated man whose efforts were not devoted to the fur trade. The public school system, no longer tied to the finances and administration of the parish church after 1871, catered to the needs and demands of Manitoba's burgeoning non-Native population.

In the early 1860s, the Church Missionary Society had sought new ways to increase its funds for the development of missions in the north. The society suggested that it begin to decrease funding to the old Protestant parishes in Red River and that the congregations there be asked to provide increased contributions toward the maintenance of their own churches. When Bishop Machray arrived in the settlement in 1865, one of his chief goals was to make Red River a self-supporting diocese. His creation of parish vestries, the diocesan synod, and the offertory, were aimed at raising the necessary funds among the various Anglican churches to help place them in a financially independent position.[100] His scheme, however, met with little support among some of the Red River clergy. Gardiner, in particular, opposed the bishop's plan. He felt it unfair to ask the poor farmers at the Rapids to offset the expenses of the church in the settlement. The plagues of grasshoppers and crop failures that occurred in 1860 had resulted in increasing poverty and, in some cases, starvation at the lower settlement. In 1868, Gardiner described how many of the families who resided on the east side of the river (or what he referred to as the "Indian part of my parish") "have scarcely an article of furniture in their houses– some of which are not more than 12 ft. by 10 ft. [in which] 6 or 7 persons ... are living, an old robe or blanket being all the bedding some of them have."[101] Gardiner's refusal to turn over the offertory from St. Andrew's widened the rift between the minister and his bishop.

At the first conference of the diocese of Rupert's Land in 1866, Machray emphasized the need for a self-supporting independent church in Red River. Three years later, at the first diocesan synod, Machray reiterated his plea, stating that "nothing is wanting to make this a great and prosperous country but a sufficient population and easy access to the outer world."[102] With Gardiner's departure from St. Andrew's in 1872, Machray found his successors, Cowley, Grisdale, and Young, to be sympathetic to the cause of self-support. Richard Young, in particular, proved tireless in his efforts to raise sufficient funds to support the Clergy Endowment Fund, the Widow and Orphan Fund, and other parish activities.[103] Young hoped that a salary of $1,000 could be raised by the parish vestry. The sale of subscriptions throughout the parish, the rental of some church property, and the sale of timber rights, he argued, could help the parish meet this goal. In 1877, Young organized the parish into a number of districts. Resident vestrymen canvassed these areas selling subscriptions toward the "Maintenance Fund." Though £700 was initially promised by the parishioners of St. Andrew's, only a fraction of this land speculation amount was ever collected.[104] In 1878, Young explained to the society that "there is a willingness on their part but more from want of economy and managing than from want of ability they don't fulfill their promises."[105] In 1881, in an open letter to his parishioners, Young chided the congregation for its failure to raise the necessary monies. Between 1878 and 1881, contributions toward the parish fund actually dropped from $316.94 to $225.38. "Surely so large and important a Parish as this," he wrote, "can raise £100, or say $500 a year for their pastor. There are at least 120 families, members of the Church of England, in this parish who are able to pay five dollars a year."[106]

178

Church picnic at St. Andrew's Rectory, c.1880 (Provincial Archives of Manitoba).

By 1881, Bishop Machray was frustrated with the failure of the Red River churches to become self-supporting. According to Machray, the character of the lower parishes had remained for the most part Métis. Grain liens and speculation, however, were resulting in the gradual departure of the former residents of the Métis parishes. While the bishop was no doubt pleased with this development, he cautioned that "the purchasers of these lots are simply keeping them unoccupied [hoping] to obtain a sufficient accumulation of neighbouring lots to form a proper farm."[107]

Beginning in 1882, the amount of CMS funding for the Red River parishes was decreased by one fifth each year over a five-year period. At St. Andrew's, this amounted to a decrease of £60 a year from a high of £300 in 1882.[108] On December 31, 1887, the Church Missionary Society terminated its connection with the church in Red River. St. Andrew's, like the other Protestant parishes, was now forced to rely upon local contributions, though it remained at least partly subsidized by diocesan endowments and monies from the Home Mission Fund.

The years between 1850 and 1887 were critical ones for the Anglican Church in Red River. During that period, it evolved from a remote mission outpost to an institution well-entrenched in an increasingly non-Native community. The mission at St. Andrew's, at one time critical to the Anglican presence in Red River, was, by 1887, a rural parish geographically and economically distant from the growing subcentre of population at the forks of the Red and Assiniboine, in the young city of Winnipeg. The decision to route the CPR closer to the forks, and the growth of trade, manufacturing, retailing, and financial services there, left St. Andrew's on the periphery of urban development. In a period of tremendous change in Red River, which saw increasing pressures for Canadian annexation, as well as the Resistance of 1869-70, the arrival of English-speaking Ontarian settlers, land speculation, the decline of the old economy, and the departure of many Métis families from the parish, the role of the church was more than peripheral and was, in fact, a driving influence in the evolution of St. Andrew's from a Métis settlement to an increasingly non-Native, rural Anglo-Protestant community.

Chapter Eight

Conclusion

In the years following Manitoba's entry into Confederation, immigrants poured into the young province, heading either for homesteads on the prairies or to the new city of Winnipeg for work in its rapidly growing supply and commercial enterprises. St. Andrew's parish, no longer a CMS mission after 1887, was now removed from the mainstream of Anglican activity in Rupert's Land, as the church moved quickly to secure the new setters' allegiance, especially those arriving from Ontario, Great Britain, and the United States.

Responsibility for the day-to-day organization and maintenance of the church in the lower community fell to the diocese and the local parish vestry. The vestry consisted of five or six laymen and two church wardens and was chaired by the incumbent rector. It was responsible for the financial and administrative operation of the church. After 1887, this duty consisted primarily of raising money within the community for the salary of the minister and the maintenance of the church and rectory.

With the Provincial Municipalities Act of 1880 and the re-organization of the old parishes in 1883, a municipal council was established in St. Andrew's. The new district encompassed the area west of the Red River and extended from the southern boundary of the old parish to Winnipeg Beach on Lake Winnipeg.[1] The municipality of St. Clement's now included the old riverlots of the east bank of the Red. Although the council was founded in 1881, the council minutes do not appear until 1884.[2] The elected body consisted of a reeve along with six elected councillors nominated from three wards within the parish. John James Bird served as the first reeve, while Charles Johnstone, E. B. Kett, George Ross, Andrew Truthwaite, George Kingsbury, and John McLeod were elected as councillors.[3] Samuel Smalley was appointed municipal treasurer at an annual salary of $250. John Norquay, the premier of Manitoba, represented the parish in the provincial assembly.

· Municipal councils in the province were given responsibility for many of the functions formerly carried out by the church, the Hudson's Bay Company, and the Council of Assiniboia. These included the allotment of school monies, the administration of script and Métis land claims, road allowances, wood-cutting privileges, and the letting of contracts for ferry operations. At St. Andrew's, expenditures for 1884 totalled almost $3,000. Six hundred and twelve dollars of that sum were used for bridge construction and $150 went towards ferry maintenance. A large percentage of the budget was used to pay the salaries of council members, the municipal clerk, and the treasurer.[4] The balance went towards council overhead and the parish schools. There were five schools in the district by this time – Parks Creek, Central St. Andrew's, North St. Andrew's, Mapleton, and Clandeboye. The former CMS school at St. Andrew's received the largest grant, about $280.[5] Elections for council were held in January of each year. As few people were nominated for the seven available positions, the composition of the group changed little over the years. E. B. Kett still served on the board in 1890, as did four of the original six councillors.[6]

The history of the church in the period after 1887 comes mainly from information contained in the minutes of the St. Andrew's parish vestry. Although a vestry was first established around 1877, a record of its activities exists only after 1890.[7] In 1884, Richard Young left St. Andrew's to take up his new position as bishop of Athabaska. His successor, the Rev. A. L. Fortin, supervised the transition of St. Andrew's from a CMS-sponsored mission to a self-supporting parish. Fortin's three-year tenure was uneventful. Unlike his predecessors, no correspondence exists between Fortin and the Church Missionary Society. No doubt a good deal of his efforts in the parish went towards fundraising, as he was without the contribution from the society in London. Fortin left in 1890 and was replaced by the Rev. W. D. Barber from Ontario. In October of 1890, less than a year after his arrival, Barber also left. "On account of the severity of the Winters in Manitoba," the minister informed his congregation, "I am compelled to resign in order to benefit my health."[8] After interviewing a number of candidates, Bishop Machray appointed the Rev. B. McKenzie to take temporary charge of the parish over the winter of 1890-91. McKenzie was paid a small stipend of only $5 per week.

In April of 1891, Rev. John William Matheson was appointed to St. Andrew's. He stayed four years at the parish, later becoming a lecturer in theology at St. John's and, in 1922, the dean of the college.[9] Matheson taught at St. John's until 1944. One of the new minister's first actions was to criticize his parishioners for the "conduct of the young people after evening services."[10] He delivered a series of evening lectures on the proper behaviour of the congregation in church and their conduct while travelling to and from the service. Moreover, at a special meeting of the vestry, the straightlaced minister asked that "every officer [vestryman] of the Parish ... take for the year of office a pledge against either drinking or treating over the bar, or drinking or treating by the roadside."[11] Though the motion was carried, it was never made clear whether the vestrymen held to their pledge.

The lack of operating capital was the greatest problem faced by the parish in this period. Without the contribution from the CMS, the church at St. Andrew's experienced difficulties in raising needed funds from a less-than-wealthy rural population. In July of 1892, a finance committee, comprised of vestrymen from St. Andrew's, St. Stephen's, and the church at Little Britain (the latter two were referred to as "chapels of ease"), was formed to explore new methods of fundraising for the parish.[12] Money was needed for repairs to the church and rectory, as well as for the salary of the incumbent minister.[13] Matheson introduced a scheme whereby money was to be raised by voluntary subscription. Under this new system, money collected toward the minister's salary was to be separate from those funds raised for repairs to buildings or for parish activities. Evidently, the committee's efforts were less than successful as in 1894 Matheson noted that this group had "failed in the fulfillment of [its] duties."[14] Matheson left St. Andrew's in 1895 and was succeeded by the Rev. Walter Johnson, who remained in the parish until the turn of the century. Although Johnson continued his predecessor's fundraising schemes, money remained a problem throughout his five-year tenure. When the Rev. Howard King came to the parish in 1900, the vestry was exploring the

St. Andrew's Church and Rectory as seen from the north, 1899 (Provincial Archives of Manitoba).

possibility of selling off "excess" church property from what was referred to as the "missionary lot," or most of lots 62 and 214 of the original CMS grant.[15] An offer of $6 an acre for the land on both sides of the river was made by a Mr. Cowie; however, the decision to sell was left with the church diocesan office. Nothing was done about Cowie's offer at that time and it eventually lapsed.

Financial problems continued. In 1908, the chapels at Lockport and Parkdale were temporarily closed because the church could not afford to keep them maintained.[16] Expenses, including the cost of repairs, salaries, supplies, and general maintenance, were mounting. In 1909, the parish was unable to meet the salary of the Rev. George Brownlee, the incumbent minister, falling short by approximately $200.[17] In 1910, Brownlee left the parish and the diocese after becoming involved in a dispute with the archbishop, Samuel P. Matheson.[18] He was followed by the Rev. Arthur Warwick, who was able to negotiate a salary of $1,000 per annum (about double Brownlee's stipend) from the parish vestry. Warwick reopened the possibility of selling off church property at St. Andrew's to help alleviate the parish debt. In 1912, it was recommended that the church put up for sale at $100 an acre that portion of their lot that lay west of the

St. Andrew's School, 1907 (Provincial Archives of Manitoba).

highway.[19] Approval was finally given by the diocese for the sale of "land lying west of the main highway and being north 10 chains of lot 62, inner and outer two miles."[20] Apparently, finding a buyer for the property proved difficult as the provincial synod was still collecting rent from farmers who were leasing part of the land as late as 1924. After becoming the rector at St. Andrew's in 1921, the Rev. Charles Saunders, though anxious to sell the 600 acres held in trust for the parish, was afraid the land might end up in the hands of speculators. While the church's financial plight would be alleviated, he argued to the vestry, it might bring an "unsuitable population" into the parish.[21] Six hundred acres, Saunders believed, could accommodate a large number of families who would attend and support the church. Absentee land owners would not provide the financial contributions necessary for the church's survival in the parish. Eventually, the land was sold on a piecemeal basis to local farmers. The money, which was controlled by the provincial synod, went initially to pay off back taxes on the property. In 1924, the synod passed a motion whereby income from the property was not to be applied against tax arrears for a period of two years and was instead to be handed over to the rector of St. Andrew's.[22]

By the beginning of the World War I, the population at St. Andrew's was in decline. Over the years, riverlots in the parish had been continually redivided, resulting in narrow strips of farmland that were unsuitable for large-scale agriculture. As land became available elsewhere in the West, many left St. Andrew's for other communities or for work in the new manufacturing industries in Winnipeg. A large number of adult males in the parish were killed in Europe between 1914 and 1918.[23] As well, the polio epidemic of 1918-19 took its toll in St. Andrew's. The Rev. Harry Hodspith remarked that the number of funerals (34) held at the church that year was up dramatically from previous years.[24]

In early 1920, Hodspith characterized the financial situation at St. Andrew's as "very serious." Declining attendance was cited as the primary reason behind the fall in income. For the year 1919, the church was forced to run a deficit of $328.56. Figures from the rector's yearly report show that attendance that year at services was down significantly.[25] Meanwhile, attendance was increasing at St. Thomas' in Lockport and St. Matthew's in Cloverdale. The number of people attending services at St. Andrew's for 1919 totalled 2,044, with an average congregation of thirty-nine. While St. Andrew's still ranked ahead of the church at Cloverdale, St. Thomas' in Lockport was attracting almost double the number of people as the old stone church.[26] The growth of these two rural communities attracted an increasing population of the Anglican parishioners. To help alleviate the financial burden, the St. Andrew's vestry undertook another campaign to canvas the district in order to "obtain a financial guarantee from every household," calling their plan the "Forward Movement."[27] The new initiative proved successful for, at the vestry meeting early in 1921, the finances of the church were now described as being in "good shape."[28]

In August of that year, Hodspith left St. Andrew's, and the vestry offered the position to Rev. Swalwell at $1,700 a year. Swalwell refused and the Rev. Charles Wesley Saunders from Unity, Saskatchewan, described as being "a very capable clergyman as well as of robust physique," was given the position as rector.[29] The new minister was awarded a stipend of $1,500 a year along with $200 in travel funds. Saunders proved to be an active minister in the parish. In his first sermon to the assembled congregation, he criticized their farming techniques and declared that "this district, 14 miles from Winnipeg, is more backward from a standpoint of agriculture than the Saskatchewan prairies."[30] It was not the kind of beginning that would endear Saunders to his flock. He told his parishoners that "we cannot rest upon tradition," and that extensive repairs to the church, rectory, and cemetery were needed.[31] The rectory, in particular, was in a bad state of repair (Saunders described the building as resembling Goldsmith's *The Deserted Village)* and in the 1920s the verandah was replaced.[32] In 1922, the vestry approved the erection of a memorial arch at the church to commemorate parishioners who had died in the war. The raising of funds for the project, estimated to cost about $1,300, was undertaken by the recently formed St. Andrew's Old Timer Association.[33] By the fall of 1922, the association had raised $850. The balance was collected over the winter and the arch was constructed the next year.[34] It still stands today near the entrance to the church. In 1928, Saunders left the parish. Archbishop Matheson decided to replace him with a deacon, Mr. Rupert Taylor, who was given a salary of $1,200 a year.[35] Taylor was ordained as a minister in June of 1929 and remained at St. Andrew's until the fall of 1930.

By its eighth decade, the old stone church was badly in need of repair. The east wall of the church had deteriorated so badly by 1930 that the building was declared unsafe and forced to close. Early the next year, a committee was formed to help raise funds from individual subscriptions for restoration work on the church. Architect Gilbert Parfitt recommended to the parish vestry that the walls be repointed and waterproofed at grade, the gable wall be dismantled and rebuilt, portions of the other walls be rebuilt, new window arches and frames be installed, damaged sills replaced, new woodwork be installed in the tower, and new eavestroughing be set. The cost of repairs was estimated at $5,000. Money for the project was raised by the vestry with the help of the St. Andrew's Oldtimers Association, and local men who helped in the work donated sixteen percent or more of their wages. The restoration work was carried out in 1931, as was repair on the balcony and interior walls. During the course of the restoration, partitions were erected under the balcony to create a small chapel that could accommodate up to sixty people for services. The cost of the repair work actually came in $1,000 under budget. One year later, in October of 1932, the southeast corner of the building collapsed, and the church was once more forced to close. A 1934 parish memo outlined the problem:

The stone work which has now failed was not touched during the course of the [1931] repairs, owing to the lack of funds and partly the fact that it was not considered necessary. Early in July 1932, however, it began to show signs of movement and it gradually became worse. In the following October [of 1932] it was thought that footings should be put under it and concrete beams extended beyond the walls to spread the weight. It was during the carrying out of this work that the corner finally gave way and induced the movement of the east wall.[36]

The cost to repair the southeast corner was estimated at $1,500, and funds were once again sought from the local community. Large beams were used to temporarily shore up the wall while the memorial window was removed. Money for the project was eventually raised (not an easy task given the poor state of the parish and the impact of the depression), and repair piles were put under the southeast, southwest, and northwest corners at a cost of $600. Later, in the 1950s, the narthex floor was replaced with new boards laid over concrete pads and beams. Further structural work on the church in the 1960s included replacement of the wooden spire, as well as repairs to the tower and balcony. But, despite these limited interventions, the disintegration of the masonry and the buckling of the stonework continued. In 1966, the St. Andrew's Restoration Committee was formed under the guidance of Bishop Anderson with a view to raising money to fund major repairs to the church on the 150th anniversary of the diocese in 1970. Architects Libling, Michener and Associates were hired in 1967 to assess the structural condition of the church. They recommended that steel trusses be installed in the roof, along with new shingles, that the walls be dismantled at the bulging sections, the foundation be underpinned, and the floor replaced. They also suggested the installation of new heating and electrical systems. Unfortunately, problems arose with the fundraising efforts of the committee and its ambitious restoration plans were put on hold.

In 1974, St. Andrew's Church – known generally as St. Andrew's-on-the-Red – was commemorated by the federal government as a national historic site. With the signing of the Canada-Manitoba "Agreement for Recreation and Conservation" (ARC) in 1978, it was hoped that government funds could be allocated for structural repairs to the church. Monies were not available at that time, so in 1979 the Anglican Diocesan Memorial Building Fund was used to repair cracks in the walls, repair the roof and chimney, paint the spire, and enlarge the furnace room. In 1983, ARC funds were allocated to replace the roof with cedar shingles and reinforce the roof trusses. A four-foot crawl space was excavated beneath the nave and the floor was re-installed on an independent foundation. Work on the interior of the church was also carried out at this time and included the installation of new carpeting and a natural gas furnace. However, the structural work that had been carried out to this point had only served to slow down the deterioration and buckling of the exterior walls. Temporary repairs, such as patching the larger cracks, were carried out in 1987-88, and a parish restoration committee was re-formed at that time to solicit government assistance. Under the National Historic Sites Cost-Share Program, a total of $423,000 was provided to the parish of St. Andrew's for the conservation of the church, matching the funds raised by the diocese and the local community. Additional money was provided to the church, now a provincial heritage site, by the Manitoba Department of Culture, Heritage and Citizenship. Work on the church, which began in September of 1993, included the stabilization of the foundation and tower, as well as conservation work on the historic masonry, windows, church interior, and cemetery. The stabilization of the church was completed in 1995, and, on 14 May of that year, the oldest stone church in the West was rededicated in a service conducted by Rev. Patrick Lee, the Lord Bishop of Rupert's Land, and St. Andrew's rector, Rev. Steven Sharman.

As for the old parish community, St. Andrew's experienced a period of significant decline in the decades after the turn of the century. It had become by that time a small rural parish with an aging congregation. The arrival of the railway, the departure of a number of the district's old Métis families after 1880, and the growth of Winnipeg as a major urban transportation centre drained off some of the population from the parish. Within the lower district itself, the development of communities such as Lockport, Clandeboye, Little Britain, and Selkirk helped deplete the population that had one inhabited the riverlot farms surrounding the old church.

Recent years, however, have seen a resurgence of "settlement" in the old parish, largely the result of exurban growth beyond the periphery of urban Winnipeg. In the early 1980s, under the federal-provincial ARC agreement mentioned above, the heritage of one of Manitoba's oldest parishes was recognized by the creation of the River Road Parkway commemorating the history of the old Métis and European community of the lower settlement. Various stone buildings, including St. Andrew's Rectory, Scott House, and Kennedy House were restored, and a series of viewing areas and interpretive signs were created to interpret the history of settlement in the parish. The River Road Parkway stands today as a fitting memorial to the original residents of one of Manitoba's oldest settlements, a "physical expression of a history encompassing many centuries and not a little conflict." [37]

* * *

Since its beginnings in the 1820s as a struggling settlement of fur-trade émigrés, St. Andrew's Parish was much changed by the early decades of the next century. The nature of this transformation was influenced by many factors: the evolving character of the Anglican mission and the impact of evangelical Protestantism, the changing nature of the parish's relationship to the fur trade, the development of a mixed economy, the pattern of kinship networks, and the emergence of an economic class structure. The traditions of the fur trade played a key role in the development of St. Andrew's, as the "Bay tradition" helped shape the response of the English-speaking Métis to the new community at the Rapids and ultimately influenced social, economic, and religious life there. The hierarchical traditions of the fur trade – the ranking of officers and men – was brought to this new community by retiring HBC servants and their families. The stratification that had once separated tripmen from chief factors would be reflected in the division between buffalo hunters and farmers, and between minor agriculturalists and major landowners, though these divisions were often blunted by an extensive kinship network with roots in the society of the fur post.

The Anglican Church played a major role in the development of the English Métis community in Red River. The Hudson's Bay Company, through the skillful negotiations of George Simpson, effectively confined CMS activity to the settlement and its growing population of Métis émigrés. William Cockran, who in 1829 established his mission among these new settlers at the Rapids, hoped to eradicate the traditions of the trading post among the members of his congregation by establishing an agricultural community that was beyond the economic influence of the fur trade. The communication of practical farming skills to a population familiar only with the life of the hunt and the trading post formed the cornerstone of the CMS message at the Rapids. An evangelical approach informed the religious values of the mission, an approach that missionaries like Cockran believed better suited a congregation unconcerned with high church principles and formal ritual. In order for "civilization" to triumph over "barbarism" at St. Andrew's, the church sought to create a society and culture patterned on an Anglo-British model, in essence a "little Britain in the wilderness."

In many respects, the success of the CMS mission was dependent upon an alliance of church and company in Red River. Although the HBC frequently attempted to undermine the goals of the church, and Simpson employed his influence to restrict CMS efforts to within the confines of the settlement, the two concerns shared a common view of Red River. For the HBC, the Anglican Church represented an instrument for social order through a zealous promotion of agriculture, education, and religious culture. The considerable number of Métis, both French- and English-speaking, who relocated to Red River in the early decades of the nineteenth century posed a threat to the company's monopoly in Rupert's Land. Both the Anglican and Roman Catholic churches in the settlement were agents of acculturation and were viewed by the HBC as means by which potential competitors could be effectively controlled and channeled into such supportive pursuits as agriculture and the provision of contract labour. Though critical of the fur trade, CMS missionaries realized that, not only could the company facilitate their work in the settlement, in fact, its monopoly helped promote the creation of a more or less stable population of congregants. While the two concerns clashed over the establishment of new missions outside Red River, they shared a common vision of how that particular community was to be structured and regulated. Both church and company considered themselves the colony's natural elite, providing direction for the large Métis population. Through representation of the Council of Assiniboia, the Anglican clergy were able to exercise social and political control and help the HBC and the "principal settlers" in their attempts to regulate the minor land holders, tripmen, and buffalo hunters who made up the community's lower classes.

The alliance of church and company in Red River was most evident in the context of the free-trade dispute. Rather than aligning themselves with their Métis parishioners, the Anglican clergy considered the dispute an unlawful challenge to authority in Red River; a challenge that might ultimately undermine their own influence within the community. The church's decision to side with the company, thereby alienating its traditional basis of support, set the mission upon a new course in St. Andrew's, one that would see the evangelical cause effectively abandoned in favour of a more formal and more traditional religious approach and strategy within the parish.

When, by 1860, it had become evident to the Anglican clergy that the Hudson's Bay Company could no longer effectively govern Red River (a fact that had become apparent to the Métis of the colony almost twenty years earlier), the church threw its support behind the Canadian party and the annexationist cause. David Anderson, Robert Machray, James Hunter, and Joseph Gardiner all realized that an influx of Anglo-Ontarian settlers would accelerate the church's influence both in Red River and throughout the West. The Anglican Church actively sought the displacement of the old order in Red River and helped promote the myth among the English-speaking Métis of the settlement that their interests would be better served by the incoming constitutional authority.

The character of the community at St. Andrew's was in large part based upon the nature of its economy. Along with agriculture, many settlers pursued such activities as buffalo hunting, tripping, fishing, haying, and for some the private trade in furs. Others, like settler Samuel Taylor, furnished services to the community in the form of stonemasonry and milling. It was a complementary rather than exclusive economy, and one that provided a practical solution to the problem of scarcity, a problem that had plagued the community since its inception. The inherent difficulties faced by farmers in Red River – a harsh climate, limited markets and primitive technology – meant that, for many, survival depended upon a varied exploitation of available resources. Limited resources also dictated building styles and materials in the parish. The use of Red River frame typified the cottages and farm outbuildings of St. Andrew's, though limestone was employed in the construction of the more imposing stone residences and churches that were located in the lower settlement.

River Road, 1922 (Provincial Archives of Manitoba).

As its architecture would suggest, St. Andrew's was not a homogeneous community, either racially or economically. European heads of mixed-blood families, such as James Sutherland and William Pruden possessed an economic advantage over many of their Métis fellow parishioners. Census records from the early years of the parish indicate that these "principal settlers" owned more livestock, implements, and cultivated acreage than the greater constituency of St. Andrew's settlers, who maintained only a few farm animals and engaged in a limited cultivation of what were, for the most part, only garden plots. Later, as commercial opportunities declined, St. Andrew's residents became more involved in farming, especially when compared to the level of agricultural activity found in other parts of Métis Red River. Wealthier farmers in the parish, however, continued to enjoy greater access to such things as superior education and the political power that went hand-in-hand with their favoured status within the community. They came to view themselves as the natural elite in Red River and, along with the church and the company in the settlement, a force for the establishment of an Anglo-Christian civilization on the frontier.

193

With the transition to a new political order after 1870, and the influx of Ontarian settlers to Red River, the character of the community underwent considerable change. Some Métis settlers departed the parish to seek new economic opportunities elsewhere or left as the result of dispossession. Those who remained found their power and influence usurped by the new settlers under a federal policy that encouraged massive immigration to Manitoba and the Northwest Territories. Agricultural colonization beyond the borders of the old settlement, and the subsequent development of Winnipeg as a quickly growing distribution and supply centre, relegated St. Andrew's to a peripheral role in the transition to a large-scale commercial agricultural economy in western Canada.

After the decades of decline that followed the turn of the century, St. Andrew's has recently become an exurban home for a gentrified community of landowners attracted to the rural ambience of riverside properties. Today, though a few historic limestone buildings remain, and here and there one can find a crumbled old barn, new upscale homes and manicured lawns have largely replaced the vestiges of the old riverlot pattern and the cultural landscapes that defined the unique character of one of Manitoba's oldest parishes. Once a muddy cart track, River Road is now a paved drive, a vague reminder of a time when for the people of St. Andrew's and the Red River settlement it was the "road to the Rapids."

Notes

Chapter One
Introduction

1. Gerald and Jean Friesen, "River Road," in *River Road: Essays on Manitoba and Prairie History*, by Gerald Friesen (Winnipeg: University of Manitoba Press, 1996), 4.

2. A number of these works have become the standard sources in fur trade and Red River studies. See, for example, Sylvia Van Kirk, *Many Tender Ties: Women in Fur Trade Society, 1670-1870* (Winnipeg: Watson and Dwyer, 1980); Jennifer S. H. Brown, *Strangers in Blood: Fur Trade Company Families in Indian Country* (Vancouver: UBC Press, 1980); and Jacqueline Peterson and Jennifer S. H. Brown, eds., *The New Peoples: Being and Becoming Métis in North America* (Winnipeg: University of Manitoba Press, 1985).

3. For an elaboration of this point, see D. N. Sprague, "The Cultural Bias of Métis Studies," *Prairie Fire* 8, no. 2 (Summer 1987): 66-67.

4. See Frits Pannekoek, "The Historiography of the Red River Settlement, 1830-1868," *Prairie Forum* 6, no. 1 (Spring 1981): 83-89.

5. Cornelius Jaenan, "Missionary Approaches to Native Peoples," in *Approaches to Native History in Canada* (Ottawa: National Museum of Man, Mercury Series, 1977), 5.

6. J. M. Bumsted, *The Red River Rebellion* (Winnipeg: Watson and Dwyer, 1996), 17.

7. Gerhard Ens, *Homeland to Hinterland: The Changing Worlds of the Red River Metis in the Nineteenth Century* (Toronto: University of Toronto Press, 1996), 12.

Chapter Two
CMS Ideology and the Red River Mission

1. R. F. Berkhofer, Jr., *Salvation and the Savage, An Analysis of Protestant Missions and the American Indian Response, 1787-1862* (Louisville: University of Kentucky Press, 1965); *The White Man's Indian* (New York: Random House, 1979); Francis Jennings, *The Invasion of America* (New York: Norton Press, 1976); James Axtell, *The European and the Indian: Essays in the History of Colonial North America* (New York: Oxford University Press, 1981); and *The Invasion Within: The Contest of Cultures in Colonial North America* (New York: Oxford University Press, 1985).

2. Bruce Trigger, *The Children of Aataentsic* (Montreal: McGill-Queen's University Press, 1976); *Natives and Newcomers: Canada's Heroic Age Reconsidered* (Montreal: McGill-Queen's University Press, 1985); Cornelius Jaenan, *Friend and Foe: Aspects of French-Amerindian Cultural Contact in the Sixteenth and Seventeenth Centuries* (Toronto: McClelland & Stewart, 1976); Jean Usher, "Apostles and Aborigines: The Social Theory of the Church Missionary Society," *Social History* 7 (1971): 28; *William Duncan of Metlakatla* (Ottawa: National Museum of Canada, 1974); John Webster Grant, *Moon of Wintertime: Missionaries and the Indians of Canada in Encounter since 1534* (Toronto: University of Toronto Press, 1984); Olive Dickason, *Canada's First Nations: A History of Founding Peoples from Earliest Times* (Toronto: McClelland & Stewart, 1992).

3. Frits Pannekoek, *A Snug Little Flock: The Social Origins of the Riel Resistance of 1869-70* (Winnipeg: Watson and Dwyer, 1991); Kerry Abel, *Drum Song: Glimpses of Dene History* (Montreal: McGill-Queen's University Press, 1993); Martha McCarthy, *From the Ends of the Earth* (Edmonton: University of Alberta Press, 1994); Raymond Huel, *Proclaiming the Gospel to the Indians and the Métis: The Missionary Oblates of Mary Immaculate in Western Canada, 1845-1945* (Edmonton: University of Alberta Press, 1996); Robert Choquette, *The Oblate Assault on the North-West* (Ottawa: University of Ottawa Press, 1995); Winona Stevenson, "The Journals and Voices of a Church of England Catechist; Askenootow (Charles Pratt), 1851-1884," in *Reading Beyond Words: Contexts for Native History*, ed. Jennifer S. H. Brown and Elizabeth Vibert (Peterborough: Broadview Press, 1996); Earle Waugh, *Dissonant Worlds: Roger Vandersteene Among the Cree* (Waterloo: Wilfred Laurier Press, 1996).

4. Thomas C. B. Boon, *The Anglican Church from the Bay to the Rockies* (Toronto: Ryerson Press, 1962); *These Men Went Out* (Toronto: Ryerson Press, n.d); "The Archdeacon and the Governor," *The Beaver* (Spring, 1968); Frank A. Peake, "Fur Traders and Missionaries: Some Reflections on the Attitudes of the Hudson's Bay Company Towards Missionary Work Among the Indians, *Western Canadian Journal of Anthropology* 3, no. 1 (1972): 72-93; "From the Red River to the Arctic: Essays on Anglican Missionary Expansion in the Nineteenth Century, *Journal of the Canadian Church Historical Society* 31, no. 3 (1989): 1-47; Arthur N. Thompson, "John West: A Study of the Conflict Between Civilization and the Fur Trade," *Journal of the Canadian Church Historical Society* 12 (1970): 44-57.

5. Frits Pannekoek, "'Insidious' Sources and the Historical Interpretation of the Pre-1870 West," in *The Anglican Church and the World of Western Canada, 1820-1870*, ed. Barry Ferguson (Regina: Canadian Plains Research Centre, 1991), 29-37.

6. See Barry Ferguson, "Secular History and Church History: A Introduction," in *The Anglican Church and the World of Western Canada, 1820-1870,* ed. Barry Ferguson (Regina: Canadian Plains Research Centre, 1991), 1.

7. Foster and Pannekoek's differing ideas on the influence of the Anglican Church in Red River are contained in a number of books, theses, and articles. A handful of these are: John Foster, "The Anglican Clergy in the Red River Settlement, 1820-1826" (MA thesis, University of Alberta, 1966); "The Country-Born in the Red River Settlement, 1820-1850" (PhD dissertation, University of Alberta, 1973); "Missionaries, Mixed-Bloods and the Fur Trade: Four Letters of the Rev. William Cockran, 1830-1833," *Western Canadian Journal of Anthropology* 3, no. 1 (1972): 94-125; "William Cockran," *Dictionary of Canadian Biography,* vol. 9 (Toronto: University of Toronto Press, 1976), 134-137. Pannekoek's ideas are also put forward in a number of publications including *A Snug Little Flock: The Social Origins of the Riel Resistance, 1869-1870;* "The Anglican Church and the Disintegration of Red River Society, 1818-1870," in *The West and the Nation,* ed. Carl Berger and Ramsay Cook (Toronto: McClelland & Stewart, 1976), 72-90; "The Rev. Griffiths Owen Corbett and the Red River Civil War of 1869-70," *Canadian Historical Review* 58, no. 2 (1976): 133-150.

8. Foster, "The Anglican Church and the Red River Settlement, 1820-1826," 1.

9. Ibid.

10. Pannekoek, *A Snug Little Flock,* 208.

11. Jean Usher, "Apostles and Aborigines: The Social Theory of the Church Missionary Society," *Social History* 7 (1971): 28. Robert Berkhofer, who studied American missionary activity in the eighteenth and nineteenth centuries, viewed the Indian-missionary contact experience within the context of "directed" and "non-directed" models of cultural contact. Under the former model, the culture of the society in the subordinate position is drastically modified to conform to that of the dominant group. See R. F. Berkhofer, *Salvation and the Savage,* xi.

12. Ibid., 29.

13. Ian Bradley, *The Call to Seriousness* (London: Jonathan Cape, 1976), 15.

14. Walter F. Houghton, *The Victorian Frame of Mind, 1830-1870* (New Haven: Yale University Press, 1957), 125.

15. Ibid.

16. Ian Bradley, *The Call to Seriousness,* 18.

17. The Clapham Sect took its name from a village near London where a number of its members lived. Although not the first pietist evangelical group to be formed, it soon became the largest and most influential within the movement.

18. Walter Houghton, *The Victorian Frame of Mind, 1830-1870,* 131.

19. Frits Pannekoek, "Protestant Agricultural Missions in the Canadian West to 1870" (MA thesis, University of Alberta, 1970), 7. For more information on the CMS and its history, see Eugene Stock, *The History of the Church Missionary Society,* 4 vols. (London: Church Missionary Society, 1899).

20. Eugene Stock, *The History of the Church Missionary Society,* 245.

21. Hal Guest, "The Historic Landscape of the Parsonage at St. Andrew's," Parks Canada, Manuscript Report Series, no. 443, 1981, 60.

22. Provincial Archives of Manitoba (hereafter PAM), MG7. A1, Ecclesiastical Archives of the Province of Rupert's Land, *Church Missionary Society Regulations and Instructions to Missionaries.*

23. Jean Usher, "Apostles and Aborigines," 29.

24. H. A. Cairns, *The Clash of Culture. Early Race Relations in Central Africa* (New York: F. A. Praeger Ltd., 1965), 54.

25. PAM, MG7, A1, Ecclesiastical Archives of the Province of Rupert's Land, *Church Missionary Intelligencer*, 1863, 3.

26. Henry Bowden, *American Indians and Christian Missions* (Chicago: University of Chicago Press, 1981), 164.

27. Cornelius Jaenen, "Missionary Approaches to Native People," in *Approaches to Native History in Canada*, ed. D. A. Muise (Ottawa: National Museum of Man, Mercury Series, 1977), 6-7.

28. Jean Usher, "Apostles and Aborigines," 32.

29. *Church Missionary Intelligencer* (1855): 243, as quoted in ibid., 32.

30. Christine Bolt, *Victorian Attitudes to Race* (Toronto: University of Toronto Press, 1971), 208.

31. E. B. Tylor, *Researches into the Early History of Mankind and the Development of Civilization* (Chicago: University of Chicago Press, 1964), 232.

32. J. W. Burrow, *Evolution and Society: A Study in Victorian Social Theory* (London: Cambridge University Press, 1966), 263.

33. Ibid., 281.

34. PAM, Church Missionary Society Archives (hereafter CMSA), A78, Journal of William Cockran, April 28, 1840.

35. Ibid.

36. W. B. Heeney, *Leaders of the Canadian Church* (Toronto: Mission Book Company, 1920), 21.

37. *Church Missionary Intelligencer* (1849): 76, as cited in Jean Usher, "Apostles and Aborigines," 33.

38. PAM, CMSA, A77, William Cockran to Secretaries, n.d.

39. PAM, MG7, A1, *Ecclesiastical Archives of the Province of Rupert's Land,* "Regulations and Instructions to Missionaries," 22.

40. Public Archives of Canada (hereafter PAC), MG19, E6, *John Smithurst Papers*, Richard Davies to John Smithurst, March 31, 1846.

41. Egerton Young, *The Apostle of the North* (Toronto: no publisher listed, 1900), 233-35.

42. Church historian Vera Fast suggests that "these early [CMS] missionaries generally differed in background, outlook and expectation from their successors in the second half of the 19th century." She argues that, before 1850, the CMS placed little stress upon communicating the basic tenets of "civilization" to the aboriginal peoples of Rupert's Land. However, the journals and correspondence of early Red River missionaries such as John West, John Smithurst, William Cockran, and Robert James indicate that, in fact, their view of Christianity was closely allied with the notion of the establishment in Red River of a self-sufficient and predominantly agricultural community. Although, in some respects, an argument can be made for the assertion that these clerics might have been "less doctrinaire [than their successors] insofar as cultural compliance was concerned," their intention was to certainly do more than build what Fast calls a community of "faith, saving grace [and] good works," See Vera Fast, "The Protestant Missionary and Fur Trade Society: Initial Contact in the Hudson's Bay Territory, 1820-1850" (PhD dissertation, University of Manitoba, 1984), i, 300.

43. PAM, CMSA, A77, William Cockran to Secretaries, August 7, 1828.

44. PAC, MG19, E6, John Smithurst Papers, 6 June, 1840.

45. Ibid., 11, May,1840.

46. *Church Missionary Intelligencer* (1860): 2, as cited in Jean Usher, "Apostles and Aborigines," 40.
47. W. B. Heeney, *Leaders of the Canadian Church*, 21.
48. A growing body of literature exists on the domestic traditions of the fur trade and the origins of the French and English Métis in the West. A handful of the better known sources include: John Foster, "The Origins of the Mixed Bloods in the Canadian West," in *Essays in Western History*, ed. L. H. Thomas (Edmonton: University of Alberta Press, 1976); Jennifer S. H. Brown, *Strangers in Blood: Fur Trade Company Families in Indian Country* (Vancouver: UBC Press, 1980); Sylvia Van Kirk, *Many Tender Ties: Women in Fur Trade Society, 1670-1870* (Winnipeg: Watson and Dwyer, 1980); Jacqueline Peterson and Jennifer S. H. Brown (ed.), *The New Peoples: Being and Becoming Métis in North America* (Winnipeg: University of Manitoba Press, 1985); and Diane Payment, "The Métis," in vol., *The Handbook of North American Indians* (Washington: The Smithsonian Museum, forthcoming).
49. The history of the Métis in the Red River Settlement can be found in a wide range of sources including a number of the those listed above. Others include: John Foster, "The Country-Born in the Red River Settlement, 1820-1850" (PhD dissertation, University of Alberta, 1973); Gerald Friesen, *The Canadian Prairies: A History* (Toronto: University of Toronto Press, 1984), chapters 5 and 6; D. N. Sprague and R. P. Frye, *The Genealogy of the First Métis Nation* (Winnipeg: Pemmican Publ., 1983); Gerhard Ens, *Homeland to Hinterland: The Changing Worlds of the Red River Métis* (Toronto: University of Toronto Press, 1996); Frits Pannekoek, *A Snug Little Flock: The Social Origins of the Riel Resistance, 1869-70*; as well as a whole host of journal articles on various aspects of Red River history and society. Consult the bibliography for a more complete list of these sources.
50. John Foster, "The Country-Born in the Red River Settlement, 1820-1850," iv.
51. PAM, CMSA, A101, Abraham Cowley to Secretaries, 14 December,1874.
52. PAM, CMSA, A77, William Cockran to Secretaries, 25 July, 1833.
53. Ibid., 29 July, 1830.
54. PAM, CMSA, A78, Robert James to Rev. Davies, 6 August, 1847.
55. A. S. Morton, *A History of the Canadian West to 1871* (Toronto: University of Toronto Press, 1973), 631.
56. N. Jaye Goossen, "The Relationship of the Church Missionary Society and the Hudson's Bay Company in Rupert's Land, 1821-1860, with a case study of Stanley Mission under the Direction of Rev. Robert Hunt" (MA thesis, University of Manitoba, 1975), 34-35.
57. David Thompson, in the narrative of his explorations between 1784 and 1812, had warned of this problem at the end of the eighteenth century. In the midst of a struggle for control of the trade, however, neither company was willing to address the growing problem. David Thompson's *Narrative of his Explorations in Western America, 1784-1812*, ed. J. B. Tyrell (Toronto: Champlain Society, 1916), 205-06.
58. Governor and Committee of the Hudson's Bay Company to George Simpson, 27 February, 1822, in *Minutes of Council, Northern Department of Rupert's Land, 1821-1831*, ed. E. E. Rich and R. H. Fleming (London: Hudson's Bay Record Society, 1940), vol. III, 311.
59. Ibid., March 8, 1822.
60. Hudson's Bay Company, *Charters, Statutes, Orders in Council Relating to the Hudson's Bay Company* (London: Hudson's Bay Company, 1931), 95.
61. Andrew Colvile to George Simpson, 11 March, 1824, in *Fur Trade and Empire*, ed. Frederick Merk (Cambridge: Harvard University Press, 1968), 205.

199

62. Hal Guest, "The Historic Landscape of the Parsonage at St. Andrew's," 66.

63. John West, *The Substance of a Journal During a Residence at the Red River Colony* (New York: Johnson Reprint Corp., 1966), 12.

64. Ibid., 13.

65. Ibid., 15.

66. Ibid.

67. Ibid., 21-22.

68. Ibid., 37.

69. George Simpson to Andrew Colvile, 20 May, 1822, in *Fur Trade and Empire*, ed. Frederick Merk, 181.

70. Arthur N. Thompson, "John West: A Study of the Conflict Between Civilization and the Fur Trade," *The Journal of the Canadian Church Historical Society*, 12, no. 3 (September, 1970): 47.

71. George Simpson to Andrew Colvile, 8 September, 1823, in Frits Pannekoek, *A Snug Little Flock*, 66.

72. John West, *Substance of a Journal*, 51.

73. Ibid., 122.

74. Ibid., 152.

75. Ibid.

76. Ibid., 91.

77. Ibid., 151.

78. PAM, HBCA, D. 4/3, 75, George Simpson to Benjamin Harrison, 1 August, 1824.

79. George Simpson to Andrew Colvile, 2 August, 1824, in Frederick Merk, *Fur Trade and Empire,* 181.

80. Ibid.

81. John Foster, "The Anglican Clergy in the Red River Settlement, 1820-1826," 126.

82. Historian Hal Guest has suggested that part of the antipathy Simpson felt for West stemmed from the former's feelings of insecurity as a result of his humble birth. (Simpson was born out of wedlock.) Simpson perhaps resented West, Guest surmises, because of his higher station. See H. Guest, "The Historic Landscape of the Parsonage at St. Andrew's," 71.

83. T.C.B. Boon, *The Anglican Church From the Bay to the Rockies*, 23.

84. PAM, CMSA, A77, J. Pratt to David Jones, 10 March, 1824.

85. Ibid., Journal of David Jones, 14 January, 1824.

86. Ibid., Dandison Coates to David Jones, 24 February, 1826.

87. John Foster, "The Anglican Clergy in the Red River Settlement," 38.

88. PAM, CMSA, A77, Journal of David Jones, 17 November, 1823.

89. Ibid., George Simpson to David Jones, 24 July, 1824.

90. Ibid., David Jones to George Simpson, 4 June, 1825.

91. Ibid., Journal of David Jones, 19 August, 1824.

92. Ibid., 19 August, 1824.

93. A self-supporting school was also established at a point approximately six miles down the river from the Upper Church (later St. John's) within the area known as Image Plain and later as St. Paul's Middlechurch. Joseph Bunn, a Rupert's Land Métis who had been educated in England was engaged in the summer of 1825 as the new teacher. See PAM, CMSA, A77, Journal of David Jones, 2 July, 1825.

94. Ibid., David Jones to D. Coates, 10 July, 1824.

95. See John Foster, "Program for the Red River Mission: The Anglican Clergy 1820-1826," *Social History* 4 (November, 1969): 61.
96. PAM, CMSA, A77, David Jones to Secretaries, July (n.d.), 1827.
97. John Foster, "Program for the Red River Mission," 67.
98. Frits Pannekoek, "The Anglican Church and the Disintegration of Red River Society, 1818-1870," 74.
99. As quoted in John Foster, "William Cockran," *Dictionary of Canadian Biography*, vol. 9 (Toronto: University of Toronto Press, 1976), 134.
100. Raymond Beaumont, "The Rev. William Cockran: The Man and the Image," *Manitoba History* 33 (Spring, 1997): 2-15.
101. Alexander Ross, *The Red River Settlement: Its Rise, Progress, and Present State* (London: Smith, Elder and Co., 1856, reprinted by H. Doherty, 1984), 183.
102. Colin Inkster, "William Cochran," in *Leaders of the Canadian Church,* ed. William Heeney (Toronto: Musson Book Co., 1920), 60-61, as quoted in Raymond Beaumont, "The Rev. William Cockran: The Man and the Image," 3.
103. T.C.B. Boon, *The Anglican Church from the Bay to the Rockies*, 35, and "The Archdeacon and the Governor: William Cockran and George Simpson at the Red River Colony, 1825-65, *The Beaver* (Spring, 1968): 41.
104. See Raymond Beaumont, "The Rev. William Cockran: The Man and the Image," 3-9.
105. Ibid., 9-12.
106. See ibid., 12. Although Beaumont effectively disputes the use of sources in the works of Pannekoek and van der Goes Ladd, and convincingly argues that they have distorted Cockran's image into caricature, he does not offer much of his own assessment of the missionary's impact within the community except to agree with Foster's assertion regarding Métis adaptation and an implied sympathy with the positive perspectives of Garrioch and Boon.
107. As quoted in Hal Guest, "The Historic Landscape of the Parsonage at St. Andrew's," 74.
108. PAM, CMSA, A77, William Cockran to the CMS Secretaries, 29 July, 1826.
109. Ibid., William Cockran to Rev. Bickersteth, 3 August, 1829. Cockran described to Bickersteth how: "A great deal of odium has been attached to me by my colleague [Jones] from time to time, but I have persevered in well-doing until I have lived down the prejudices which he has raised against me, and my example of industry is as valuable in its way as the preaching of the Gospel."
110. Ibid.
111. Aside from their dispute over the farm, Cockran also accused Jones of not involving himself enough in the spiritual welfare of his people and of being overly concerned with the goings on at the Fort Garry dinner tables. See ibid., William Cockran to CMS Secretaries, 7 August, 1828.

Chapter Three
Establishing the Mission at St. Andrew's

1. George Simpson to Andrew Colvile, 15 May, 1833, in Frederick Merk, *Fur Trade and Empire,* 190.
2. PAM, CMSA, A77, William Cockran to Secretaries, 25 July, 1833.
3. John Foster, "The Country-Born in the Red River Settlement, 1820-1850," 157-58.
4. PAM, CMSA, A77, William Cockran to Secretaries, 29 July, 1830.
5. Ibid., 5 August, 1829.
6. Ibid.
7. "William Cockran's Deed of Purchase," as reproduced in Appendix A, Rodger Guinn, "St. Andrew's Parsonage, Red River: A Structural and Land Use History" (Manuscript Report Series, no. 251, Ottawa: Parks Canada, 1978), 79.
8. PAM, CMSA, A77, William Cockran to Secretaries, 29 July, 1830.
9. Ibid.
10. Ibid.
11. Journal entries regarding work on the church continue between 21 September, 1831 and 21 April, 1832. See PAM, CMSA, A77, Journal of William Cockran, 21 September, 1831 to 21 April, 1832.
12. PAM, CMSA, A77, Journal of William Cockran, 7 September, 1831.
13. Ibid., William Cockran to Secretaries, 20 July, 1831.
14. Ibid., Journal of William Cockran, 23 December, 1831.
15. Ibid., 1 May, 1832.
16. Ibid., David Jones to Secretaries, August, 1835.
17. Ibid., William Cockran to Secretaries, 25 July, 1833.
18. Ibid.
19. Ibid., 5 August, 1833.
20. PAM, CMSA, A77, Journal of William Cockran, 29 July, 1830.
21. Ibid., November 12, 1833.
22. Ibid., October 17, 1831.
23. Ibid., July 30, 1833.
24. Ibid., September 8, 1834.
25. Ibid., September 2, 1833.
26. Ibid., A78, Journal of William Cockran, September 28, 1837.
27. Ibid., October 4, 1839.
28. Ibid., September 14, 1837.
29. Ibid., September 3, 1845.
30. Ibid., A77, William Cockran to Edward Bickersteth, August 7, 1828.
31. Ibid., William Cockran to Secretaries, August 11, 1828.
32. Ibid., Journal of William Cockran, October 16, 1833.
33. Ibid., William Cockran to Secretaries, August 20, 1835.
34. Ibid., William Cockran to Lay Secretary, August, n.d., 1832.
35. As cited in Frits Pannekoek, "Protestant Agricultural Missions in the Canadian West to 1870," 92.

36. Ibid.
37. Ibid., 92-93.
38. PAM, MG2, B2, Red River Census, 1838 and 1848.
39. PAM, CMSA, A78, Journal of David Jones, n.d.
40. Ibid. According to Jones, Peguis asked that the Society never allow Cockran to leave the Indian settlement as "he is now well-customed with our oily and fishy smell, and all our bad habits."
41. Frits Pannekoek, *A Snug Little Flock: The Social Origins of the Riel Resistance of 1869-70*, 99.
42. Hal Guest, "The Historic Landscape of the Parsonage at St. Andrew's," 125.
43. Laura Peers, "Aboriginal People and Lower Fort Garry" (unpublished manuscript on file with Parks Canada, Winnipeg, 1995), 60.
44. Ibid., 67.
45. PAM, CMSA, A85, John Smithurst to the Secretaries, October 27, 1847.
46. PAM, CMSA, A78, Robert James to Rev. Davies, August 6, 1847.
47. Ibid.
48. Frits Pannekoek, "Protestant Agricultural Missions in the Canadian West to 1870," 97.
49. HBCA, B.135/c/2, fol. 65, George Simpson to J. G. McTavish, April 10, 1831.
50. PAM, CMSA, A77, William Cockran to Secretaries, July 20, 1831.
51. Ibid., William Cockran to Rev. Woodriff, August 3, 1831.
52. PAM, Ecclesiastical Archives of the Province of Rupert's Land, *Proceedings of the Church Missionary Society, 1832-33*, W. K. Smith to Secretaries, 64.
53. PAM, CMSA, A77, William Cockran to Secretaries, July 30, 1833.
54. CMSA, CC1/039, George Simpson to David Jones, 14 July 1832, as quoted in Sylvia Van Kirk, *Many Tender Ties: Women: Women in Fur Trade Society, 1670-1870*, 148. For a history of the Red River Academy, see Thomas Bredin, "The Red River Academy," *The Beaver* (Winter, 1974): 12.
55. PAM, CMSA, A77, William Cockran to Secretaries, August, 1835.
56. CMSA,CC1/039, George Simpson to David Jones, 14 July 1832 as quoted in Sylvia Van Kirk, *Many Tender Ties*, 148
57. Letitia Hargrave to Mrs. Dugald McTavish, 16 September, 1843, in Letitia Hargrave, *The Letters of Letitia Hargrave*, ed. M. McLeod (Toronto: Champlain Society, 1947), 177.
58. Letitia Hargrave to Mrs. Dugald McTavish, 1 September, 1845, ibid., 206.
59. Thomas Bredin, "The Red River Academy," 17.
60. PAM, CMSA, A77, William Cockran and David Jones to Secretaries, "Report on the State of Religion," August, 1835.
61. Ibid., A78, Journal of William Cockran, 19 October, 1837.
62. Ibid., 31 October, 1837.
63. Ibid., 21 June, 1835.
64. Ibid., A77, William Cockran to Secretaries, 25 July, 1833.
65. Ibid.
66. Ibid.
67. Ibid., A78, 4 August, 1841.
68. Ibid.
69. Ibid., A77, Journal of William Cockran, 17 December, 1834.
70. Ibid., A78, Abraham Cowley to Secretaries, January 4, 1842.

71. Ibid., Journal of William Cockran , September 19, 1839.

72. Ibid., December 4, 1838.

73. Ibid., William Cockran to Lay Secretary, August 7, 1843.

74. Ibid.

75. Ibid., Journal of William Cockran, September 19, 1839.

76. Ibid., William Cockran to Secretaries, August 2, 1838.

77. Ibid.

78. Ibid., Journal of William Cockran, August 16, 1838.

79. Ibid., William Cockran to Secretaries, August 4, 1838.

80. Ibid., Journal of William Cockran, August 27, 1845.

81. Ibid., December 31, 1844.

82. Ibid.

83. Ibid., William Cockran to Secretaries, July 30, 1845.

84. Anglican Diocesan Archives of Rupert's Land, St. Andrew's Account Books, 1849-1852, *Materials furnished by Subscribers towards Payment of their Subsciptions.*

85. Ibid., Journal of William Cockran, June 10, 1846.

86. Ibid., A92, Robert James to Secretaries, August 2, 1848. "The new stone Church is not completed," he wrote, "but [is] proceeding fast under the superintendence of Mr. Cockran."

87. Ibid.

88. Ibid., August 6, 1849.

89. Ibid., November 28, 1849.

90. HBCA, D.5/18, folios 327-28, Adam Thom to George Simpson, November 11, 1846.

91. PAM, CMSA, A78, Robert James to Benjamin Davies, November 12, 1846.

92. HBCA, D.5/18, folios 327-28, Adam Thom to George Simpson, November 11, 1846.

93. PAM, CMSA, A78, Robert James to Benjamin Davies, August 6, 1847.

94. Ibid., Journal of Robert James, May 30, 1847.

Chapter Four
Church and Company in Red River

1. Arthur Thompson, "John West: A Study of the Conflict Between Civilization and the Fur Trade," *The Journal of the Canadian Church Historical Society* 12, no. 3 (September, 1970): 47.

2. Jaye Goossen, "The Relationship of the Church Missionary Society and the Hudson's Bay Company in Rupert's Land, 1821-1861," 1.

3. Frits Pannekoek, "The Rev. James Evans and the Social Antagonisms of Fur Trade Society," 1-15.

4. Jaye Goossen, "The Relationship of the Church Missionary Society and the Hudson's Bay Company in Rupert's Land, 1821-1861," 13.

5. John Grant, *Moon of Wintertime*, 108.

6. Ibid., 109.

7. Frits Pannekoek, "The Churches and the Social Structure in the Red River Area, 1818-1870" (PhD dissertation, Queen's University, 1973), 154.

8. John West, *Substance of a Journal*, 92.

9. PAM, CMSA, Journal of John West. September 16, 1823.

10. PAM, HBCA, D.4/3, folio 141, Simpson to Benjamin Harrison, n.d.

11. John Foster, "The Country-Born in the Red River Settlement, 1820-1850," 115-16.

12. *Minutes of Council of the Northern Department of Rupert's Land, 1821-1831,* ed. R. H. Fleming (Toronto: Champlain Society, 1940), 90-95.

13. E. E. Rich, *The History of the Hudson's Bay Company, 1670-1870,* vol. 3 (Toronto: McClelland & Stewart, 1970), 528.

14. Jaye Goossen, "The Relationship of the Church Missionary Society and the Hudson's Bay Company in Rupert's Land, 1821-1861," 60.

15. John Foster, "The Anglican Clergy in the Red River Settlement, 1820-1826," 82.

16. J. J. Hargrave, *Red River* (Altona, Manitoba: Friesen Printers, 1977), 104.

17. PAM, CMSA, A78, William Cockran to Secretary, August 4, 1838.

18. Ibid., A77, William Cockran to Secretaries, July 30, 1831.

19. Ibid., July 25, 1833.

20. Ibid., A78, August 4, 1838.

21. Ibid., A77, July 24, 1834.

22. Ibid., August n.d., 1832.

23. Ibid., July 25, 1833.

24. Ibid.

25. Country marriages, or marriage "à la façon du pays," and the role of women in fur trade society, have been researched extensively by Sylvia Van Kirk in her book *Many Tender Ties* (Winnipeg: Watson and Dwyer, 1980). Van Kirk discusses the evolution of fur trade marriage practices from the establishment by traders of liaisons with Native women to the arrival of European women in Rupert's Land after 1831. The role of the missionaries in Red River and the promotion of church marriage is also examined.

26. Before 1830, Simpson actually encouraged country marriages. In contemplation of the move into New Caledonia in the early 1820s, for instance, Simpson recommended that the officers form alliances with the principal families immediately upon their arrival as "the best security we can have of the goodwill of the Natives," as quoted in *Simpson's Athabaska Journal, 1820-1821,* ed. E. E. Rich (London: Hudson's Bay Record Society, 1938), 392.

27. Sylvia Van Kirk has written that; "For a woman to be left without a male protector was deemed undesirable and accounts for the incessant pressure that mixed-blood women felt to remarry. Those who were recently widowed, unless too old, were expected to marry again, while the custom of "turning off" may have remained a means of, at least, ensuring that mixed-blood wives, whose husbands were leaving them in the Indian Country, would continue to be maintained at fur-trade posts. The exigencies of fur-trade life were such that it was not uncommon for a mixed-blood woman to have two or three husbands in her lifetime." See *Many Tender Ties,* 120.

28. See Brian Gallegher, "A Re-Examination of Race, Class, and Society in Red River," *Native Studies Review* 4, nos. 1/2 (1988): 25-54.

29. For a description of the scandal, see Sylvia Van Kirk, "'The Reputation of a Lady': Sarah Ballenden and the Foss-Pelly Scandal," *Manitoba History* 11 (Spring, 1988): 4-11, and Van Kirk, *Many Tender Ties,* 220-30.

30. Sylvia Van Kirk, "'The Reputation of a Lady,'" 10.

31. PAM, CMSA, A77, William Cockran to Secretaries, August, 1832.

32. Ibid., A78, August 7, 1840.
33. Ibid.
34. Ibid., William Cockran to Lay Secretary, August 4, 1841.
35. Pannekoek, "The Reverend James Evans and the Social Antagonisms of Fur Trade Society," 1.
36. In a letter dated December of 1845, Cockran wrote that: "The Weslyians have been into the colony three times during the past summer to endeavour to proselytize from our Church and Establish themselves amongst us." PAM, CMSA, A78, William Cockran to Secretaries, December 29, 1845.
37. HBCA, D.4/5, folio 27, George Simpson to Benjamin Harrison, March 10, 1825.
38. Ibid., D.4/3, 76, George Simpson to Benjamin Harrison, August 1, 1824.
39. PAM, CMSA, A77, William Cockran to Secretaries, July 25, 1833.
40. E. E. Rich, *Hudson's Bay Company*, 508-14.
41. See W. L. Morton, *Manitoba: A History* (Toronto: University of Toronto Press, 1957), 73-75.
42. Alexander Ross, *The Red River Settlement* (Edmonton: Hurtig, 1972), 402.
43. Gerald Friesen, *The Canadian Prairies: A History* (Toronto: University of Toronto Press, 1984), 101.
44. Frits Pannekoek, "The Churches and the Social Structure in the Red River Area. 1818-1870," 86.
45. Ibid., 98.
46. HBCA, D.5/26, folio 553, William Cockran to George Simpson, November 21, 1849.
47. Frits Pannekoek, "The Churches and the Social Structure in the Red River Area, 1818-1870," 99.
48. HBCA, D. 5/25, folios 327-28, John Smithurst to George Simpson, June 29, 1849.
49. Ibid.
50. Frits Pannekoek, "The Churches and the Social Structure in the Red River Area, 1818-1870," 90.
51. Between the spring of 1842 and the arrival in Red River of Bishop Mountain of Montreal on June 23, 1844, the ordination dispute created a flurry of letters among Thom, Smithurst, Simpson, Cockran, the CMS Secretaries, and the Governor and Committee of the HBC in London. During his seventeen-day stay in the settlement, Mountain ordained Cowley and McCallum (Roberts had departed), preached thirteen times to large congregations and claimed to have confirmed a total of 846 people. In his journal, Mountain stated that at the Rapids mission he confirmed 192 girls and women and 150 men and boys. Bishop G. J. Mountain, *The Journal of the Bishop of Montreal During a Visit to the Church Missionary Society's North-West America Mission* (London: Seeley, Burnside and Company, 1846), 51.
52. More than likely, the difficulties of Thom, Smithurst, and James in 1847 over possession of Cockran's property at the Rapids were a result of the earlier ordination dispute.
53. Eden Colvile to the Governor and Committee of the Hudson's Bay Company, July 21, 1852, in *The Letters of Eden Colvile, 1849-1852*. ed. E. E. Rich and Alice Johnson (London: Hudson's Bay Record Society, 1956), 194.
54. Ibid., Eden Colvile to George Simpson, February 7, 1851, 205.
55. Ibid., May 22, 1851, 214.
56. HBCA, D.5/34, folio 21, Donald Ross to George Simpson, July 2, 1852.
57. Ibid., D.5/32, folio 324, Donald Ross to Eden Colvile, February 27, 1851.
58. National Archives of Canada, H.P. 4873, John Black to James Hargrave, November 25, 1851.
59. PAM, MG1, D.20, Donald Ross Papers, George Simpson to Donald Ross, December 15, 1851.
60. For evidence of this fact, one has only to scan Eugene Stock, *The History of the Church*

Missionary Society (London: Church Missionary Society, 1899), the official history of the CMS, to see that of the three lengthy volumes only a handful of pages are devoted to Rupert's Land.

61. Frits Pannekoek, "The Churches and the Social Structure in the Red River Area, 1818-1870," 88.

62. Hal Guest, "The Historic Landscape of the Parsonage at St. Andrew's," 86.

63. Frits Pannekoek, "The Anglican Church and the Disintegration of Red River Society, 1818-1870," in *The West and the Nation*, ed. C. Berger and R. Cook, 83.

64. Gerald Friesen, *The Canadian Prairies, A History*, 110.

65. Frits Pannekoek, "The Anglican Church and the Disintegration of Red River Society, 1818-1870," 83-84.

66. Ibid., 83.

67. Ibid., 86-87.

68. Gerald Friesen, *The Canadian Prairies: A History*, 115.

Chapter Five
The Mission and the Community

1. John Foster, "The Country-Born in the Red River Settlement," 91.

2. Archer Martin, *The Hudson's Bay Company's Land Tenures* (London: William Clowes, 1898), 223.

3. PAM, HBCA, D.4, George Simpson to Andrew Colvile, May 20, 1822.

4. John Foster, "The Country-Born in the Red River Settlement," 131.

5. PAM, CMSA, A77, William Cockran to Secretaries, July 29, 1830.

6. Ibid.

7. Ibid., "Report of the State of Religion, August 10, 1835."

8. PAM, CMSA, A77, William Cockran to Secretaries, July 29, 1830.

9. Ibid.

10. Ibid., A78, Journal of William Cockran, November 15, 1838.

11. Ibid., A77, Journal of David Jones, January 28, 1828.

12. Ibid., A77, Journal of William Cockran, May 15, 1829.

13. John Foster, "The Country-Born in the Red River Settlement," 153.

14. Ibid., 161.

15. PAM, CMSA, A77, William Cockran to Secretaries July 30, 1833. While Cockran's comment would seem to indicate that the church served as a broker in the provision of community assistance, no doubt the practice was carried on privately among Métis families at the Rapids.

16. Ibid., July 25, 1833.

17. Ibid., August 3, 1838.

18. Ibid., A78, August 7, 1840.

19. PAM, MG1, D.20, Donald Ross Papers, Donald Ross to James Hargrave, March 12, 1835.

20. PAM, CMSA, A77, Journal of William Cockran, August 2, 1832. According to the 1835 census families at the Rapids had a mean average of 4.5 children. The average number of children per household in Red River increased until 1843. Due to such factors as disease and

occasional food shortages, this average declined between 1843 and 1849. See Frits Pannekoek, "A Probe Into the Demographic Structure of Nineteenth Century Red River," in *Essays on Western History,* ed. L. H. Thomas (Edmonton: University of Alberta Press, 1976), 92.

21. Sylvia Van Kirk, *Many Tender Ties,* 106.

22. Sylvia Van Kirk, "What if Mama was an Indian, The Cultural Ambivalence of the Alexander Ross Family," in *The Developing West,* ed. J. Foster (Edmonton: University of Alberta Press, 1983), 125-35.

23. Ibid.

24. John Foster, "The Country-Born in the Red River Settlement," 184.

25. PAM, CMSA, A77, Journal of William Cockran, April 5, 1833.

26. Ibid.

27. John Foster, "The Country-Born in the Red River Settlement," 184.

28. See James Sutherland to John Sutherland, August 10, 1842, as quoted in John Foster, "The Country-Born in the Red River Settlement," 185.

29. D. N. Sprague and R. P. Frye, *The Genealogy of the First Métis Nation* (Winnipeg: Pemmican Publ., 1983). See Table 2 "Family Size, Personal Property, and Geographical Location and Land Owners, 1835," n.p.

30. E. E. Rich, *The Hudson's Bay Company, 1670-1870,* vol. 2, 315.

31. PAM, MG7, B4-1, M274, St. Andrew's Parish Records, Register of Marriages, 1835-1910.

32. PAM, MG2, B2, Red River Census, 1835.

33. Ibid.

34. Sylvia Van Kirk, *Many Tender Ties,* 106.

35. John West, *The Substance of a Journal,* 136.

36. James Sutherland to John Sutherland August 7, 1838, as quoted in Sylvia Van Kirk, *Many Tender Ties,* 200.

37. D. N. Sprague and R. P. Frye, *The Geneology of the First Métis Nation,* Table 3, "Contract Employees of the HBC Recruited From or Retired to the Red River Colony, 1821-1870," n.p.

38. PAM, MG2, B2, Red River Census, 1835.

39. Ibid.

40. Ibid., 1843.

41. Irene M. Spry, The Métis and Mixed-Bloods of Rupert's Land before 1870," in *The New Peoples:Being and Becoming Métis in North America,* ed. Jacqueline Peterson and Jennifer Brown (Winnipeg: University of Manitoba Press, 1985), 112.

42. Rodolfo Stavenhagen, *Social Classes in Agrarian Societies* (New York: Anchor Press, 1975), 40-52.

43. See Gerhard Ens, *Homeland to Hinterland,* 28-56, 93-122.

44. Frits Pannekoek, Review of *Homeland to Hinterland: The Changing Worlds of the Red River Métis,* H-Canada@msu.edu, September, 1997.

45. A total of sixteen censuses where taken in Red River before 1870. Censuses that included the Rapids and later St. Andrew's were carried out in 1831, 1832, 1833, 1835, 1838, 1840,1843, 1846, 1847, and 1849. Only a partial census has survived from 1856.

46. PAM, CMSA, A78, William Cockran to the Secretaries, October 25, 1836.

47. Ibid., Journal of William Cockran, September 2, 1842.

48. Ibid., MG7, B4-1, M274, St. Andrew's Parish Records, Register of Burials, 1846-87. This fact corresponds to the decline in the number of children per household in Red River in the

1840s. See Frits Pannekoek, "A Probe into the Demographic Structure of Nineteenth Century Red River," 82.

49. Ibid. While the age of death has been recorded for registered burials in the parish, a simple statistical average of these ages will not shed light on trends occurring within the community. Moreover, the limited number of yearly entries (47 in 1846) does not allow for a conclusive computation. A quick scan of the data, however, reveals that 22 of the 47 deaths recorded in 1846 occurred in infants two years of age and under.

50. Frits Pannekoek, "The Churches and the Social Structure in the Red River Area, 1818-1870," 192.

51. Ibid., 193-94.

52. PAM, CMSA, A78, Robert James to Rev. Davies, August 7, 1847.

53. Ibid.

54. Ibid., A92, Journal of James Hunter, March 29, 1864.

55. In his journal for October 1864, St. Andrew's resident Samuel Taylor wrote: "The Scarlet Fever is all through the Settlement now this while back." PAM, MG2, C13, Journal of Samuel Taylor, October, 1864.

56. Gerald Friesen, *The Canadian Prairies*, 116.

57. PAM, CMSA, A98, Journal of J. P. Gardiner, n.d.

58. F. A. Peake, "The Achievements and Frustrations of James Hunter," *Journal of the Canadian Church Historical Society* 19 (1977): 158.

59. Ibid., A91, James Hunter to the Secretaries, April 8, 1857.

60. See, for instance, the writings of Rev. Gardiner at St. Andrew's, who wrote to the CMS in 1870 that "there is little doubt now that the instigation of the Rebellion was intended to make this a Roman Catholic colony." PAM, CMSA, A99, J. P. Gardiner to the Secretaries, November 30, 1870.

61. Ibid. See, for example, Bishop Machray's contention in a letter to Sir John Young that the "1,400,000 acres [to be given] to the Half-breed part of the community is a most dangerous provision," in *Alexander Begg's Red River Journal,* ed. W. L. Morton (Toronto: Champlain Society, 1956), 559.

62. Ibid., 558.

63. Ibid., 108. It should also be noted that the Christian Indians at St. Peter's and the handful living at St. Andrew's opposed Riel's government, primarily due to the influence of John Shultz and Colonel John Dennis. See ibid., 101.

64. PAM, MG3, B1-2, Thomas Bunn Papers, Donald Gunn to Thomas Bunn, February 11, 1870.

65. See Frits Pannekoek, *A Snug Little Flock*, 181-187.

66. As quoted in Gerald Friesen, "River Road," in *River Road, Essays on Manitoba and Prairie History* (Winnipeg: University of Manitoba Press, 1996), 8.

67. D. N. Sprague and P. R. Mailhot, "Persistent Settlers: The Dispersal and Resettlement of the Red River Métis, 1870-1885," *Canadian Ethnic Studies* 17, no. 2 (1985): 2-3.

68. The term "corporate rights" has been used to describe rights other than those expressed by simply land or religion. The concerns of the Métis in 1869-70 went beyond these individual rights. They demanded the right to a kind of "collectivity of culture" as defined by language, faith, kinship networks, education and the socialization of parish and neighbourhood.

In the years following the events of 1869-70, the Manitoba land question became the single most contentious issue to face the new Canadian administration. Section 31 of the Manitoba Act promised "one million four hundred thousand acres ... for the benefit of the families of Halfbreed residents." This acreage (given in the form of $160 worth of scrip that could be used to purchase Dominion land) was to be initially divided amongst the children of Métis heads of families. The legislation, however, was changed in 1874 to also include the parents of these Métis children. As well, the descendants of the original Selkirk settlers were offered approximately 140 acres of land per head. But through mismanagement, or a deliberate attempt by the federal government to allow speculators to disenfranchise the Manitoba Métis in favour of incoming Canadian settlement, only a portion of the grant, estimated at less than 600,000 acres in 1882, was ever allotted. The rest ended up in the hands of speculators and eastern Canadian squatters, who were attempting to turn Red River into an Anglo-Ontarian settlement. Early in 1871, the new Lieutenant Governor of Manitoba, Adams G. Archibald, proposed to the Dominion government that local legislation be framed in order to administer Section 32 of the Act, that part of the law that ensured that land already occupied would not be jeopardized by the transfer. The federal government rejected Archibald's proposal. Instead, Ottawa considered the whole of the province to be Dominion land and in effect made no distinction between occupied parish lots and the open territory outside the settlement belt. This interpretation had serious ramifications for the Métis parishes along the Red and Assiniboine, including St. Andrew's. New legislation was used to bar anyone who had not made sufficient "improvements" to their land, which might include a minimum number of cultivated acres, or the existence of an acceptable dwelling. The result of the legislation was to drive from the colony those settlers the government felt were indifferent farmers, or those who cultivated only a few acres while engaged in other types of economic activity. Gerhard Ens has argued, however, that it was the collapse of the HBC monopoly in the 1840s and the development of a new "proto-industrial" Métis economy based largely on the exploitation of the buffalo robe trade in the western interior that led to the abandonment of agriculture, the creation of *hivernant* communities on the plains, and eventually to emigration from Red River. But other historians, including Diane Payment and D. N. Sprague, maintain that the Red River Métis were driven from their lands by government dispossession, the violence of the troops sent to control the settlement, and the racism of incoming Ontario settlers. Approximately 1,200 families in Manitoba lost all chance of obtaining patent on their land because they could not meet the government's stipulation for ownership. And while the "pull" of the buffalo robe trade may have provided economic alternatives for some Red River Métis after 1850, it was the "push" of dispossession that ultimately changed Red River from a Native settlement to an Anglo-Canadian province of the new Dominion.

69. PAM, MG2, B3, District of Assiniboia, Census of Manitoba, 1870.
70. Gerald Friesen, *The Canadian Prairies*, 202.
71. See, for example, *Beyond the Gates of Lower Fort Garry* (Municipality of St. Andrew's, 1982), a local history of the parish and municipality.
72. Gerald Friesen, "River Road," 11.
73. Laura Peers, *The Ojibwa of Western Canada, 1780 to 1870* (Winnipeg: University of Manitoba Press, 1994), 123-139.
74. Ibid., 182.

75. Peter Grant, "The Saulteaux Indians about 1804," vol. II in *Les Bourgeois de la Compagnie du Nord-Ouest,* ed. L. R. Masson (New York: Antiquarian Press, 1960), 329, as quoted in Laura Peers, "Aboriginal People and Lower Fort Garry" (Winnipeg: Parks Canada, 1995), 33.

76. David Butterfield, *Architectural Heritage of the Selkirk and District Planning Area* (Winnipeg: Historic Resources Branch, Manitoba Department of Culture, Heritage and Citizenship, 1988), 18-19.

77. For a discussion of the influence of architectural style on historic commemoration, see Robert Coutts, "Stone Symbols of Dominance: The River Road Parkway and the Bias of Architectural Commemoration," *NeWest Review,* August, 1986.

78. David Butterfield, *Architectural Heritage of the Selkirk and District Planning Area,* 19-20.

79. S. H. Scudder, *The Winnipeg Country,* as quoted in ibid., 21.

80. Ibid., 29

81. Ibid., 29-32.

82. George Ingram, "The Big House, Lower Fort Garry," in Canadian Historic Sites, *Occasional Papers in Archaeology and History,* no. 4 (Ottawa: National Historic Sites Service, 1970), 114.

83. PAM, CMSA, A78, William Cockran to Secretaries, October, 1845.

Chapter Six
St. Andrew's and the Agricultural Economy

1. See Alexander Ross, *The Red River Settlement: Its Rise, Progress and Present State* (Edmonton: Hurtig, 1972), especially Chap. 10, 108-18.

2. Ibid., 195.

3. H. Y. Hind, *Narrative of the Canadian Red River Exploring Expedition of 1857,* 222.

4. Marcel Giraud, *The Métis in the Canadian West,* vol. II, translated by George Woodcock (Edmonton: University of Alberta Press, 1986. First published in 1945), 123-125.

5. W. L. Morton, "Agriculture in the Red River Colony," *Canadian Historical Review* 30, no. 4 (December, 1949): 316.

6. Stanley considered the Métis of Red River to be "Indolent, thoughtless and improvident, unrestrained in their desires, restless, clannish and vain." G.F.G. Stanley, *The Birth of Western Canada* (Toronto: University of Toronto Press, 1961), 8.

7. Barry Kaye, "'The Settlers' Grand Difficulty:' Haying in the Economy of the Red River Settlement," *Prairie Forum* 9, no. 1 (Spring, 1984): 1-11; and W. L. Clarke, "The Place of the Métis Within the Agricultural Economy of Red River During the 1840s and 1850s," *The Canadian Journal of Native Studies* 3, no. 1 (1983): 69-84.

8. See, for example, W. L. Morton, "Agriculture in the Red River Colony," 315.

9. Gerhard Ens, *Homeland to Hinterland,* 172-175.

10. Anthropologist G. H. Sprenger has argued that the Selkirk settlers in Red River were slavishly wedded to agricultural practices that more often than not resulted in poor crop yields or complete failures. G. H. Sprenger, "An Analysis of Selective Aspects of Métis Society 1810-1870" (MA thesis, University of Manitoba, 1972), 56-86.

11. W. L. Morton, "Introduction," in *The Letters of Eden Colvile, 1849-1852* (London: Hudson's Bay Record Society, 1956), xxv.

12. Barry Kaye, "'The Settlers' Grand Difficulty:' Haying in the Economy of the Red River Settlement," 5.

13. W. L. Morton, "Agriculture in the Red River Colony," 309-311. Morton uses a number of sources to support his argument that wheat grown in Red River matured in 110 to 120 days. He also cites Donald Gunn who wrote in 1856: "wheat sown in the beginning of May was above the ear on the 13th of July, and ripe on the 20th of August."

14. Barry Kaye, "Some Aspects of the Cultural Geography of the Red River Settlement, 1827-1850" (MA thesis, University of Manitoba, 1967), 165.

15. Ibid., 174.

16. In most histories of Red River, including this text, the term "lower settlement" refers to the parishes of St. Paul's, St. Andrew's, and St. Peter's at the "lower," or downstream, end of the colony. However, in the Red River censuses (excluding that of 1849), "lower settlement" had a broader designation and referred to all of Red River except for Grantown and the Indian settlements.

17. Unfortunately, while the 1870 census provided the parish affiliation of individuals in Red River, it did not record information as to land under cultivation, livestock, or other agricultural possessions. In *Homeland to Hinterland,* Gerhard Ens reconstitutes nineteenth-century families in the parishes of St. Andrew's and St. François Xavier using a methodology that provides statistical data on cultivation and livestock, as well as a number of other demographic patterns related to birth rates, mortality rates, and marriage trends. For an explanation of his approach, see *Homeland to Hinterland,* Appendix A: "Family Reconstitution Methodology," 177-181. Differences between the totals given for St. Andrew's households in 1835 and 1849 in this study and those arrived at by Ens for the same dates can be traced to differences in the assignation of parish affiliation from the census data of 1835 and 1849. These discrepancies have affected attributed cultivated acreage in the parish (especially for 1849), although we both show that the average cultivated acreage for St. Andrew's residents had clearly increased between 1835 and 1849 vis-à-vis other farmers in Red River.

18. Alexander Ross, *The Red River Settlement*, 112-113.

19. PAM, MG2, C13, Samuel Taylor Diary, May, 1866.

20. PAM, CMSA, A77, William Cockran to Secretaries, July 25, 1833.

21. H. Y. Hind, *Narrative of the Canadian Red River Exploring Expedition of 1857*, 150.

22. Barry Kaye, "Some Aspects of the Cultural Geography of the Red River Settlement," 172.

23. Archives of the Archdiocese of St. Boniface, file no. 269, Alexander Christie to Henry Fisher, March 2, 1847, as quoted in W. L. Morton, *Manitoba: A History* (Toronto: University of Toronto Press, 1957), 513.

24. Marcel Giraud, *Le Métis Canadien; Son Role dans l'Histoire des Provinces de l'Ouest* (Paris: Institut d'Ethnologie, 1945), 836.

25. See livestock totals contained in the Red River census, primarily the censuses of 1835, 1838, 1843, 1847, and 1849. PAM, MG2, B3, Red River Census.

26. Alexander Ross, *The Red River Settlement*, 150-151. Ross discusses the Company's attempts to bring cattle into the settlement as part of Simpson's scheme to create a "Tallow Company."

27. PAM, MG2, B3, Red River Census, 1849.

28. Ibid.

29. W. L. Morton, "Introduction," in Eden Colvile, *The Correspondence of Eden Colvile, 1849-1852*, xxxi.

30. PAM, MG2, B3, Red River Census, 1849.

31. Barry Kaye, "The Trade in Livestock between the Red River Settlement and the American Frontier, 1812-1870," *Prairie Forum* 6, no. 2 (1981): 163.

32. Ibid.

33. PAM, MG2, C13, Samuel Taylor Diary, March, 1859.

34. Ibid. See entries for November, December, and January, 1860.

35. Barry Kaye, "Some Aspects of the Cultural Geography of the Red River Settlement, 1827-1870," 193.

36. Writing in 1856, Alexander Ross commented: "Sheep are declining fast in number for the ravages of dogs and wolves ... [and] were fewer by 1,000 than the year before." Alexander Ross, *The Red River Settlement*, 391.

37. W. L. Morton, "Introduction," in Eden Colvile, *The Correspondence of Eden Colvile, 1849-1852*, xxvi.

38. Barry Kaye "Some Aspects of the Cultural Geography of the Red River Settlement, 1827-1870."

39. Barry Kaye, "Flour Milling at Red River: Wind, Water and Steam," *Manitoba History* 2 (1981): 12.

40. Marcel Giraud, *Le Métis Canadien*, 779.

41. John Bunn to Thomas Bunn, August 10, 1857, cited in G. H. Sprenger, "An Analysis of Selective Aspects of Métis Society, 1810-1870," 84.

42. PAM, MG2, C13, Samuel Taylor Diary, September, 1860.

43. Ibid., July 1863.

44. The first water-powered mill in St. Andrew's was constructed by John Tait at Parks Creek near the southern boundary of the parish. In 1854, John Gunn built a water mill on the east side of the Red at Gunn's Creek. Windmills in the parish were owned by Donald Gunn on lot 109, Thomas Sinclair on lot 59, Edward Mowat on lot 90, William Taylor on lot 28, and Richard Thomas on lot 54.

45. Legislative Library of Manitoba, *The Nor'Wester*, August 18, 1864.

46. H. Y. Hind, *Narrative of the Canadian Red River Exploring Expedition of 1857*, 223.

47. PAM, MG2. C13, Samuel Taylor Diary, July, 1859.

48. *The Nor'Wester*, May 14, 1860.

49. The Anglican Bishop in Rupert's Land, Robert Machray, believed that the protection and extension of the traditional system of land tenure in Red River would not facilitate the re-settlement of the colony by Anglo-Protestant farmers from Ontario. In a letter to Sir John Young, Machray maintained that the "1,400,000 acres [to be reserved] for the half-breed part of the community is a most dangerous provision." Quoted in *Alexander Begg's Red River Journal*, ed. W. L. Morton (Toronto: Champlain Society, 1956), 559.

50. HBCA, B.239/K/2-3, Minutes of Council of the Northern Department of Rupert's Land, 1832-1870.

51. Provincial Archives of Manitoba, William Lane papers, A. Buchanan to William Lane, September 2, 1852.

52. Greg Thomas, "The North West Bastion Bakehouse, Lower Fort Garry: A Structural and Furnishing Study," Manuscript Report Series, no. 297, Environment Canada, Parks, 1979.

53. PAM, CMSA, A77, William Cockran to Rev. Bickersteth, August 3, 1829.

54. See, for example, Taylor's entry for April of 1859, PAM, MG2, C13, Samuel Taylor Diary.

55. Barry Kaye, "The Trade in Livestock between the Red River Settlement and the American Frontier, 1812-1870," 173.

56. Duncan Finlayson to H. H. Sibley, October 31, 1840, as quoted in ibid., 173.

57. Ibid., 174.

58. Glenbow Alberta Archives, Sutherland Correspondence, James Sutherland to John Sutherland, August 10, 1840.

Chapter Seven
Anglican Mission to Rural Church

1. Frits Pannekoek, "The Churches and the Social Structure in Red River," 157.

2. See M. P. Wilkinson, "The Episcopate of the Right Rev. David Anderson, 1849-1864," (MA thesis, University of Manitoba), 1950.

3. PAM, EAPR, *Church Missionary Society Record*, Report for the Year 1851, vol. 22, 13.

4. Ibid.

5. See Hal Guest, "The Historical Landscape of the Parsonage at St. Andrew's," 88, as well as F. A. Peake, "The Achievements and Frustrations of James Hunter," *Journal of the Canadian Church Historical Society* 19, no. 2 (1977): 143.

6. Sylvia Van Kirk, *Many Tender Ties*, 179.

7. Letitia Hargrave, *The Letters of Letitia Hargrave,* ed. M. McLeod, 185.

8. T.C.B. Boon, *The Anglican Church from the Bay to the Rockies*, 82.

9. PAM, CMSA, A78, Robert James to Secretaries, August 6, 1849.

10. For more information regarding the construction of the stone parsonage at St. Andrew's, see Rodger Guinn's, "St. Andrew's Parsonage, Red River: A Structural and Land-Use History," 251.

11. PAM, CMSA, A92, William Cockran to Secretaries, December 6, 1853.

12. Ibid., August 4, 1854.

13. Ibid., December 29, 1854.

14. Ibid., A92, William Kirkby to Rev. Venn, July 13, 1854.

15. PAM, HBCA, D.5/11, folios 294-95, "The Petition of the Presbyterian Inhabitants of Red River Settlement, Rupert's Land," n.d.

16. A total of about 300 people left the Anglican parishes in Red River and joined the new Presbyterian Church at Kildonan. Of that number, approximately 100-120 people quit services at St. Andrew's in 1851.

17. Frits Pannekoek, "The Churches and the Social Structure in the Red River Area," 181.

18. PAM, HBCA, D.5/32, folio 384, Donald Ross to George Simpson, December 18, 1851.

19. Ibid.

20. Frits Pannekoek, *A Snug Little Flock: The Social Origins of the Riel Resistance of 1869-70*, 134-136.

21. PAM, CMSA, A91, Journal of James Hunter, n.d., 1861.

22. Ibid., A99, Rev. J. P. Gardiner to Secretaries, November 18, 1871. Since 1852, a number of Presbyterians in St. Andrew's had held services in the home of Donald Gunn. Eventually, fourteen families built a log "meeting house" at a site north of the rapids. In 1863, the

Presbyterians received a grant of land from the HBC one-half mile south of the lower fort. Construction of the Little Britain Presbyterian Church was started that year and was completed in 1873. The Rev. John McNabb served as its first minister.

23. T.C.B. Boon, *The Anglican Church from the Bay to the Rockies*, 83.

24. Ian A. L. Getty, "The Failure of the Native Church Policy of the CMS in the Northwest," *Canadian Plains Studies* 2 (1974): 21.

25. T.C.B. Boon, *The Anglican Church from the Bay to the Rockies*, 85-87.

26. Ian A. L. Getty, "The Failure of the Native Church Policy of the CMS in the Northwest," 19-20.

27. Henry Youle Hind, *Narrative of the Canadian Red River Exploring Expedition of 1857* (Edmonton: Hurtig, 1971), 197.

28. PAM, CMSA, A92, James Hunter to Rev. Chapman, December 19, 1855.

29. Ibid., November 7, 1856.

30. PAM, MG19, E6, James Hunter to John Smithurst, July 2, 1857.

31. Ibid.

32. H. Y. Hind, *Narrative of the Canadian Red River Exploring Expedition of 1857*, 197.

33. PAM, CMSA, A92, James Hunter to Rev. Chapman, December 19, 1855.

34. H. Y. Hind, *Narrative of the Canadian Red River Exploring Expedition of 1857*, 197.

35. Ibid.

36. Ibid.

37. Ibid.

38. Ibid., 199. In a letter written in 1854, William Lane, the postmaster at Lower Fort Garry, commented that the average congregation "cannot much exceed 400 individuals," PAM, MG19, A40, William Lane Correspondence, Lane to Mrs. G. Lane, August 22, 1854.

39. Ibid., 195-96.

40. PAM, CMSA, A91, James Hunter to Henry Venn, August 11, 1856.

41. Ibid.

42. PAM, HBCA. D.5/32, folio 761, Adam Thom to George Simpson, November 8, 1851.

43. PAM, CMSA, A91, James Hunter to the Secretaries, January 1, 1861.

44. Ibid.

45. Ibid., February 14, 1862.

46. Ibid.

47. PAM, Rev. John Black Papers, John Black to James Black, April 3, 1862.

48. HBCA, D.4/50, folio 119, George Simpson to David Anderson, June 28, 1855.

49. PAM, CMSA, A91, James Hunter to Secretaries, April 8, 1857.

50. F. A. Peake, "The Achievements and Frustrations of James Hunter," 154-55.

51. As quoted in Eden Colvile, *Letters of Eden Colvile,* ed. E. E. Rich, Eden Colvile to George Simpson, August 3, 1848, 225.

52. PAM, EAPR, *Proceedings of the Church Missionary Society, 1859-60*, 207.

53. PAM, CMSA, A92, copy of *The Nor'Wester*, June 14, 1860. In his journal for March 29, 1864, Hunter makes reference to the selling of subscriptions in order to raise money for the parish. He wrote: "Attended our yearly meeting for the election of Church wardens and Vestry men ... subscriptions amounting in all to £28.10.6 which with £9.16.5 Meetings and Sermons, makes the total £38.6.11. This is very far short of the amount collected last year, but the harvest was a partial failure [due to drought and insects], causing much want and

distress in our midst." PAM, CMSA, A92, Journal of James Hunter, March 29, 1864. Hunter used much of the money raised to provide assistance in the form of food and clothing to those parishioners who suffered the heaviest from crop failures throughout the settlement.

54. Ibid., James Hunter to Secretaries, June 19, 1860.

55. Ibid., James Hunter to Richard Davies, January 18, 1864.

56. Ibid., James Hunter to Secretaries, March 7, 1863.

57. PAM, MG7, Register of births, Marriages and Deaths, St. Andrew's Parish, 1864.

58. PAM, CMSA, A92, James Hunter to Secretary Venn, December 1, 1864.

59. Ibid.

60. Ibid., January 28, 1865.

61. Ibid., December 1, 1864.

62. Ibid., December 1, 1864.

63. Ibid.

64. Ibid., January 28, 1865.

65. Ibid., December 1, 1864.

66. Ibid., January 28, 1865.

67. Ibid., December 1, 1864.

68. PAM, EAPR, MG7, A1, *Church Missionary Intelligencer* (1867): 33.

69. Ibid.

70. CMSA, A98, Journal of J. P. Gardiner, November 27, 1869. "The Committee for Public Safety reported 302 men in the parish and 203 Guns.... A Company of Volunteers are to be enrolled and the men are to drill every day."

71. Ibid., December 4, 1869.

72. Ibid., A99, J. P. Gardiner to Secretaries, November 30, 1870.

73. In the aftermath of the Resistance, a curious incident involving Gardiner and the wife of Captain William Kennedy occurred at the Rapids. In a letter to Bishop Machray dated October 10, 1870, Mrs. Kennedy accused Gardiner of spreading rumours that she was attempting to get up a petition in the parish to spare the life of Louis Riel should he be apprehended. Mrs. Kennedy refused to attend St. Andrew's until the minister apologized. Eventually, after being urged by Machray, Gardiner did apologize to Mrs. Kennedy but insisted he could not remember making the remark. The episode could indicate that if there was not some support for Riel in the settlement, the Anglican clergy at least suspected that there was. Soon after, according to Mrs. Kennedy, an Eastern newspaper got wind of the story and wrote an editorial describing how she "counseled and insisted on the murder of poor young Scott." PAM, MG2, C2, Kennedy Correspondence, October 10 and 26, 1870.

74. Ibid., August 1, 1871.

75. Ibid.

76. While most of the Anglican clergy in Rupert's Land were staunchly anti-Catholic, Cowley was particularly vociferous in his opposition to the Church of Rome. In praising a certain anti-Catholic tract to a friend in England, Cowley wrote: "What a marvelous refutation of Roman Catholic doctrines! What an awful exposure of popish practices ... could you send further tracts, especially the one called: *The Priest, the Woman and the Confessional.*" Cowley continued, "I hear the priest goes among our people in the night seeking to turn them from

the practice of Bible Christianity to the idolatry of Mary and saint worship.... The Romish priest distributes pictures for adoration in the way of Maryolotry." Ibid., A100, Abraham Cowley to Rev. Smith, June 1, 1887.

77. Ibid., Arabella Cowley to Secretaries, March 10, 1873.
78. Ibid.
79. Ibid., John Grisdale to Secretary Hutchinson, December 26, 1873.
80. Ibid., John Grisdale to Secretary Wright, February 20, 1874.
81. Ibid., A101, Richard Young to Secretary Wright, July 5, 1875.
82. Ibid.
83. Ibid., A103, Richard Young to Secretaries, December 17, 1878.
84. Ibid.
85. Ibid.
86. Ibid., A109, January 3, 1881.
87. T.C.B. Boon, *The Anglican Church from the Bay to the Rockies*, 215-16.
88. PAM, CMSA, A78, Robert James to Secretaries, August 6, 1847.
89. In 1853, Kirkby ordered the following books for the school at St. Andrew's:
    Rev. W. B. McKenzie's Sermons
    The Bible and the Working Classes
    Reeds' Conversions
    Martin's Illustrated Natural Philosophy
    Cornwall's Young Composer
    Tate's Euclid's Elements
    Tate's Principles of Geometry
    Tate's Elements of Mechanism
    Heley's Grammar Exercises
    Hughes Explanatory Arithmetic
    Source: ibid., A92, William West Kirkby to Major Straith, October 17, 1853.
90. According to Kirkby, construction began in 1851 and was not completed until the fall of 1853. Ibid., Journal of W. W. Kirkby, November 8, 1853.
91. Ibid., W. W. Kirkby to Secretaries, December 9, 1852.
92. Ibid., W. W. Kirkby to Secretaries, August 4, 1854.
93. *The Nor'Wester*, June 14, 1860.
94. PAM, CMSA, A101, R. Young to Secretary Wright, July 5, 1875.
95. Mary Perfect, "One Hundred Years of History of the Rural Schools of Manitoba: Their Formation, Reorganization and Dissolution, 1871-1971" (MA thesis, University of Manitoba, 1978), 8.
96. See Alexander Gregor and Keith Wilson, *The Development of Education in Manitoba* (Dubuque, Iowa: Kendall and Hunt), 1984.
97. W. L. Morton, *Manitoba: A History*, 186. Morton argues that the Schools Act and the establishment of other local institutions indicated that "intimate and inner modes of community life were taking shape in the late 1870s." His view reinforces the notion that the Métis of Red River were part of a one-dimensional, unsophisticated society balanced between the hunt and the farm. In fact, the parish system, the interrelationship between kinship groups, the economic diversity in the settlement, and its relation to the HBC demonstrated a complex and mature society uniquely adapted to the environment in the Northwest.

98. PAM, CMSA, A101, Richard Young to Secretary Wright, July 5, 1875.

99. Ibid.

100. Frits Pannekoek, "The Churches and the Social Structure in the Red River Area," 216.

101. CMSA, A98, Journal of John P. Gardiner, December 7, 1868.

102. T.C.B. Boon, *The Anglican Church from the Bay to the Rockies*, 99.

103. CMSA, A102, Richard Young to Secretary Wright, June 18, 1877.

104. Ibid., A103, December 2, 1878.

105. Ibid., Young argued that the fundraising drive had met with little success because of poor economic conditions within the parish. "The [crop] yield has been very poor," he stated, "... and there is literally no market for produce."

106. Ibid., A110, Richard Young to the Parishioners of St. Andrew's, n.d., 1881.

107. Ibid., "Draft Report by the Bishop of Rupert's Land with regard to relieving the cost of Expenses of the Pastoral Stations," October, 1881.

108. Ibid.

Chapter Eight
Conclusion

1. St. Andrew's was part of the federal county of Lisgar and represented by member of parliament John Christian Shultz until 1883.

2. PAM, MG15, Minute book of Council, Municipal Records of St. Andrew's Parish, January 8, 1884–June 13, 1887.

3. Ibid., January 8, 1884.

4. Ibid., January 5, 1885.

5. Ibid.

6. Ibid., January, n.d., 1890.

7. Diocese of Rupert's Land Archives (hereafter DRA), Vestry Minutes of the Parish of St. Andrew's, April 4, 1890.

8. Ibid., July 21, 1890.

9. T.C.B. Boon, *The Anglican Church from the Bay to the Rockies*, 270.

10. DRA, Vestry Minutes, November 25, 1891.

11. Ibid.

12. Ibid., July 21, 1892.

13. For a detailed discussion of repairs to the rectory in this period, see Rodger Guinn, "St. Andrew's Parsonage, Red River: A Structural and Land-Use History," 30-37.

14. DRA, Vestry Minutes, March 12, 1894.

15. Ibid., December n.d., 1901.

16. Ibid., April 20, 1908.

17. Ibid.

18. Ibid., April 4, 1910. The Vestry Minutes do not elaborate upon the nature of the dispute.

19. Ibid., April 2, 1912.

20. Ibid.

21. DRA, Vestry Minutes, n.d., 1921.

22. Rev. Canon Jeffrey to Mr. Lyall, Warden of St. Andrew's Vestry, October 24, 1924, DRA, Vestry Minutes of St. Andrew's Parish, 1919-1930.

23. According to Rev. Harry Hodspith, the Rector at St. Andrew's between 1917 and 1921, almost ninety percent of the adult males in the parish were killed in the war. This figure, however, does seem exaggerated. Vestry Minutes of St. Andrew's parish, October, n.d., 1920.

24. Ibid., February 4, 1919.

25. Ibid., February 22, 1920.

26. Ibid., Twenty-seven children attended Sunday School at St. Andrew's that year. Seventy-eight attended at St. Thomas.'

27. Ibid., February 9, 1920.

28. Ibid., February 17, 1921.

29. Ibid., October 4, 1921.

30. Copy of Address by the Rev. C. W. Saunders to the Congregation of St. Andrew's, n.d., ibid., 1921.

31. Ibid.

32. Ibid., A detailed outline of renovations to the rectory after 1900 is contained in Rodger Guinn's "St. Andrew's Parsonage, Red River: A Structural and Land-Use History," 35-45.

33. Ibid., February 3, 1922.

34. Ibid., September 8, 1923.

35. Ibid., May 15, 1929.

36. Diocese of Rupert's Land Archives, Vestry Minutes of the Parish of St. Andrew's, August, 1934.

37. Gerald Friesen, *River Road*, 11.

Bibliography

Unpublished Sources

Canada, Public Archives
MG19, E6, John Smithurst Papers.

Archives of the Diocese of Rupert's Land
Vestry Minutes of the Parish of St. Andrew's.
Account Book of St. Andrew's Parish, 1849.

Hudson's Bay Company Archives, Provincial Archives of Manitoba
B.235/d/46-212b, Red River Settlers' Accounts, 1830-65.
B.235/z/2, Pay Lists and Accounts with Missions, Red River.
B.235/z/3, Red River Miscellaneous.
B.239/k/7-12, Minutes of the Northern Council of the Hudson's Bay Company, 1840-52.
D.4, The Correspondence of Governor George Simpson, Inward and Outward, 1821-60.
E.6/1-2, Red River Settlement, Land Register Book.
E.6/7-8, Memoranda Respecting Grants of Land.
E.6/9, Red River Settlement, Land Sales Memoranda.
E.18/4-7, Parliamentary Select Committee on the Hudson's Bay Company, Copies of Proceedings, 1857.

Provincial Archives of Manitoba
MG1, D20, Donald Ross Papers
MG2, B2, Red River Census, 1832-1849.
MG2, B3, District of Assiniboia, Census of Manitoba, 1870.
MG2, B5, Alexander Christie's Letterbook.
MG2, C1, William Kennedy Papers.
MG2, C2, Eleanor Kennedy Correspondence.

MG2, C10, Jacob Truthwaite Papers.

MG2, C12, Hudson's Bay Company Correlation Book.

MG2, C13, Samuel Taylor Diary.

MG2, C14, Alexander Ross papers.

MG2, C15, William Cowan Diary.

MG3, B1-2, Thomas Bunn Papers.

MG7, Register of Births, Marriages and Deaths, St. Andrew's Parish.

MG7, A1, Ecclesiastical Archives, Province of Rupert's Land.

Church Missionary Society Gleaner.

Church Missionary Society Intelligencer.

Church Missionary Society Regulations and Instructions to Missionaries.

Proceedings of the Church Missionary Society.

MG7, B2, Archives of the Church Missionary Society.

Journals and Correspondence of William Cockran

Journals and Correspondence of Abraham Cowley

Journals and Correspondence of Joseph Gardiner

Journals and Correspondence of James Hunter

Journals and Correspondence of Robert James

Journals and Correspondence of David Jones

Journals and Correspondence of William West Kirkby

Journals and Correspondence of John Smithurst

Journals and Correspondence of John West

Journals and Correspondence of Richard Young

MG8, Minutes of Council, District of Assiniboia.

MG9, A76, Margaret McLeod Collection.

MG13, C2, John Norquay Papers.

MG14, C23, Charles Napier Bell Collection.

MG15, Municipal Records, Parish of St. Andrew's.

RG17, D.2, Mines and Natural Resources, Land Branch Files, St. Andrew's Parish.

Legislative Library of Manitoba
The Nor'Wester, 1859-75.

Published Sources

Anderson, David. *The Net in the Bay,* London: S. R. Publishers, 1967.

Axtell, James. *The European and the Indian: Essays in the History of Colonial North America,* New York: Oxford University Press, 1981.

Axtell, James. *The Invasion Within: The Contest of Cultures in Colonial North America,* New York: Oxford University Press, 1985.

Beaumont, Raymond. "The Rev. William Cockran: The Man and the Image," *Manitoba History 33* (Spring, 1997): 2-15.

Begg, Alexander. *Alexander Begg's Red River Journal,* ed. W. L. Morton, Toronto: Champlain Society, 1956.

Berkhofer, R .F. *Salvation and the Savage,* University of Kentucky Press, 1965.

Bolt, Christine. *Victorian Attitudes to Race,* Toronto: University of Toronto Press, 1971.

Boon, T.C.B. *The Anglican Church from the Bay to the Rockies,* Toronto: Ryerson Press, 1962.

——— "The Archdeacon and the Governor," *The Beaver* (Spring, 1968) 41-49.

———. *These Men Went Out,* Toronto: Ryerson Press, n.d.

———. "William West Kirkby," *The Beaver* (Spring, 1965): 36-43.

Bowden, H. W. *American Indian and Christian Missions: Studies in Cultural Contact,* Chicago: University of Chicago Press, 1981.

Bradley, Ian. *The Call to Seriousness,* London: Jonathan Cape, 1976.

Breden, Thomas F. "The Red River Academy," *The Beaver* (Winter, 1974): 10-17.

Brown, Jennifer S. H. "A Colony of Very Useful Hands," *The Beaver* (Spring, 1977): 39-45.

———. *Strangers in Blood: Fur Trade Company Families in Indian Country,* Vancouver: University of British Columbia Press, 1980.

———. "Ultimate Respectability: Fur Trade Children in the Civilized World," *The Beaver* (Winter, 1977): 4-10 and (Spring, 1978): 48-55.

Brown, Jennifer S. H., and Elizabeth Vibert (eds.). *Reading Beyond Words: Contexts for Native History,* Peterborough: Broadview Press, 1996.

Brown, R. G. "Missions and Cultural Diffusion," *American Journal of Sociology* 50 (1944-45): 31-42.

Bumsted, J. *The Red River Rebellion,* Winnipeg: Watson and Dwyer, 1996.

Burrow, J. W. *Evolution and Society, A Study in Victorian Social Theory,* Cambridge: Cambridge University Press, 1966.

Cairns, H. A. *The Clash of Culture: Early Race Relations in Central Africa,* New York: F. A. Praeger, 1965.

Choquette, Robert. *The Oblate Assault on the North-West,* Ottawa: University of Ottawa Press, 1995.

Clarke, J. *Population and Economic Activity – A Geographical and Historical Analysis based upon Selected Censuses of the Red River Valley in the Period 1832 to 1856,* M.A. thesis, University of Manitoba, 1966.

Clarke, W.K.L. *A Short History of the S.P.C.K.,* New York: Macmillan and Company, 1919.

Clarke, W. L. "The Place of the Métis within the Agricultural Economy of Red River During the 1840s and 1850s," *Canadian Journal of Native Studies* 3, no. 1 (1983): 69-84.

Colvile, Eden. *The Letters of Eden Colvile, 1849-52,* London: Hudson's Bay Company Record Society, 1956.

Coutts, Robert. "Anglican Missionaries as Agents of Acculturation: The Church Missionary Society at St. Andrew's Red River, 1830-1870," in Barry Ferguson (ed.), *The Anglican Church and the World of Western Canada,* 1820-1870, Regina: Canadian Plains Research Centre, 1991.

———. "The Role of Agriculture in an English-Speaking Halfbreed Economy: The Case of St. Andrew's, Red River," *Native Studies Review* 4, nos.1/2 (1988): 67-94.

Davidson, C. B. *The Population of Manitoba,* Winnipeg: Economic Survey Board, 1938.

Dawson, S. J. *Report on the Exploration of the Country Between Lake Superior and the Red River Settlement,* Toronto: Macmillan and Company, 1968.

Dickason, Olive. *Canada's First Nations: A History of Founding Peoples from Earliest Times,* Toronto: McClelland and Stewart, 1992.

Ens, Gerhard. *Homeland to Hinterland: The Changing World of the Red River Metis in the Nineteenth Century,* Toronto: University of Toronto Press, 1996.

———. "Métis Lands in Manitoba," *Manitoba History* 5 (1983): 2-11.

Fast, Vera. *The Protestant Missionary and Fur Trade Society: Initial Contact in the Hudson's Bay Territory, 1820-1850,* Ph.D. dissertation, University of Manitoba, 1983.

Ferguson, Barry (ed.). *The Anglican Church and the World of Western Canada, 1820-1970,* Regina: Canadian Plains Research Centre, 1991.

Fleming, R. H. (ed.). *Minutes of Council of the Northern Department, 1821-31,* London: Hudson's Bay Company Record Society, 1940.

Foster, John. *The Anglican Clergy in the Red River Settlement, 1820-26,* M.A. thesis, University of Alberta, 1966.

———. *The Country-Born in the Red River Settlement,* Ph.D. dissertation, University of Alberta, 1973.

———. *The Developing West: Essays on Canadian History in Honor of Lewis H. Thomas,* Edmonton: University of Alberta Press, 1983.

———. "Missionaries, Mixed-Bloods and the Fur Trade; Four Letters of the Rev. William Cockran, Red River Settlement, 1830-33." *Western Canadian Journal of Anthropology,* vol. 3, no. 1, 1972): 94-125.

Fowke, V. C. "The Myth of the Self-Sufficient Canadian Pioneer," *Transactions of the Royal Society of Canada,* 56, Series 3 (June, 1962): 23-37.

Friesen, Gerald. *The Canadian Prairies, A History,* Toronto: University of Toronto Press, 1984.

———. *River Road: Essays on Manitoba and Prairie History,* Winnipeg: University of Manitoba Press, 1996.

Gallegher, Brian. "A Re-Examination of Race, Class, and Society in Red River," *Native Studies Review* 4, nos 1/2 (1988): 25-54.

Getty, Ian. "The Failure of the Native Church Policy of the CMS in the North-West," *Canadian Plains Studies* 2 (1974): 19-32.

Giraud, Marcel. *Le métis canadien, son rôle dans l'histoire des provinces de l'Quest,* Paris: Institute d'Ethnologie, 1945.

Goldring, Philip. *Papers on the Labour System of the Hudson's Bay Company,* Manuscript Report Series, #362, Parks Canada, 1979.

Goossen, Jaye. "Missionary-Indian-Trader; the Triangular Nature of Contact in Rupert's Land," in *Approaches to Native History in Canada* (Ottawa: National Museum of Man, paper no. 25, 1975), 30-43.

———. *The Relationship of the Church Missionary Society and the Hudson's Bay Company in Rupert's Land, 1821-1861 with a Case Study of Stanley Mission under the Direction of the Rev. Robert Hunt,* M.A. thesis, University of Manitoba, 1975.

Guest, Hal. *The Historic Landscape of the Parsonage at St. Andrew's With Some Comment on the Role of the Church Missionary Society at Red River, 1822-87,* Manuscript Report Series #443, Parks Canada, 1981.

Guinn, Rodger. *St. Andrew's Parsonage, Red River: A Structural and Land-Use History,* Manuscript Report Series #251, Parks Canada, 1978.

Grant, John W. *The Moon of Wintertime; Missionaries and the Indians of Canada in Encounter since 1534,* Toronto: University of Toronto Press, 1984.

Gregor, Alexander, and Keith Wilson. *The Development of Education in Manitoba,* Dubuque, Iowa: Kendell, Hunt, 1984.

Gunn, Donald. *History of Manitoba from the Earliest Settlement to 1835,* Ottawa: Maclean, Roger and Co., 1880.

Hargrave, J. J. *Red River, Altona,* Manitoba: Friesen, 1977.

Hargrave, Letitia. *The Letters of Letitia Hargrave, Ed. M. A. Macleod,* Toronto: Champlain Society, 1947.

Heeney, William Bertal. *Leaders of the Canadian Church,* Toronto: Misson Book Company, 1920.

Hind, Henry Youle. *Narrative of the Canadian Red River Exploring Expedition of 1857,* Edmonton: Hurtig, 1971.

Houghton, Walter E. *The Victorian Frame of Mind, 1830-1870,* New Haven, Conn.: Yale University Press, 1957.

Huel, Raymond. *Proclaiming the Gospel to the Indians and the Métis: The Missionary Oblates of Mary Immaculate in Western Canada, 1845-1945,* Edmonton: University of Alberta Press, 1996.

Jaenen, Cornelius. *Friend and Foe: Aspects of French-Amerindian Cultural Contact in the Sixteenth and Seventeenth Centuries,* Toronto: McClelland and Stewart, 1976.

———. "Missionary Approaches to Native Peoples," in *Approaches to Native History in Canada* (Ottawa: National Museum of Man, paper no. 25, 1975), 5-15.

Kaye, Barry. "Flour Milling at Red River: Wind, Water and Steam," *Manitoba History* 2 (1983): 12-20.

———. "Flour Mills in the Fur Trade," *Alberta History* 30, no. 2 (Spring, 1982): 1-8.

———. "The Settlers' Grand Difficulty, Haying in the Economy of Red River," *Prairie Forum* 9, no. 1 (Spring, 1984): 1-11.

———. *Some Aspects of the Historical Geography of the Red River Settlement, 1827-70,* M.A. thesis, University of Manitoba, 1967.

———. "The Trade in Livestock between the Red River Settlement and the American Frontier, 1812-1870," *Prairie Forum* 6, no. 2 (1981): 163-81.

Machray, Robert. *The Life of Robert Machray,* Toronto: Macmillan and Company, 1909.

Manitoba, Province of. *Report of the Department of Agriculture: Statistics and Health,* Winnipeg, Queen's Printer, 1884.

Martin, Archer C. *The Hudson's Bay Company's Land Tenures,* London: William Clowes, 1898.

Mason, Philip. *Patterns of Dominance,* London: Oxford University Press, 1971.

McBeath, R. G. "Farm Life in the Selkirk Colony," *Transactions of the Historical and Scientific Society of Canada* 50 (1897): 1-4.

McCarthy, Martha. *From the Ends of the Earth,* Edmonton: University of Alberta Press, 1994.

Merk, Frederick. *Fur Trade and Empire, George Simpson's Journal 1824-25,* Cambridge, Mass.: Harvard University Press, 1968.

Morton, A. S. A *History of the Canadian West to 1871,* Toronto: University of Toronto Press, 1973.

Morton, W. L. "Agriculture in the Red River Colony," *Canadian Historical Review* 30, no. 4 (December, 1949): 305-21.

———. *Manitoba: A History,* Toronto: University of Toronto Press, 1957.

———. "The Red River Parish and its Place in the Development of Manitoba," *Manitoba Essays,* Toronto: Macmillan Co. of Canada, 1937.

Mountain, G. J. *The Journal of the Bishop of Montreal During a Visit to the Church Missionary Society's North-West America Mission,* London: Seeley, Burnside and Col., 1846.

Nute, Grace Lee (ed.). *Documents Relating to the North-West Mission, 1815-1827,* St. Paul: Minnesota Historical Society, 1942.

Ossowski, Stanislaw. *Class Structure in the Social Consciousness,* London: Routledge and Kegan Paul, 1963.

Pannekoek, Frits. "The Anglican Church and the Disintegration of Red River Society, 1818-1870," in Carl Berger and Ramsay Cook (eds.), *The West and the Nation* (Toronto: McClelland and Stewart, 1976), 133-50.

———. *The Churches and the Social Structure in the Red River Area,* Ph.D. dissertation, Queen's University, 1973.

———. "A Probe into the Demographic Structure of Nineteenth Century Red River," in L. H. Thomas (ed.), *Essays on Western History* (Edmonton: University of Alberta Press, 1976): 83-97.

———. *Protestant Agricultural Missions in the Canadian West to 1870,* M.A. thesis, University of Alberta, 1970.

———. "Protestant Agricultural Zions for the Western Indian," *Journal of the Canadian Church Historical Society* 14, no. 3 (1972): 55-66.

———. "The Rev. Griffiths Owen Corbett and the Red River Civil War of 1869-70," *Canadian Historical Review* 57 (1976): 133-49.

———. "The Rev. James Evans and the Social Antagonisms of Fur Trade Society, 1840-46," *Prairie Forum* 3 (1974): 1-16.

———. *A Snug Little Flock: The Social Origins of the Riel Resistance of 1869-70,* Winnipeg: Watson and Dwyer, 1991.

Peake, F. A. "The Achievements and Frustrations of James Hunter," *Journal of the Canadian Church Historical Society* 19 (1977): 138-63.

Peers, Laura. *Aboriginal People and Lower Fort Garry,* unpublished report, Winnipeg: Parks Canada, 1995.

———. *The Ojibwa of Western Canada,* Winnipeg: University of Manitoba Press, 1994.

Peterson, Jacqueline, and Jennifer S. H. Brown, The New Peoples: Being and Becoming Métis in North America, Winnipeg: University of Manitoba Press, 1985.

Rempel, Arthur. *The Influence of Religion on Education For Native People in Manitoba Prior to 1870,* M.Ed. thesis, University of Manitoba, 1973.

Rich, E. E. *The Hudson's Bay Company, 1670-1870* (2 vol.), Toronto: McClelland and Stewart, 1960.

Ross, Alexander. *The Red River Settlement: Its Rise, Progress and Present State,* London: Smith, Elder and Company, 1856, republished by Hurtig, 1972.

Sprague, D. N. "The Cultural Bias of Métis Studies," Prairie Fire 8, no. 2 (Summer, 1987): 66-67.

———. "Government Lawlessness in the Administration of Manitoba Land Claims, 1870-87," *Manitoba Law Journal* 10, no. 3 (1980): 415-41.

———. "The Manitoba Land Question," *Journal of Canadian Studies* 15, no. 3 (Autumn, 1980): 74-84.

Sprague, D. N., and R. P. Frye, *The Genealogy of the First Métis Nation,* Winnipeg: Pemmican Publications, 1983.

———, and R. P. Frye, "Manitoba's Red River Settlement: Manuscript Sources for Economic and Demographic History," *Archivaria* 9 (Winter 1979-80): 139-146.

Sprague, D. N., and P. R. Mailhot, "Persistent Settlers: The Dispersal and Resettlement of the Red River Métis, 1870-1885," *Canadian Ethnic Studies* 17, no. 2 (1985): 1-30.

Sprenger, G. H. *An Analysis of Selective Aspects of Métis Society, 1810-1870,* M.A. thesis, University of Manitoba, 1972.

Stanley, G.F.G. *The Birth of Western Canada,* Toronto: University of Toronto Press, 1960.

Stavenhagen, Rudolfo. *Social Classes in Agrarian Societies,* New York: Anchor Press, 1975.

Stevenson, Winona. *The Church Missionary Society Red River Mission and the Emergence of a Native Ministry, 1820-1860, with a Case Study of Charles Pratt of Touchwood Hills,* M.A. thesis, University of British Columbia, 1988.

———. "The Journals and Voices of a Church of England Catechist; Askenootow (Charles Pratt), 1851-1884," in Jennifer S. H. Brown and Elizabeth Vibert (ed.), *Reading Beyond Words: Contexts for Native History* (Peterborough: Broadview Press, 1996): 304-329.

Stock, Eugene. *History of the Church Missionary Society,* London: The Church Missionary Society, 1899.

Taylor, W. H. "W. H. Taylor's Journal, Assiniboia, 1851," *Journal of the Canadian Church Historical Society* 12, no. 2 (June, 1970): 28-34.

Thomas, L. G. "Churches and Church Records in the History of the Canadian West," *Newsletter of the Bibliographical Society in Canada* 3, no. 1 (September, 1959): 6-14.

Thomas, L. G. (ed.). *The Prairie West to 1905,* Toronto: Oxford University Press, 1975.

Thompson, Arthur N. "John West: A Study of the Conflict Between Civilization and the Fur Trade," *Journal of the Canadian Church Historical Society* 12 (1970): 44-57.

———. "The Wife of the Missionary," *Journal of the Canadian Church Historical Society* 15 (1973): 35-44.

Troeltsch, Ernst. *The Social Teachings of the Christian Churches,* New York: Harper and Row, 1960.

Tucker, Sarah. *The Rainbow in the North,* London: James Nisbett and Company, 1858.

Usher, Jean. "Apostles and Aborigines: The Social Theory of the Church Missionary Society," *Social History* .7 (April, 1971): 28-52.

Van Kirk, Sylvia. *Many Tender Ties; Women in Fur Trade Society, 1670-1870,* Winnipeg: Watson & Dwyer, 1980.

———. "What if Mama was an Indian: The Cultural Ambivalence of the Alexander Ross Family," in J. Foster (ed.), *The Developing West* (Edmonton: University of Alberta Press, 1983): 123-36.

Warkentin, John, and Richard Ruggles. *Historical Atlas of Manitoba, 1612-1969,* Winnipeg: Manitoba Historical Society, 1970.

Waugh, Earle. *Dissonant Worlds: Roger Vandersteene Among the Cree,* Waterloo: Wilfrid Laurier Press, 1996.

West, John. *The Substance of a Journal During a Residence at the Red River Colony,* New York: Johnson Reprint Corp., 1966.

Wilkinson, Maurice P. *The Episcopate of the Right Rev. David Anderson,* M.A. thesis, University of Manitoba, 1950.

Williams, Glyndwr. *London Correspondence Inward from Sir George Simpson,* London: Hudson's Bay Record Society, 1973.

227

Index

Page numbers in italic type refer to illustrations.

Abel, Kerry, 11

aboriginal people. *See* Assiniboine (people); Cree; Métis; Ojibwa

Aborigines Protection Society, 18-9

Act for Regulating the Fur Trade, and Establishing a Criminal and Civil Jurisdiction.... (1821), 26

Act to Establish a System of Public Education in Manitoba, 177

Agreement for Recreation and Conservation (1978), 188-9

agriculture, 54, 57, 94, 103, 131-2, 192
    animal husbandry, 141-4
    buildings and implements of, 144-5
    as civilizing agent, 3-4, 21-2, 29, 36, 44, 49, 79, 94
    commercial, 148-9
    crops, 45-6, 134-6, 176-8, 215n53
    HBC's views on, 21, 91, 192
    mission farms, 36, 44-51
    See also economy, mixed; land use

Allan, James, x

Allen, Miss (governess, Red River Academy), 53

Anderson, David, 59, 61, 66, *66*, 84-7, 125, 156
    accused of slandering James Hunter, 168-9
    annexation favoured by, 192
    appointed bishop, 153-4
    cemetery consecration dispute and, 158-9

Anglican Church
    annexation favoured by, 87, 89, 107, 165, 192
    clergy's attitudes to Catholic Church, 28, 81-2, 87, 89, 107-8
    community life role of, 104-5
    free trade opposed by, 81
    historiography of, 197n7
    immigration favoured by, 87
    and Native clergy, 160-1
    Red River Resistance opposed by, 107-8, 170
    relations with Presbyterians, 28, 33, 84-6, 157-9, 163, 169, 214n16
    social order maintained by, 192
    See also Church Missionary Society

The Anglican Church from the Bay to the Rockies (Thomas Boon), 12

Anglican Diocesan Memorial Building Fund, 189

animal husbandry. *See under* agriculture

annexation by Canada
    clergy's support for, 87, 89, 107, 165, 192
    immigration to Manitoba following, 181

architecture in Red River
    aboriginal, 112-4
    church, 61-2, 118
    climate influence on, 112, 121-2

as evidence for human history, 111, 129
French-Canadian influence on, 114, 123-4
interior designs, 120-1
Lower Fort Garry, 9, 118-9, 119, 124
Red River frame construction, 114-8, 117, 121, 192
Scottish influence on, 123-4
St. Paul's, 126
stone construction in, 116, 123-9
See also under St. Andrew's
Assiniboia, District of, 4
Assiniboia, General Quarterly Court of, and Sayer trial, 80-1
Assiniboia, Governor and Council of, 7-8
membership of, 68
Métis appointed to, 54
Assiniboine (people), 6
Assiniboine Wool Company, 144
distillery at Lower Fort Garry, 79-80
Axtell, James, 11

Baie St Paul Parish (Wabassong), 7
Baillairgé, Thomas (architect), 125
Ballenden, John, 76, 80
Ballenden, Sarah, 76
Bannatyne, A.G.B., 96
barley, 136, 139
Barnley, George, 78
Beaumont, Raymond
on William Cockran, 34, 201n106
Berkhofer, Robert, 11
Bickersteth, Rev., 36
Bird, James, 53
Bird, John James, 182
biscuit, production of at Lower Fort Garry, 148-9
Black, John (Presbyterian clergyman), 158, 159, 164
Black, John (trader), 85
Bliss, Michael, 12
Bompas, William, 174
Boon, Thomas C. B., 12, 34, 35, 155-6
Bradley, Ian, 14-6
Brooks, J. W., 35

Brownlee, George, 184
Budd, Henry, 159-60, 160
buffalo hunt
decline of, 54, 63, 103, 105, 113, 143, 150, 153
missionaries disapprove of, 24
in mixed economy, 131-4, 150, 192
robe trade, 103, 105, 132
Buffalo Wool Company, 79
Bulger, Andrew, 91
Bunn, Joseph, 200n93

Cairns, H. A., 17
Caldwell, Lt-Col. W., 87
Cardwell, Major (Chelsea Pensioners), 83
Catholic Church
Anglican attitudes to, 28, 81-2, 87, 89, 107-8
first mission and church (1818), 6-7, 28, 118
HBC attitudes to, 78
cattle, 141, 142
censuses of Red River Colony, 137-40, 142-3, 208n45
data as evidence, 136-7, 145
Chelsea Pensioners, 83
children
mortality among, 105, 209n49
numbers per household, 207n20, 208n48
rearing of, 98-9
Choquette, Robert, 11
Christie, Alexander, 140
Church Missionary Intelligencer (CMS house journal), 17
Church Missionary Juvenile Association, 174
Church Missionary Society
calibre of its missionaries, 86
evangelicalism in, 16, 17
expansion plans of, 153
free trade opposed by, 81-2
historiography of, 3-4, 198n42
Native Church Policy of, 160
ordination crisis in, 83, 206n51
relations with HBC, 4, 66-72

support for Red River missions
withdrawn, 175, 176-7, 177-9, 179
views on: agriculture and education as
civilizing agents, 21-2; Métis peoples,
22-4; Native peoples, 17-20, 160-1
worldview of, 13-5, 16-20
See also Anglican Church
Church of England Temperance Society, 174
Clapham Sect, 15-6, 25, 197n17
Clarke, John, 91
Clarke, Leland, 132
class and status, 92, 100-1, 102-4, 191
changing attitudes to in Red River, 68
endogamous marriage as result of, 75
Marxist theory of, 103
role of in Red River Resistance, 109
clergy, Native, 32-3, 53-4, 159-61
clergymen, salaries of, 26, 35, 44, 163, 183-4
Cochrane, Henry, 160
Cochrane, Thomas, 156
Cockran, Ann (wife of William), 35, 51
Cockran, William, 17, 34-7, *35*, 39, 41-2, 55,
153, 156
builds church, 42-4, 58-9
daily work of, 55
described, 34, 84, 97
health of, physical and mental, 56-7
historiography relating to, 34, 201n106
influence on Métis, 64
and mission farm, 36, 44-6
and orphanage, 157
popularity of, 97
Portage La Prairie settlers and, 105
relations with David Jones, 44, 201n111
and schools, 36, 51-2, 175
State of Religion report (1835), 53-4
views on: Catholic francophone Métis, 84;
child rearing, 100; 'civilizing' agents,
21-2, 46; CMS, 43-4; country
marriage, 73-4; free trade, 69, 81-2; fur
trade and traders, 71-4, 93-4; George
Simpson, 77; HBC land grant policy,
40; Methodism, 77; Native peoples,
19, 20, 24, 72, 93, 94-6

Colonial and Continental Church Society, 156
Colonial Service Act (1819), 16
Colvile, Andrew, 25, 26
promises HBC aid to CMS, 41
Colvile, Eden, 83-4, *84*
and dispute over cemetery consecration,
158-9
Committee for Public Safety (St. Andrew's
1869-79), 170
Connolly, William, 74
Cook, Joseph (Métis catechist at St. Peter's),
53-4
Corbett, Griffith Owen, 88, 156, 167
Corrigal, James, 59, 176
Cowley, Abraham, 23-4, 81, 83, 86, 168, 172
arrives at The Rapids, 56
self-supporting missions favoured by, 178
views on Catholic Church, 216n76
Cowley, Arabella (wife of Abraham), 172, 177
crafts and trades
grist milling, 149|
mills, 213n44
Cree, 6, 7, 46
Cree, architecture of. *See* architecture,
aboriginal
Cree (language)
religious texts translated into, 86, 154
crops. *See under* agriculture
cultural evolution theory, 18-20

Davis, Matilda, 128, 177
school of, *128*, 129, 176
Davis, Richard, 21
Demers, Jérome, 125
Demeurons (regiment)
settle in Red River, 6
depression, economic, 105, 106
Dickason, Olive, 11
Douglas, Thomas. *See* Selkirk, 5th Earl of
drought (1860s), 106
Dumoulin, Father, 118

East India Company, 25-6
economy of Red River
    historiography of, 131-2
    mixed, 49, 54, 57, 94, 103, 131-3, 148, 192
education
    as civilizing agent, 3-4, 21-2, 28-9, 51-2
    importance of to English Métis, 101
    See also school(s)
Ellice, Edward, 87
Ens, Gerhard, 103, 132
Ethnological Society of London, 18-9
evangelicalism
    architectural expression of, 61
    in Clapham Sect, 15-6, 25, 197n17
    individualism in, 15, 40-1
    revival of in Britain, 14-6
    See also under Church Missionary Society
Evans, James, 83
    accusations against, 78
    relations with fur traders, 67

family life, 98
    See also children; marriage
Fast, Vera, 198n42
fertilizer, use of, 146-7
Finlayson, Duncan, 149
fire, prairie, 45
First Furrows (A. C. Garriock), 34
fishery at Grand Marais, 149
Flett, Jane (Mrs. James Sutherland), 101
Flett, John, 147
flood(s)
    in 1826, 6, 39, 105
    in 1852, 146, 156
Fortin, A. L., 182-3
Foss-Pelly scandal and trial (1850), 76-7
Foster, John, 13, 23, 34-5, 71
free trade, 54, 69, 79-82
    HBC opposes, 80
    in mixed economy, 150-1
French-Canadians
    settle at the Forks, 6

Friesen, Gerald, 88
    on British government and HBC
    relations, 87
Frye, R. P., 137
Gallagher, Brian, 75
Gardiner, Joseph Phelps, 106, 108, 159, 168
    annexation favoured by, 192
    ministry of, 170
    rumour mongering accusations against,
    216n73
    self-supporting missions opposed by,
    172, 177-8
Garrioch, A. C., 34, 35
Garrioch, Peter (school teacher), 53
Garrioch, William, 32
Garry, Nicholas, 25
Genealogy of the First Métis Nation (D. N.
    Sprague & R. P. Frye), 137
Gibeault, Belonie (stonemason), 119
Giraud, Marcel, 12, 65, 131, 140, 146
Goossen, Jaye, 67
Granatstein, J. L., 12
The Grand Rapids. *See* St. Andrew's;
    The Rapids
Grant, James Webster, 11
Grant, Peter, 114
grasshoppers, infestation of, 106, 146, 176,
    177-8
Grisdale, John, 172
    self-supporting missions favoured by, 178
Gunn, Donald, 53, 101, *108*, 149
    Riel's government supported by, 108
Gunn, John, 149

Harbidge, George, 27, 29-30, 33, 51
Hargrave, Letitia
    on: Miss Allen, 53; Red River Academy, 53
Harrison, Benjamin, 25, 78
Hay, Edward, 108
haying privilege, 134
Heeney, William, 20
Hillyer, Charles, 166, 176
Hime, H. L., 113, 161

Hind, Henry Youle, 161
    on Métis, 131; Red River potatoes, 139;
    St. Andrew's mission, 162-3
Hodspith, Harry, 186
Home Mission Fund, 179
horses, 141, 143
Houghton, Walter, 15
Hudson's Bay Company
    farms of, 148
    as governing body, 7-8, 66-7, 87
    government investigation of, 87
    land grants policy of, 40
    missionary activity encouraged by, 70
    relations with churches and missionaries,
        4, 21-2, 66-72, 77-8, 85, 190-2
    views on: agriculture, 21, 89, 191; John
        West, 28, 30; missionaries, 24-6
Huel, Raymond, 11
Hunter, James, 86, 107, *155*, 156, 161-2
    annexation favoured by, 165, 192
    career of, 154-5, 163-9
    investigates charges against G. O.
        Corbett, 167
    neutral stand of in cemetery dispute, 159
    requests annual indent to come from St.
        Paul, 166
Hunter, Mrs. (2nd wife of James). See Ross, Jean
Hunter, Mrs. (1st wife of James), 154

Image Plain (Middlechurch), 40
    school at, 53
immigration, 87, 109-10, 192, 194
    and architectural styles, 123-4
Indian House (orphanage) at St. Andrew's,
    157, 162
individualism, in evangelical view, 15, 40-1
influenza (1836), 54
Inkster, Colin, 34, 35
itinerant Christianity
    approved by Simpson, 77, 78

Jaenen, Cornelius, 11, 18
James, Mrs. (wife of Robert), 63
    described by John Black, 85

James, Robert, 49-50, 57, 59, 81-2, 86, 154
    educational program of, 175-6
    parsonage dispute and, 62-3
    views on: aboriginal people, 24; Métis,
        106; mission farming, 50
Jennings, Francis, 11
Johnson, Walter, 183
Johnstone, Charles, 182
Jones, David, 30-1, 39, 48-9, 51, 56, 125
    Cockran's farm plans opposed by, 36
    on Métis, 94-6
    Red River Academy founded by, 52
    and Red River schools, 32-3
    relations with HBC, 70
    State of Religion report (1835), 53-4
Jones, Mrs. (wife of David), 49, 51

Kaye, Barry, 132, 149
Kennedy, Aggathas (wife of Alexander), 107
Kennedy, Alexander, 107
Kennedy, George, 176
Kennedy, Phillip, 145
Kennedy, William, 107, *107*
Kennedy, Mrs. William, 216n73
Kett, E. B., 182
Kildonan Parish, 7
Kildonan Presbyterian Church, 126, *128*
King, Howard, 183
Kingsbury, George, 182
kinship
    and community life, 96-7, 100, 104-5
    See also children; marriage
Kirkby, William West, 155-7, *156*, 163, 168
    mission in Mackenzie district established
        by, 165
    as superintendent of schools, 176
Kittson, Norman, 80
Kitty (HBC supply ship), lost in Hudson
    Strait, 166

labour market, 149
land grants in Red River, 40
land use
    cultivated acreage statistics, 138-40,
        214n17
    patterns of: infield/outfield, 134, *135*;
    park lot, 146; river lot, 40, 147, 186
Leaders of the Canadian Church (William
    Heeney), 20
LeBlanc, Pierre (stonemason), 74, 124, 126
Letitia (Métis woman), *93*
Libling, Michener and Associates (architects), 188
limestone, quarrying of, 126-9
Linklater, Andrew, 101
Little Britain Presbyterian Church, 214n22
livestock. *See* agriculture, animal husbandry
Logan, Robert, 158
London Missionary Society, 16
Lower Fort Garry, *89*, *119*, *124*
    buildings at, 118-9
    transportation centre at, 148
Lowman, Mary (governess, Red River
    Academy), 52

Macallum, John (master, Red River Academy),
    52-3, 59
Machray, Robert, *169*
    annexation favoured by, 192
    ecumenicism opposed by, 170
    Riel's government opposed by, 170
    self-supporting missions planned by,
        172, 177-8, 179
    views on English Métis, 108
Mackay, John, 166
MacKay, John Alexander, 160
MacKenzie, Donald, 91
MacKenzie, Roderick, 74
Manitoba
    demographic analysis of, 110-1
    Land Question, 209n68
Marion, Narcisse, 80
marriage, country, 69, 73-6, 205n25-7
Martyn, Henry, 16
Mason, William, 78

Matheson, John William, 183
Matheson, Samuel P., 184
Mayhew, Caleb, 176
McBeath, Mary, 155
McCarthy, Martha, 11
McDermot, Andrew, 80, 85, *85*, 96
McDermot, Annie (Mrs. A.G.B. Bannatyne), *96*
McDonald, Donald, 59
McKay, John, *95*
McKenzie, B., 183
McLeod, John, 182
McNab, Sarah, 76, *76*
McNabb, John, 214n22
McRae, Duncan (stonemason), 58, 63, *63*,
    124, 156
McTavish, J. G., 74
Methodist Church
    clergy, 78
    Cockran's views on, 77
    missionary agenda of, 21
    relations with HBC, 77
Métis
    attitude of CMS to, 22-4
    Cockran's influence on, 64
    corporate rights claimed by, 209n68
    as de facto constabulary, 8
    described by: William Cockran's, 24, 57,
        72, 93-6; Alexander Ross, 131; George
        Simpson, 30; Richard Young, 174
    designation of, xiii-xiv
    economic diversity among, 103-4
    ethnic solidarity of, 88-9, 109
    HBC monopoly opposed by, 54
    historiography of, 12-3, 22-3, 131-2,
        195n2, 199n48-9
    occupations of, 7, 94, 103, 131, 133
    religious solidarity among breaks down,
        110-1
    settle at The Rapids, 39-40
Métis (English-speaking)
    alienation from Anglican Church, 154
    assimilation of, 111
    attitude to 1869 Resistance, 107, 108-9
    child rearing among, 98-9

cultural formation of, 99-100
farming at St. Andrew's, 44-5, 63-4
HBC attitude to, 25
historiography of, 35
immigration favoured by, 110
kinship support systems of, 96-7
leave St. Andrew's, 148, 179-80, 189, 194
mixed economy of, 57, 133-4, 150
origins of, xiii, 2-3, 22-3
religious attitudes of, 94-6
settle at The Rapids, 6, 37, 39-40
Métis (French-speaking)
origins of, 23
settle near the Forks, 6
Le Métis Canadien (Marcel Giraud), 140
Middleton, Rev. (CMS bishop), 16
Miles, Robert, 74, 78
Miller, Elizabeth (Mrs. John Norquay), 94
missionaries in Rupert's Land, historiography
of, 65-6
missions, self-supporting, 172, 174-5, 177-8,
179, 200n93
missions and missionaries, Christian, in North
America, historiography of, 11-3
Moody, W. D., 50
Morton, A. S., 12
Morton, W. L., 65, 217n97
Mountain, George Jehosaphat, 83
municipal councils, 182

Nahovway (Mrs. William Sinclair), 74
*Narrative of the Canadian Red River Exploring
Expedition of 1857* (H. Y. Hind), 162-3
National Historic Sites Cost-Share Program, 189
Native Church Policy. *See under* Church
Missionary Society
Native clergy, 200n93
Nolin, Augustin, 80
Norquay, John, 110-1, 174, 176, 182
Norquay, Thomas, *94*

oats, 136, 139
O'Donnell, James (architect), 61
Ojibwa, architecture of. *See* architecture,
aboriginal
Ojibwa (Anishinabe), 6, 7
settle at Sugar Point, 46
ordination crisis, 83, 208n51-2
orphanage (Indian House) at St. Andrew's,
157, 162
oxen, 141, 143

Pannekoek, Frits, 11, 12, 13, 34, 35, 81
on: agricultural missions, 50; Corbett
scandal, 88; James Evans, 67; John
Smithurst, 49; race relations in Red
River, 88; Red River Resistance
(1869-70), 88, 109; missionaries in
Red River, 33
Parfitt, Gilbert (architect), 187
Partridge Crop (Fairford) mission, 172
Peake, Frank, 12
Peers, Laura, on St. Peter's mission and social
change, 49
Peguis, Chief (William King)
letter to CMS, 48
settles at Sugar Point (St. Peter's), 46
Pelly, Andrew, 31
Pelly, Robert (governor of Assiniboia)
evangelical sympathies of, 71
pigs, 141, 143
ploughs, 144
polio epidemic (1918-19), 186
Portage La Prairie, settlement of, 105
potatoes, 136, 139
Pratt, Josiah, 31
Presbyterians
campaign for own church, 84-5, 158,
164, 214n22
clergy salaries of, 163
Kildonan Church, 126, *128*
relations with Anglicans, 28, 33, 84-6,
157-9, 163, 169, 214n16
Pritchard, John (schoolteacher at Frog Plain), 53

Provencher, Joseph-Norbert (Catholic
     clergyman), 6-7, 78, 125
     builds first Catholic church, 118
Provincial Municipalities Act (1880), 181
Pruden, William, 193

Quebec Rifles, 167
quern(s), 144-5

race and race relations in Red River, 88-9
     among Métis, 109
     changing attitudes to, 68
     Pannekoek theory of, 88
     statistics on, 93
Rae, John, 87
railway, 109-10
The Rapids, 1-2
     Cockran settles at, 36-7, 41-2
     community life at, 100
     described by Smithurst, 50
     English Métis at, 36-7, 39-40, 55, 92, 94
     family life at, 98
     mission farm at, 44-6, 50
     schools at, 42, 51-2, 53-4
     See also St. Andrew's
Red River Academy, 61
     founding of, 52-3
Red River Colony, 5 map
     demographic analysis of, 137-9
     economic and social change (1830-50),
          54-5, 105
     geographical organization of, 6-7
     government of, 7-8
     mission personnel at, 55-6
     mixed economy of, 94
     origins of, 4-6
     settlement plan of, 173 map
Red River Resistance (1869-70), 88, 107-9, 170
Red River Settlement (Alexander Ross), 131
religion. See evangelicalism; Tractarianism
Rich, E. E., on Simpson's religious beliefs, 70
Rindisbacher, Peter, 113
river lots, 40
River Road, 1-2

Roberts, John, 83
Ross, Alexander, 35, 84, 111, 121-2
     describes Métis, 131
     petitions for Presbyterian clergy, 158
     views on Cockran, 34
Ross, Donald, 78, 85, 154, 159
     views on William Cockran, 97
Ross, George, 182
Ross, James, 99, 99
Ross, Jean (2nd wife of James Hunter), 154-5,
     155
Rundle, Robert, 78

Saunders, Charles, 184, 186-7
Sayer, Guillaume, 80-1
scarlet fever, 106
school(s)
     CMS withdraws from, 176-7
     confessional, 177
     death of pupils at, 32
     declining enrollment (1840s), 54
     at Frog Plain, 53
     at Image Plain, 36
     John West's, 27-30, 31
     Miss Davis's, 128, 129, 176
     pupil racial origins (1835), 93
     in Red River, 27-30, 32-3, 36, 51
     Red River Academy, 52-3
     State of Religion report on, 53-4
     at Sugar Point, 46
     tuition charged at, 175-6
     See also education; See also under
          St. Andrew's
school(s), industrial
     Cockran's plans for, 51-2
Schultz, John Christian, 109
Selkirk, 5th Earl of (Thomas Douglas), 4
Selkirk settlement, 9 map
Selkirk Settlers
     arrive in Red River, 6, 7
Settee, James, 160
Setter, Andrew, 138, 142
Setter, George, 145
sheep, 141, 143-4, 147

Simpson, Frances, 74

Simpson, George, 7, 66, *66*, 87, 149

economic strategy for Red River, 79

missionary expansion opposed by, 70, 190-91

and ordination crisis, 83

views on: David Jones, 32; education in Red River, 30; John West, 28, 69-70, 202n82; missionaries, 21, 41, 85; native women, 53; temperance movement, 164

Sinclair, Betsy, 74

Sinclair, James, 80, 107, 158

Sinclair, Thomas, *92*, 149

supports Riel's government, 108

Sinclair, William, 74

Sixth Regiment of Foot, 80, 83

provide market for local produce, 140, 149

Slater, John, in 1835 census, 142

Smalley, Samuel, 182

Smith, John (Métis catechist at St. Peter's), 53-4

Smith, W. K. (schoolmaster), 51

Smithurst, John, 21, 22, 47-9, 56-7, 63, 81, 83-4, 86, 156, 161

Society for the Propagation of the Gospel, 163

criticized by CMS, 16

Spence, Andrew, 129

Spence, Anne (wife of William), 102

Spence, Margaret, 129

Spence, William, 102

Sprague, D. N., 109, 137

Spry, Irene, 102

St. Andrew's, *115*

agriculture at, 63-4, 134-6, 138-48, *147*

architectural styles at, 61-2, 111-22, 123-7, 126, 192

churches at, *60, 171, 184*: financial affairs of, 178-9, 182-5, 187-8, 215n53; heritage and historic site, 188-9; log, 42-4, 118; stone, 58-62, *60*, 153, 156, 161-2, *171*, 182, 187-9

class and status at, 190

economic activity at, 133-4, 149-51, 192-3

ethnic diversity of, 193

heritage and historic sites, 129

historiography of, 2-4, 182

land use patterns at, 134, *135*, 146

mission at, *31, 62*

municipal council established at, 181-2

orphanage (Indian House) at, 157, 162

parish, 7, 162-3

population statistics at, 55, 162-3, 186

Presbyterian church at, 214n22

rectory at, *60*, 156, 157, 162, *179, 184*, 187: dispute over, 62-3

schools at, 36, 42, 51-2, 93, 155, 175-6, *185*: industrial, 175; Miss Davis's, *128*, 129, 176

See also The Rapids

St. Andrew's Old Timer Association, 187

St. Andrew's Restoration Committee, 188

St. Boniface, 6

St. Boniface Cathedral, 124-5

St. Clement's Mapleton parish, 167

St. Clement's municipality, 181

St. John's, 7, *125*

St. John's Cathedral

construction of, 125-6

St. John's Church, 125

dispute over cemetery consecration at, 158-9

St. John's Collegiate, 173

St. Matthew's (Cloverdale), 186

St. Paul's Church, 126, *126*

St. Peter's, 7

as agent of social change, 49

church and school at, 46-7

farm at, 47-8

mission at, *36*, 46-8

Ojibwa settle at, 46-7

rectory at, *127*

St. Thomas's (Lockport), 186

St. Vital, 7

St Boniface, 118

Stanley, George F. G., 12, 65, 132

State of Religion report (1835)

race statistics in, 93

schools described in, 53-4

Stevens, Richard (school teacher at Image
    Plain), 53
Stevenson, Winona, 11
Stewart, John, 74
Substance of a Journal (John West), 27
Sutherland, James, 101-2, 111, 138, 193
Sutherland, Sally, 101
Swalwell, Rev., 186

Tait, Elizabeth, 129
Tait, John, 59, 109, 129, 149, 167
tallow company, 79-80
Taylor, George, Red River survey of (1835), 137
Taylor, Margaret, 74
Taylor, Samuel (stonemason), 139, 142-3,
    146-7, 149, 167, 192
temperance movement, 164, 174
Thom, Adam, 62-3, 82, 83, 163
Thompson, Arthur, 12, 28, 65
Thompson, David, 199n57
Tractarianism, 61-2
Trigger, Bruce, 11
Truthwaite, Andrew, 182
Truthwaite, Catherine, 75, *75*
Tylor, Edward, 19

"Upper" Church (St. John's), 40
Usher, Jean, 11

van der Goes Ladd, George, 34, 35
Van Kirk, Sylvia, 74, 76
vegetable crops, 136, 139
Venn, Henry, drafts CMS Native Church
    Policy, 160
Venn, John, 16
Warwick, Arthur, 184
Waugh, Earle, 11
weather and climate in Red River, 105, 106,
    145-6
    architecture influenced by, 112, 121-2
    crops damaged by, 45-6, 215n53
    winter's daily problems, 56
Wesleyans. *See* Methodist Church
West, John, 7, 24, 26-30, *27*
    builds first Protestant church, *31*, 118
    on Catholic Church, 28
    enemies of in Red River, 28, 69-70
    HBC criticized by, 69-70
    home of, *29*
    schools established by, 27-30
wheat, 134-6, 139
White Horse Plain (Grantown)
    settlement at, 6, 7
Whitway, James, 138, 142

Young, Richard, 174-5, 178, 182